MAGIC BUS

MAGIC BUS

ON THE HIPPIE TRAIL FROM ISTANBUL TO INDIA

RORY MACLEAN

BROOKLYN, NEW YORK

Printed in the United States of America.
10 9 8 7 6 5 4 3 2 1

Ig Publishing
178 Clinton Avenue
Brooklyn, NY 11205
www.igpub.com

Library of Congress Cataloging-in-Publication Data

MacLean, Rory, 1954-
  Magic bus : on the hippie trail from Istanbul to India / by Rory MacLean. -- 1st
American ed.
     p. cm.
  ISBN-13: 978-0-9788431-9-9
  ISBN-10: 0-9788431-9-3
  1. MacLean, Rory, 1954---Travel--Middle East. 2. MacLean, Rory,
1954---Travel--Asia,Central. 3. MacLean, Rory, 1954---Travel--India. 4.
Middle
East--Description and travel. 5. Asia, Central--Description and travel. 6.
India--Description and travel. 7. Middle East--Politics and government--1945-
8.
Asia--Politics and government--1945- I. Title.
  DS10.M23 2009
  915'.0443--dc22
                              2008045918

To the original Intrepids

"From this hour I ordain myself loos'd of limits and imaginary lines"

– Walt Whitman, *Open Road*

PREFACE

Hot wind ripples across the blood-red earth. Airy waves wash over the scorched stones, ruffle the ashen mountains, stir the fabric of elements as a pebble flicked into water. The distant, shimmering vision stops me in my tracks. I stare toward it, past the shells of burnt-out tanks and *fusilli* twists of thick armor plate. The object seems to be suspended in space like a bird or a feather. It is a camel and rider, a helicopter gunship, a levitating Valkyrie. I'm alone in this raw, empty place and it's coming toward me.

As I watch, the spectre transforms itself, reaching down to touch the boiling tarmac road, extending black legs, sprouting tyres. Its flashing eyes become a split windscreen. Its phantom limbs are the arms of men. I bend my ear toward the horizon and the familiar *tick-tick* rents the absolute stillness of the deserted valley.

The old bus rolls out of the heat haze, two dozen Afghan heads craning and calling out of its broken windows at the sight of me by the roadside. Its engine brake thunders the Blue Bird school bus to a stop, enveloping me in voices and dust. When the cloud clears, I'm staring up at the riders, responding to their invitation, about to step onboard.

Then the metal body catches my attention. On impulse, I sweep a strip of grit off its mottled surface. I see the crude "Flying Muslim Coach" logo has been painted over flaking portraits of sultry beauties, their faces scratched out years earlier by Taliban fanatics. I brush away another coat of dirt and discover Russian words beneath the portraits, faded reminders of the Soviet occupation. With both arms, I rub again, pushing back another decade, reaching deeper into the collage and discovering that the Cyrillic characters themselves efface psychedelic, Day-Glo peace symbols.

In the blazing heat, I'm looking for clues, wanting to identify the transiting dreamer who brought the vehicle from the States to Europe and then Asia in the 1960s. Then the driver sounds the horn. Arms reach out to me. Voices beg me to stop cleaning the dirty old bus, assuring me that others will do the job in Herat, asking me to honor them with my company. The conductor, a laughing man with midnight-black hair and a glass eye, pulls his *Leili Leili* jann cassette out of the old stereo. He rifles in the bottom of a chest and clicks another tape, worn and stretched, into the machine.

"Music for you! For you!" he calls in English, cranking up the volume, filling the Valley of Fear with the sound of The Who.

I'm disorientated, laughing with the other men. I hoist my pack on to a shoulder and step onboard the four-wheeled palimpsest, setting off between the war ruins on the road which so many once believed led to a better world.

Turkey

1. I GET AROUND

My wonder at that first step moves me still, that stride into the unknown, that grasping for stars; the open road before me, the Blue Mosque at my back, the Beach Boys in my ear. Ahead stretched six thousand miles, six countries, three world religions spanning West and East along the world's wildest and oldest trail. I was leaving ordered Europe, crossing Turkey and chameleon Iran, reaching through reopened Afghanistan, falling into the ferment of India and lifting myself toward the pure, clean Himalayas, to Nepal and the trail's end.

All my life I have wandered. When I was a boy, I rambled away from home after school, straying along unfamiliar streets, roaming off into parks and meadows to climb trees, build camps and talk to strangers. The world felt vast, diverse and safe. I was as free as a leaf in the wind, as long as I came back in time for supper. Day after day I discovered the wonder in my neighborhood, in the streets and fields beyond, spiralling ever further away from the familiar.

My father, too, loved to roam. Night after night, he came into my room and told me to get dressed. We climbed into the car and started out for Florida, California, even Mexico, with me aged eight or nine driving on his lap. He cranked up the radio and hurtled us on our way with "I Get Around", "Magic Carpet Ride", "Gates of Eden". Together we sang along to Dylan, the Stones, ten dozen Golden Oldie stations along the endless dark Interstates. The next morning, when I awoke, we found ourselves blinking in the sharp daylight of Times Square or the Eire shore, hundreds of miles from home.

As I grew older, the world changed. People became suspicious of unfamiliar streets and lonely parks. We no longer trusted in the kindness of strangers. We eyed our fellow man warily rather than looked out for him.

We divided society into "them" and "us", our optimistic innocence lost as we exiled ourselves from Eden at home and abroad. Those dazzling, high-volume night flights with my father had left me both enchanted by and wary of spontaneity. But I hungered for the perfect destination that he and I had never reached. I still wandered along the trail of wonders, believing in a family of man, yearning to complete the greatest journey bopping to the best songs of all time.

I knew of the historical importance of the Asia overland route: part Silk Road, part web of desert caravan tracks, above all, a critical cultural highway. For over 1,700 years the trail had been the principal link between Europe and Asia, before it was closed by sea trade and the Ming dynasty. Alexander the Great, the Persians, Mohammed and Marco Polo had all trekked along its dusty path. Last winter, I read about them and the trail's role in the interchange of ideas, spices and faith. I considered how a dozen religions – including Christianity, Judaism, Buddhism and Hinduism—had coexisted along the route until the coming of Islam. I pored over diligent tomes on British colonialism and the stupid lines drawn on maps which divide the Middle East.

Those hard, old journeys then carried me forward to the Now, or Nearly Now, to the original independent travellers, the Beats, hippies and *Intrepids,* the kids who adopted the trail in the 1960s. They were the ones whose freedom I envied, whose spontaneity attracted and haunted me, whose bewitching optimism today seems as lost as my once-safe world. I wanted to know why this route became *the* journey of their age. I needed to put my finger on the triggering events which shot them—and so us all—along the road. I had to understand how that decade affected the countries traversed, sweeping the region through extraordinary changes, casting such long shadows over our own fearful and protective era.

Then spring came, the great time of traveling, and I flew to Istanbul. I stood before the Blue Mosque and the Milion, the lone stone Roman pillar, worn and fragmented, from which all road distances were once measured. I took that first step. I didn't realize this *Journey to the East* would be my *Pilgrim's Progress* "from this World to that which is to come". I couldn't see yet that I was Goldmund cutting free of Narziss. Sal Paradise running down the razor-edge of time. A Merry Prankster *on* the bus, tootling the multitudes, rolling up for the real Magical Mystery Tour. I simply trusted that my hidden *somewhere* lay on the road ahead; the perfect place somehow always known to us. All I had to do was reach out for it, to outrun life, to follow one great red line across Asia to the wild beating of my heart.

I looked up at the blue sky into which the swallows were rising and thought: Here it began. Here I begin.

2. HIPPIE HIPPIE SHAKE

The Bosphorus surges between the tail of Europe and toe of Asia, dipping, rising, rushing from the Black Sea to a silver-mirrored Marmara. Dancing ferries defy the noon-hot current, cutting between churning tankers, skeins of shearwater and two continents. Their almond-eyed passengers wash ashore, over decaying sea-walls caked with moss and mussels, around bobbing skiffs of fishermen flogging fried-fish sandwiches, into the great, jumbled capital of three empires.

Istanbul is among the oldest inhabited cities, a metropolis founded on the advice of Apollo's oracle, the western gateway of the Silk Road since the sixth century. Its pivotal location, astride the Bosphorus, flanking the scimitar-shaped Golden Horn, was the most strategic in the ancient world. In its time, "the City" was occupied by Persia, Alexander and Rome, rising to Christian glory after Constantine, defying Muslim invaders for almost a thousand years. Under the Ottomans it held sway over territories stretching from Hungary to the Persian Gulf, from North Africa to the Caucasus. Today, this is where the modern world's fault lines meet: between rich and poor, democracy and the authoritarian, Islam and the West.

At Topkapı Palace, I'm scribbling descriptions of the rushing faces of the city. Silver sunlight flashes off the dark waters. The *muezzin* calls the faithful to prayer. I'm deep in thought, minding my own business, when an astoundingly beautiful woman limps out of the crowd and says to me, "There should be a candle..." Radiant green eyes. Purple tie-dyed blouse. Ebony walking-stick. "...an eternal flame burning where a desiccated girl first popped her cork."

"Popped her cork?" I ask, stopped in mid-sentence. The sign says no open fires are permitted near the pavilions of the Imperial Terrace, but the luminous stranger seems to spark with pyrotechnic energy.

"Use your imagination, Jack," she snorts, turning away her hoary head and letting loose a raunchy laugh.

She's pushing seventy. Her thick grey hair is the color of a seal's coat. Her long, soft features seem to have been cast in wet clay by a Cubist sculptor during a monsoon. Her gravelly London accent has been smoothed by Californian surf and sand.

"At night we'd steal over that wall, sneak through the harem garden and make love here,' she coos, stroking the sultan's divan with a lingering touch, grasping hold of one of the domed canopy's slim bronze pillars. "So the first eternal flame goes here."

I look away from her love-nest *iftariye*, dazzled by opulent sweeps of marble so white that I have to screw up my eyes, but the bright old bird points across the shallow mirror pools to the Baghdad Kiosk and goes on, "We made love there too." The Terrace of the Favorites. "And there." *Sünnet Odası*, or the Circumcision Room, built for Sultan Ibrahim in 1642 to celebrate the circumcision rites of his first son, the future Mehmet IV. "And there." I hope at least the Pavilion of the Holy Mantle—with its relics of the Prophet (Peace be upon Him) and Moses' walking stick—had been spared her enthusiasm.

"I'm working," I tell her, trying to revive my train of thought.

"There must also be lights in the park," she insists, her iridescent eyes changing color as she steadies herself on the carved balustrade. Jade green. Liquid turquoise. "As well as at the Gülhane, up the Maiden's Tower, in Cappadocia, on Mount Ararat..."

With wheeling gestures, she flings imaginary candles off the palace walls. The flames, fiery points of passion burnt in time, trace a line between the needle minarets and golden domes, over the plane trees and the fast-flowing sea, up the low stone hills of the Asian shore and away to the East.

"Everywhere," she says, excited by her memories, pulling off her feathered felt hat, embracing the vista in slender arms and pivoting on her toes.

"We named our positions after the cities of Asia: riding the Kabul, up the Khyber, doing the Bam-bam-bamiyan. Check it out, Jack; you have to figure out which one was which."

I ask her, "When was this?"

"My Summer of Love."

And she starts to cry. Great, crystal raindrop tears glinting in the sun, collecting in little pools where her spectacles rest against her cheeks, ruining her mascara, hissing on the searing white marble. I look down at my notes to cover my surprise as much as her embarrassment. Then I smell smoke. I turn back to the woman. "My name isn't Jack," I say.

But she's gone, leaving a single tea-light twinkling on the divan.

In the early sixties, the first Intrepids began arriving in Istanbul in small numbers, finding a sweet, melancholy city of ramshackle wooden houses and crumbling city walls, without tourists or touts. Old men in baggy trousers idled away afternoons in backstreet coffeehouses. Taxi drivers wore ill-cut Western suits, chewed gum and drank opiate wine. Fearsome razor-sellers worked the piers. Diesel smoke rose from weathered freighters. The oily air smelt of charcoal and mackerel. Along the cobblestone pavements, peddlers stirred steaming cauldrons of sweet corn cobs. Tailors slithered on the heels of their slippers, bent under the weight of dozens of leather jackets. The bazaar—where public letter-writers typed on Coronas—wasn't yet a gift-shop warehouse. Sultanahmet hadn't become a sightseers' ghetto. The neighboring slopes and hills were still bare of buildings. With rainbow patches on their jeans or maple leaves on their backpacks, the travelers hung out at the first hostels, played guitars together on the steps of the Blue Mosque, smoked hubble-bubbles under the cypress trees before driving their battered VW Campers and Morris Minors on to the rusty Bosphorus ferry.

To catch a clearer glimpse of those years, I take a city bus along the Golden Horn, past shattered remnants of Byzantine sea palaces and fragments of *yalı* boathouses. Ships' whistles and nasal love songs echo off the few remaining timber buildings, their blackened "gingerbread" lattices pressed and cracked between new concrete tenements.

Ersin Kalkan is a lean, fifty-five-year-old journalist with deep-set brown eyes, rough porous skin and fleshy boxer's lips. In the dusk, we sit in his compact walled garden of orange trees and damp old stones, drinking coffee beneath the darting swallows.

Istanbul, he tells me, marks the point where Asia and Europe both begin and end. The city was founded in 660 BC by colonists from Megara and Athens, he says. In AD 326 the Emperor Constantine shifted the capital of the Roman Empire here from Italy. In 1265, Princess Maria Palaeologina was sent from the church next door to Persia to wed the Great Khan of the Mongols, whom she converted to Christianity. In the 1920s, Atatürk founded the Republic out of the devastated Ottoman Empire and decreed that Turkish would henceforth be written in a modified Latin, not Arabic, script. He inaugurated an era of fervent nationalism which frustrated the cause of the caliphate until the close of the twentieth century.

In return, I tell Kalkan that the city's tangled marriage of East and West has already moved me: in Byzantium's ruins overlaid by Mehmet's serene mosques, along the narrow, cobbled streets where Janissaries once walked and now flashy European Union kiosks stand, in my fleeting, time-warp encounter on the Imperial Terrace.

"Are you sure she wasn't a ghost?" he asks me with a sudden smile. "There are many ghosts in Istanbul: Trojans, Crusaders, Californians."

I shake my head. "We didn't dwell on the spiritual. Her main interest seemed to be fornication."

Kalkan tips back his head and stares for a long moment into the sky. Then, he says in a voice filled with feeling, "To us, hippies were the fireworks of freedom. They were ... exotic."

"As you would have been to them."

"Every night I went to Sultanahmet to meet them."

"To practice your English?" I ask.

"To see what they were reading," he says, surprising me, lighting another Marlboro. "Ginsberg, for example, who had the courage to put up his head and insult the American system, a system which to us was Protestantism and God."

Allen Ginsberg was the bearded Beat poet whose enduring anti-authoritarianism made him a spokesman for the generation. His prophetic work—like the hippie trail itself—would come to link the Beats to the Beatles, *On the Road* to "The Long and Winding Road", karma to Coca-Cola, transcendence to terrorism.

"'America I'm putting my queer shoulder to the wheel,'" Kalkan quotes from memory, nodding with new enthusiasm.

"I didn't know young Turks had even heard of the Beats," I say with sharp delight.

"Come on. Ginsberg's poetry emboldened dozens of our best writers: Can Yücel, Ece Ayhan, Cemal Süreyya. Dylan inspired Erkin Koray, the father of Turkish protest music. Joan Baez played a concert here. Their example gave us courage to voice our dissent," he insists, thinking of Turkey's decade of rapacious military dictatorship. "In those hard years, words and lyrics were a vital social and intellectual resource."

"As they were in the West," I say, leaning forward and shifting my chair on the stones, indulging our shared passion. "People really believed that music could change the world."

"At times, dreams are as important as bread."

Over salted slivers of anchovy flecked with garlic and thyme, I tell Kalkan about the Grand Tourists, precursors of the Intrepids. After the Napoleonic Wars, young Englishmen, for the most part wealthy Romantics, travelled in their numbers to Rome and Greece, then the crossroads of classical and contemporary culture. On horseback, by bone-rattling carriage and in the shadow of the Pantheon, their formative experiences established the concept of travel as an adventure of the self as well as a means of gathering knowledge. Like the hippies who followed them a century and a half later, the Grand Tourists looked abroad for models for political reform and a free-love alternative to Christianity. Both groups aimed to learn and extract pleasure from "the foreign". Most of all, they travelled to be transformed.

"The Grand Tourists changed Regency society like the sixties changed the West," I tell him. 'The counterculture searched for a meaning of life outside the old institutions. Are you saying the travelers changed Turkey too?"

This is my first chance to examine the effect of the Intrepids on the peoples along the trail.

"We saw hippies as revolutionaries," replies Kalkan. "They traveled without money, rejected materialism, cut their relationship with career and government. Their objective was to know themselves."

"But most critics think they were naive and cultish," I say, at once envious and wary of their search for themselves. "Flower Power can be seen as sentimental Romanticism."

"Their liberal values were innocent," he tells me, "and they spread in a soft way throughout Turkish society. Our women began to feel they had the freedom to act as they wished. Young villagers re-evaluated their culture because of hippies' love of native clothing. They showed that there was a way of finding peaceful solutions to problems. They helped us to see that the world belongs to the people: wherever you put your feet is home."

"Many of them were stoned out of their heads."

'But all of them had flowers in their hair. Philosophical flowers,' he nods, lifting his hands as he talks, as if balancing ideas. "And their greatest effect was *after* their journey."

"On America and Europe?"

"Europe used to be just one color: white. It used to have one religion: Christianity. The West believed that world history began with Greece and Rome. As you say, the hippies were curious for different cultures. From us, they learnt that Mesopotamia – here in Turkey and the Middle East – was the mother of all civilization. They carried home with them a *kilim* woven from different beliefs: threads of Islam, sky-blue of Buddhist prayer flags, silver from Hindu temple bells."

"Like the Romantics and neo-classicism," I point out. "The frontier of the exotic was simply pushed further east, the imaginative potency of Italy replaced by India. Asia was the new touchstone of the ancient."

"Their travels made Europe aware of color, of our common heritage. In a way, humanity was reborn."

Kalkan laughs once more, perhaps at himself, perhaps at adolescent ideals, and runs his hands over his close-cropped, ink-black hair.

"For me, it was because of the hippies – not Silk Road traders or colonists – that most Westerners discovered the East."

A nightingale sings in the cedars and the evening's mist rises from the strait. Waves of cool air flow around us heavy with the scent of honeysuckle and judas blossoms. Green leaves rustle behind a wooden railing. A sleek, stray cat slips behind the pots and across the top of a wall. In the old Greek house, Kalkan's mother serves us yoghurt soup with mint. Afterwards, we return to the garden for tea and more conversation by the pale light of stars.

Some time after midnight I complete my first notebook and thank Kalkan for his time. He dips his boxer's head and thanks me for indulging his memories of flowers and fireworks. He jots down the names of friends in Ankara and Cappadocia who might be willing to help me. We shake hands at the door. I hesitate before turning away.

"How did other Turks – apart from young liberals like yourself – take to the first travellers?" I ask him. I knew that many single hitchhikers were raped and at least one German couple murdered along the road. I think of the bombs which have rocked Mediterranean resorts in recent years.

"For twenty-seven centuries, Istanbul hungered for new ideas," he answers me.

In the year Ginsberg published *Howl*, cosmopolitan Istanbul had a population of one million: Armenians, Greeks, Jews, the sons of old Byzantine families and daughters of Ottoman households.

"But today the *dağlı* – the villagers from the mountains – do not welcome change."

Turkey's years of political turmoil ended in 1983 when prime minister Turgut Özal, a former World Bank economist, liberalized the economy and stimulated a business and tourism boom. The city's population grew tenfold, the vast majority of new residents migrants from rural Anatolia. But many of the incomers – despite the influence of travellers, television and work in Germany – remained rooted in an earlier century. An angry minority grew embittered by their country's race to become Western.

"The *dağlı* are scared, by the size of the city, by liberal society, by America's ways. They retreat into insular communities. They don't want reform. Kalkan fixes his eyes on me. "They fight to survive."

I walk down the uneven streets. A line of late-night washing drifts in a roofless ruin. I cross the Golden Horn at Galata Bridge, still bristling with fishing rods despite the hour, and climb into a hilly neighborhood of stepped streets and Maritime pines cradled in the Bosphorus's arms. As I walk, I think of the Grand Tourists and the first Intrepids, about the sixties impulse to reinvent the world and today's anxious acceptance of one's place in it. Law students play backgammon under the vines. A yawning, veiled woman pushes a wakeful child on a swing. A sleepless mussel-seller mops his neck with a cloth.

Istanbul touches me in the fluid Arabic script of its Iznik tiles, in its expressways built over Roman roads, in a lamb feeding on the grass precincts of a mosque. Yet for all its richness, I'm pursued by a gnawing hollowness of heart. Part of my attraction to the sixties is that era's reverence for immediacy, for self-surprise, for the imperative to Be Here Now. Most of the time, I find it hard to seize the moment, to live every act as if it were my last. I reflect on the day, simplifying and eliminating experiences to understand exactly what stirred me, and recognize how shaken I am by the chance meeting with the dippy, weeping hippie. I worry that I lost an opportunity by letting her go.

At that moment, a flash of light catches my eye. I look up, realizing in an instant that I want to see her line of candle flames sweep across the inky sky. Instead I watch the landing lights of a descending aircraft.

I buy a kebab and crash out in my room.

3. THE TIMES THEY ARE A-CHANGIN'

The beginnings are easy to trace.

First, *On the Road* with Jack Kerouac, his soul stripped naked, his body hungry for release, his heart "mad to live, mad to talk, mad to be saved, desirous of everything at the same time".

Next, in New York on Bleeker Street at the Mills Hotel, where Allen Ginsberg, aged twenty-four, is "blowing Jack", coming out of the conformist 1950s and into the rebellious, hopeful decade.

Then, on MacDougal at the Rienzi and the Gaslight with bongo-beaters and wide-eyed runaways in turtlenecks reading frayed copies of Kierkegaard and asking, "Like, where do we go from here?" Their parents survived the Depression, came home from Normandy and Guam, took shelter in materialism and suburbia.

Now, poets like Gregory Corso and Lawrence Ferlinghetti reject the spiritual emptiness of their unexamined lives, plead for the resurrection of America's soul, rail against the "concrete continent, spaced with bland billboards, illustrating imbecile illusions of happiness".

"Beyond all laws, it is our stunted consciousness that imprisons us, and we suffer from a consequent hunger of the spirit," writes novelist John Clellon Holmes, friend of Kerouac and Ginsberg. "How are we to break out of this prison? How do we let the spirit prosper so that the blistered desert we are making of the world can flower again?"

The new generation sets out to change the world by changing itself, and not only in rich, post-war America. On the Mersey and in London, bomb-blitzed and ration-grey, down at Canning Dock and Wardour Street, ravers and hipsters begin the transformation. The Quarry Men play the Cavern Club. The Who grind out "My Generation" at the Marquee. Mods make five-bob deals at the Flamingo. Michael Horovitz launches *New Departures* "to make poetry and to realize visions in the way Blake realized his

Jerusalem". On Eel Pie Island in the Thames – once a Victorian pleasure garden – sixteen-year-old girls listen to John Mayall, buy the *International Times* at the Barmy Arms, then hurry home to finish their homework.

Teenagers are hacked off with the tired old ways and days. Economic prosperity and the welfare state have liberated them. They're casual about jobs, passionate about ideas, hungry for innovation. At Better Books on Charing Cross Road and on the BBC, they tune into Ginsberg chanting about "angelheaded hipsters burning for the ancient heavenly connection":

World world world...
Imagine the future...

London re-creates itself as a city of and for the young. East End boys sport winklepickers and drainpipe jeans. Capital punishment is suspended. National Service ends. Marianne Faithful, singer and girlfriend of Mick Jagger, writes about never renouncing youthful hedonism in favor of the insane world of adulthood. In art schools and at the 2-Is coffee bar, from dole-poor Notting Hill to hip Chelsea, kids abandon their parents' Kingdom Come of postponed pleasure to catch hold of the living, transient world. They sing love songs and never doubt the reach of their grasp. Their decade unfolds with a *feeling*, "out here at night, free, with the motor running and the adrenaline flowing," as writes Tom Wolfe. A *feeling* that it is "very Heaven to be the first wave of the most extraordinary kids in the history of the world". Kids who face no unemployment, who fear no hunger, who have the chance to imagine no boundaries; a footloose generation devoted to the acquisition of experience and self-knowledge.

At home in Minnesota, Dylan reads Kerouac's *Mexico City Blues*. "It blew my mind," he says, "because it was the first poetry which spoke my own language." That same year, Maharishi Mahesh Yogi brings his simple form of meditation from the Himalayas to the West. In Arizona the next spring, campaigner Margaret Sanger witnesses her dream become reality, the approval of the birth-control pill. Three months later, John, Paul, George and Ringo, appearing as the Beatles for the first time, play "Whole Lotta Shakin' Goin' On" at the Indra Club in Hamburg.

In Turkey, the new, searching consciousness awakes when Erkin Ko-ray sings his first protest song. In Tehran, the women's magazine *Zan-e Rooz* rejoices in youth by launching a Miss Iran competition. In Afghani-stan, the country's first democratic constitution establishes basic liberties, permitting student demonstrations and giving rise to thirty-three inde-pendent publications.

In India, young people embrace political and spiritual regeneration as well as rock 'n' roll. Nehru's socialist democracy champions an alternative Third Way that is neither dictatorial Soviet egalitarianism nor cold-hearted American capitalism. The caste system is reformed and feudal estates are discarded along with imperial subjugation. A generation adopts the Nehru jacket to celebrate the triumph of self-determination over colonialism.

In Nepal, the beginning is marked with the completion of the first road from the outside world to nirvana, in the same year that Hermann Hesse's *Journey to the East* is published in English. Two years later, the first Boeing 707 Clipper Jet lifts off from New York for Europe, doubling speed and halving fares across the Atlantic.

In 1960, Kennedy is elected, the first US president to be born in the twentieth century. This virile, attractive leader articulates the lofty values and poignant ambitions of the utopian revolution, heralding the opening of the New Frontier. At his inaugural address, he proclaims, "Let the word go forth from this time and place to friend and foe alike that the torch has been passed to a new generation." His brother Bobby helps to shine its light beyond America's shores. "There is discrimination in this world, and slavery, and slaughter and starvation," he says. "The answer is to rely upon youth – not a time of life but a state of mind, a temper of will, a quality of imagination, a predominance of courage over timidity."

Kids. Their decade begins all over Marshall McLuhan's "global vil-lage": on the Alabama bus where Rosa Parks refuses to give up her seat to a white passenger; at the first Greensboro Civil Rights sit-in when four black freshmen sing "We Shall Overcome"; in Washington with the first $5 donation to the National Organization for Women; in Greenwich Vil-lage at the gay Stonewall Inn; off Sunset Boulevard where novelist Aldous Huxley flings open the *Doors of Perception* on his first mescaline trip; on damp, impassioned Aldermaston CND marches; among the Paris Left

Bank duffel-coat clique listening to Moustaki's *Métèque*; in dreamin' California when restless pioneer Ken Kesey fires up his psychedelic school bus; and, of course, in the music.

"His voice is crude, his appearance scruffy and as a performer he lacks all traces of a professional," writes *Village Voice* of an early Dylan performance. "But one brief listening to the emotional understatement in his voice emphasizes the power of his lyrics and his genuine concern for the state of the world."

Dylan sings "The Times They are a-Changin'" at Newport. Peter, Paul and Mary record 'Leaving on a Jet Plane'. Ray Charles instructs, "Hit the Road, Jack". On both sides of the Atlantic, lyrics inspire, guide – or in some cases misguide – the search for a new way of living.

Roger McGuinn of the Byrds speaks of the camaraderie between musicians as "a sort of international code going back and forth through records". In a Manhattan coffeehouse, Dylan writes "Blowin' in the Wind", its melody derived from a black spiritual "No More Auction Block for Me". His "Talkin' New York" inspires Pete Townsend's "My Generation". After living in India, Jorma Kaukonen, Jefferson Airplane's lead guitarist, brings Asian tonality to psychedelic music. Dylan's ability to write profound songs that huge crowds can sing encourages John Lennon to pen "Give Peace a Chance". Keith Richards derives the riff of "(I Can't Get No) Satisfaction" from Martha and the Vandellas' "Dancing in the Street". When Ginsberg first hears "I Want to Hold Your Hand", he shocks his New York confrères by jumping to his feet to dance. Music and literature chronicle the generation's desire to love one another and all mankind.

"Our goal was not only the East, or rather the East was not only a country and something geographical," writes Hesse in *Journey to the East*, "but it was the home and youth of the soul, it was everywhere and nowhere, it was the union of all times."

4. I SAW HER STANDING THERE

I'm transcribing my notes, laptop surrounded by breakfast plates of honeydew melon, sweet cucumber and saffron-yolk eggs. To ease my labor, there's cherry nectar, tasting sugary and round on the back of the tongue, plus waisted glasses of strong, black Turkish tea. My binder is propped open by a chipped saucer of oregano olives so earthy that I'm tempted to spit the stones on to the grubby floor.

Modern Istanbul's complex geography renders it all but unmappable: three dozen districts swelling over seven hills, no single center, fingered by water, jumbled in time. Age dilutes its fluidity. I can't keep a grip on its currents of slippery politics, of chaotic transport, of residents drawn together to argue, talk and trade. Its light is maritime, a sea lies over each shoulder, yet the city is 2,000 miles from any ocean. A ten-minute stroll takes me from a sleepy Greek fishing village to a Hapsburg cul-de-sac reminiscent of a Klimt painting. Across the horizon surge waves of new world tower blocks. In the expanding spiral of my wandering, I find its anarchic streets, its shifting colors, its millions of voices, its dreams of a legendary past at once foreign and familiar.

I'm at the Pudding Shop, the first meeting point on the trail. In 1957, two brothers from the Black Sea, Namık and Idris Çolpan, opened the *Lâle Pastanesi* across from Istanbul's Blue Mosque. For a couple of years, well-to-do Turks stopped by for frothy black *kahve* and honey-soaked *baklava* topped with green pistachios. Then, the tiny, open-fronted patisserie attracted the attention of the early overlanders, both because of its central location and their sugar-craving munchies. Overnight, the travellers made the *Lâle* their place, renaming it the Pudding Shop. Outside its door, London double-deckers and fried-out Kombis parked along the Hippodrome. Pop music played in its garden. The well-to-do Turks stood outside, their mouths agape, watching their sons and nephews – among them Ersin Kalkan – drink coffee with paradise-bound freaks in Apache headbands and paisley waistcoats.

Today, the cafeteria is indistinguishable from a dozen of its neighbors, apart from a few faded sixties photographs tacked on the rear wall. Beneath them, a handful of Lycra-clad Danish civil servants procrastinate over desiccated pizzas and *köfte* meatballs. At the next table, a sunburnt Englishman nurses an early Troy Pilsner.

"In your book you can write that the hippies discovered Turkey," Adem Colpan tells me a few minutes later.

"And that Turkish tourism started in our *pastane*," adds Namık, as he and his nephew join me at my table.

"Our country had no tourism policy, no telephones, no information in those years," Adem explains, turning his neat, twirling moustache with long, manicured nails. "My uncle and father, because of their personalities, wanted to help our young guests to find their way. So they stuck announcements on the wall about the nearest Turkish bath and the next boat to Antalya."

"Our noticeboard was the first signpost along the trail," confirms Namık.

On it, kids traded travel advice, found the address of the Iranian Embassy and checked out the safest route through Afghanistan. "Gentle deviant, 21, seeks guitar-playing chick ready to set out for mystical East," read one message. "Anyone know where to crash in Kabul?" asked another. At times, the notices were so thickly layered that nails rather than tacks had to be used to post them on the board. Today, the messages themselves, as the first scribblings of an oral tradition, are nearly all lost.

"We in return are grateful to the hippies," concedes Adem. A mild sweetness has been instilled in him by a lifetime of serving desserts. "Because they taught us how to make Nescafé."

The Pudding Shop was probably the first café east of Dover to serve Nescafé, delivered by bus drivers who refilled the tins for the return journey with hands of Afghan Black or Lebanese Gold.

"The hippies didn't want to drink Turkish coffee," he goes on, with no hint of irony. "They wanted to eat ice cream and macaroni."

"And *sütlaç*," I remind them. Sweet baked rice pudding.

"My father always said to me, " 'If we don't live our dream, why live?'

That is why we are still here."

By 1969, the Pudding Shop was so popular that a refectory and an authentic-looking wooden façade were added. The self-service counter was introduced in the seventies. As travellers morphed into tourists, the Çol-pans started writing bus tickets and making hotel bookings, charging a dollar for each service, pioneers of a national industry which now serves 12 million visitors every year.

I ask if any of their neighbors remain from the era; Sitki Yener, for example, the self-styled Turkish "King of the Hippies" with sweeping cloak, long black locks and beard. On his *pastane's* door, he hung a bilingual sign demanding universal free love. He painted the café walls with psychedelic mandalas and waived the bills of needy pilgrims. More than once, the newspapers carried photographs of him after he had been beaten by the police.

Adem shakes his head. "Sitki worked next door for twenty-six years but, in the end, his son wanted nothing to do with the restaurant. He was evicted and died of stomach cancer in Ankara."

"Now the East has come to the West," says Namık. "Sitki's is Turkey's first Indian restaurant."

I ask Adem about business.

"Better not to say," sighs Namık.

"This year has been slow," Adem admits, speaking softly as he's drawn back to the present day. Only two other tables are in use. Tourism is down across the region since the Second Gulf War. "I am anxious for the future."

"Travelers follow guidebooks today," I say, getting him wrong. "A good recommendation can make a place. *Remake* a place. You know, in Hué in Vietnam, there are two adjacent restaurants, both with deaf-mute proprietors and both claiming to be the *Lonely Planet* original."

Adem shakes his head.

"I grew up behind that counter, learning about the world from curious tourists," he says in a sorrowful voice, looking across the street, his eyes focusing long-range. "Now, different Westerners come to Asia; first to Afghanistan, then Iraq; next, I am thinking, to Iran, to Syria and maybe even to Turkey."

I feel my heart sink.

"These visitors come not because they are open to different cultures," he goes on, "but because they are hungry for power, for oil. They turn Babylon into a military camp. They kill innocent Muslims in Kabul and Baghdad and say only 'Sorry.'" He lowers his eyes. He doesn't raise his voice. "All my life I am an atheist. Please understand this offence is the one thing which will make me go to the mosque."

I look out on the summit of Istanbul's First Hill and its monuments of past empires. I wonder how many Turks share my genial hosts' anger? How many Muslims have been alienated by the latest Western incursions in the Middle East and Central Asia?

The broad dome of Haghia Sophia, once the greatest church in Christendom, then Islam's largest mosque and now a museum, rises beyond a Softie ice-cream machine. In cellars beneath the Four Seasons Hotel, lions were kept to fight Roman gladiators. Next door stands the Spiral Column from the Delphic Temple of Apollo – in front of which limps the luminous stranger.

"Synchronicity spoken here!" wrote Tom Wolfe in *The Electric Kool-Aid Acid Test*, a resonant literary link between Beat epoch and pop culture. I'm not going to miss my chance again.

I thank the Çolpans for their time, pass on their offer of a plate of macaroni and snap shut my laptop. By the time I'm on my feet, the woman is already halfway down the hill, striking her walking stick on the cobbles with every step. I chase after her toward the park.

"Hey, Jack," she says as I fall in beside her.

"I saw you from the Pudding Shop."

"They painted out the peace symbol," she says, swinging her head, failing to prevent strands of hair escaping their purple-feather clip.

"What peace symbol?"

"The one that used to be on their back wall. They've covered it with a dollar-bill clock. I sure am glad Jill didn't see that."

"Jill?" The name doesn't mean a thing to me.

"Last month she called and asked if I wanted to come back here with her on a crusties' tour. Like, can you imagine me on a *tour*?"

"Not easily."

"I'd rather sniff around and find my own funky spots. But her call got me thinking. With all the bad shit that's gone down this year, I decided to chase my own ghosts; starting here."

Memories tend to age with people, yet the stranger's dated patter suggests strong feelings root her to the sixties. I look at her as she fixes her open, putty face on a line of dilapidated buildings. One particular dirty blue ruin – its windows barred, its metal shutters warped by vandals – holds her attention.

"That's the Gülhane," she tells me, waving a beaded wrist.

I stare in wonder at the lost Atlantis of the hippie trail. "I thought it was knocked down years ago," I gasp.

The Gülhane was the Intrepids' favored hostel for almost two decades. Here, roof space could be had for fifty cents a night and a first bout of dysentery endured. Here, also, lived junkies and prostitutes.

"In the sixties, on my first morning in town, a hand reached out of that open door and gave me a huge J. One toke and I was blasted for three hours. Magical things happened here if you went with the flow."

"Assuming you weren't busted first."

"Istanbul seemed so fantastic back then," she goes on. "Boys singing in the souks, cripples chipping away at lumps of crystalized sugar, travelers tie-dyed to the hilt. I'd walk into Sitki's, order a waterpipe, just like the Turks did, and he'd ask 'With or without?' Meaning with or without *hashash*, as they called it. All night we'd argue about Vietnam. Man," she says, "this town had good vibes."

The woman lowers her big mauve spectacles and turns her wide feline eyes on me. I notice that her long fingernails are painted purple.

"There's a karmic connection between us," she whispers, her husky voice sincere and emotional. "I don't know what it is but, for sure, by meeting twice we're in this together."

I remember her tears on the Imperial Terrace. I sense a darkness inside her. I hope her reminiscences aren't about to bring on an acid flashback. But her undiluted audacity makes me laugh out loud. I tell her my name.

"Call me Penny," she says.

Penny's soft hands are always moving, spinning her ebony stick, lighting cigarettes, twisting her purple beads and eight rings: god's-eyes, moonstones and an *I Ching* signet. Her hourglass figure has timed out into a skittle shape. Yet her slim body, though unbalanced by a replacement hip, retains a startling beauty which no puffing of flesh, no number of age lines, can erase.

"Let's check out the park," she says, reining back her feelings.

Beyond the dirty shell of the hostel, Gülhane Park spreads cool and green down to the Bosphorus. The high embankment walls of the palace, through which Penny once stole to copulate, have been rebuilt. Local couples still meet at the foot of them, under the broad-leaved plane trees, though they tend to sit a hand's width apart. Young mothers push Mamas and Papas prams along the cobbled pathways where Penny sang "Dream a Little Dream".

As we pass through the arched gateway next to the Sublime Porte, I ask her what "bad shit" has gone down this year. Instead of answering me, she says, "Jill – the friend who tried to rope me into a tour – and I used to be terrific pals. She had a shop in San Francisco full of amazing things like strobe lamps and rose-tinted glasses made with prisms."

A lopsided smile rises on her face like a sickle moon.

"I remember one morning tripping together down Haight Street. You know, at the bottom where it curves round..."

"I know it," I say, warming to her story, picturing Haight-Ashbury *circa* 1964: staggers of open bay windows, civil rights banners, customized Harley choppers and bell-bottomed bohos carrying guitars and zonked to the eyeballs.

"We'd taken a smidgen of LSD, just a tiny little bit under our tongues, homeopathically you might say, like the tip of the little finger. At the bottom of the hill there was a flower shop and a little lady with a mauve rinse selling daisies: thirty cents a bunch. They were beginning to wilt and I told her she should be giving them away, but she shook her mauve head and insisted on the full price. So we paid and, you know, it felt so good, two young chicks on a sunny Californian morning, that we started giving the flowers away. We gave one to a policeman, who put it in his cap. Jill handed a bunch to some mailmen. I gave one to a guy who was a journalist. 'Hey, what are you?' he asked us. 'Flower girls or something?'"

I stare at Penny, an original flower child.

"It was no big deal," she says without hesitation. "Lots of people were doing it. Jill and I handed out flowers again the next day. Ours was a small community and the idea spread quickly. Wasn't much later that everyone started calling it Flower Power."

A uniformed park warden shoos a clutch of children off the grass. Turkish families picnic beside spitting charcoal grills, reading newspaper reports about the "war on terror" and US troops on their border.

Penny thrusts out her cane and lowers herself on to a bench. She puts up her good leg, showing off venerable leather boots – hand-tooled in Mexico – which hurt her hip like hell when she pulls them on, but she's never giving them up. She fixes me in her gaze and asks me to tell her about myself. I've hardly begun when she interrupts.

"You're heading further east?"

"All the way to Kathmandu," I reply.

"Are you stopping in Cappadocia?"

"Didn't everyone?" I say. "It's in all the guidebooks."

Five hundred miles east of Istanbul, the strange Anatolian valley was the second essential stop along the route.

"You know, when I was young, there was no *Lonely Planet*. We travelled without guides."

"Apart from the odd guru," I remind her.

"Look at yourself, Jack," she sniggers, glowing now. "You're a good-looking boy. You've got clear eyes, supple limbs, a grace of movement and manner..."

"Sounds like *Siddhartha*."

"You *have* done your reading," she laughs. On the trail, most Intrepids read Hesse's story of the wandering ascetic's search for meaning in life. 'Like Siddhartha, you have to learn to follow your own road."

"You realize the personal quest isn't any longer a prerequisite for this journey?" I tell her. But when I see her regret, I soften my tone. "I'm writing a book. I don't have time to sit under a banyan tree reaching for enlightenment."

Without warning, Penny stretches out to touch the back of my hand. The stranger's spontaneity shakes me. "You asked me about the shit," she says, a needy tremble again in her voice. "There have been ... changes at home."

"Changes?" I ask. She holds my gaze and a shiver runs up my spine. I imagine a flash of fireworks once more. Suddenly I want to know more about her.

"I'll tell you on the bus."

"What bus?"

"I'll also tell you about Kesey."

"Ken Kesey?" I say, my voice rising an octave. Kesey was one of the dominant personalities of the hippie era. In 1964, he travelled across America in a converted school bus, staging the Acid Test dances, blowing his and the nation's minds. His journey was another of the cultural precedents for the Asian trail. "You knew Kesey?"

"I crossed the States on his magic bus."

With Neal Cassady at the wheel, on whom Kerouac--bebop Whitman, lonesome traveler--based the central character in *On the Road*.

"Jack," says Penny, "I fancy your company."

I know that the best way to discover a city is to walk it, to stop for a moment, to gaze and to listen. But I did unexpected Istanbul at a run, immersing myself in Friday prayers with Adem Colpan and the Intrepid's favorite *hamam*, taking in both the sacred tomb of Mohammed's standard-bearer and the venue of Petula Clark's 1966 concert, discussing political disaffection in Kalkan's garden and wrapping up the capital of three empires in four days. While I worked, Penny hung out at our hotel, making me humus and chive sandwiches, reading her tarot cards. She also repacked our bags.

"They're overweight with expectation," she told me, "that is, illusion."

Not long after dawn on our last morning, we walked through Beyoğlu's leafy courtyards, smelling washed cobblestones and apple tea, sharing the city with market cats and street-sweepers. Outside the Institut Français, policemen dozed in their patrol car, glasses of *cay* cooling on the roof. A spent clubber slept beneath an exhausted cash machine. Dirt-poor peasant traders from central Anatolia unpacked their meagre sacks of garden vegetables on the pavement of Taksim Square. We checked in at the Metro Express city terminal. Our bus left on time.

On a sunny Thursday morning a few months after our departure, a white van hurried by the Grand Hôtel de Londres, where we had stayed, and crashed through the wrought-iron gates of the nearby British Consulate. The explosion killed twenty-seven, including the consul general and the suicide bomber. Fatih, our deferential hotel manager, ran on to the street screaming as a cloud of yellow smoke blocked out the sun.

5.FEELING GROOVY

Spirals of dust trailed away from Istanbul, kicked up not by nomadic traders' caravans but by Hog Farm commune coaches. Ancient Austins and retired Royal Mail vans staggered on to the Silk Road. Born-again hearses were spurred east by seekers in sandals. Mountain freaks leapt towards Himalaya in rainbow-colored Jeeps. Banners fluttered from rear windows. Pop music tumbled out of open doors. Overlanders called Blossom and Wombat piloted three-ton Bedford lorries through one-mule hamlets. Aboard clapped-out Turkish coaches and converted Top Deck Routemasters, the Intrepids lit sticks of incense and settled back on Habitat cushions, riding in the weirdest procession of unroadworthy vehicles ever to rattle and rock across the face of the earth.

"Whooee, here we go."

Penny, one of the hundreds of thousands who made the singular journey, is leaning across me, staring out of our bus's tinted windows, down over the side of the new Bosphorus Bridge at the sparkling water. Behind us is Europe. Ahead a road sign reads, "Welcome to Asia."

"First time our ferry hit the shore, I yelled, 'Outasight. We're going to Kathmandu!'"

The morning sun, already hot, casts sharp shadows across Istanbul's dense eastern suburbs. A clutch of worshippers mills outside a concrete mosque, husks of sunflower seeds around their feet. Two middle-aged men, a hand on each other's shoulder, stroll along the central reservation. Beside a crash barrier, hawkers flog pirate CDs and leeches, curling in their jars, sold by the dozen for home-bleeding. When Penny first made this journey, only villages and kitchen gardens dotted the long, bare hills.

"I remember crazy colors, wild smells, camels at the side of the road," she thrills. "It was like nothing, *nothing*, I'd ever seen in my life."

In the sixties, young people grew up with the world. They came of age during a period of political and social revolution, in parallel with the space race, in step with the banishing of borders by Boeing and the fear of pregnancy with the Pill. The concurrence of historical events and individual lives convinced them that by changing themselves they could change the planet. It instilled in them a sense of shared destiny. It inspired them to break free of the shackles of bad tradition. Penny's story encapsulates the heady spirit of those times.

Her mother was a fandango-dancing refugee from Guernica. Her father was a West Country structural engineer. She was born into a comfortable north London suburb on the day civil war ended in Spain. The juxtaposition of opposing stars--dizzy leaps, solid foundations and dreamy ideals--stretched her life between the century's extremes.

"My father wanted me to be a bluestocking, God bless him. To raise his grandchildren in Welwyn Garden City," Penny tells me. "Like, get real. Why go to Girton when the whole world was mine?"

She was an independent girl at the grand opening of the teenage epic. Aged seventeen, she wore tight skirts, seamed nylons and jived in the aisles of the Odeon to "Rock Around the Clock". At eighteen, she read Kerouac and embraced his hedonistic search for fulfilment.

Like many of her contemporaries, she enrolled at art college. She worked in Marseille as a studio assistant and introduced tie-dying to Estepona. In 1961, she moved to Morocco and met the former owner of Greenwich Village's Gaslight. He had decamped with other "creative cats" to Tangier to open the first Western coffee bar in Africa. Penny rented a nearby *pasha*'s house, invited Ginsberg and Paul Bowles – author of *The Sheltering Sky* – for tea and sold her paintings to Beat writer Bill Burroughs. With an artist named Tim, she turned on the town with an exhibition called *Your Own Thing*.

"Tim and I created a cultural jam session," she says, spreading a pinch of tin tobacco along a Zig-Zag rolling paper. "With chanting poets, Berber drummers, snake charmers and me naked in a wheelbarrow. A pair of Dadaists dressed as lobsters pushed me around the gallery, smashing into the sponge rubber breast sculpture and big, pink, phallic lollipops. For the climax of the show we all pushed out the doors and ran downhill calling, 'Love! *Amore*! *Liebe*!' Tangier was my first little paradise," she laughs, lighting her rollie and dragging on it. "We wanted to give the world new meaning."

"Did you manage it?" I ask.

"I met a man," she answers, shifting in her seat.

Our coach pauses for breath at a suburban terminal, belching hot exhaust over a muddle of rag merchants and discount satellite-dish shops. A Yörük carpet-dealer, an unhurried provincial couple and two grizzled conscripts climb onboard along with a young mother in black cloak and Nikes. When the bus pulls back on to the wide highway, the mother and her toddler wave at a huddle of faceless tenements, tears in their eyes.

Penny says, "The best thing he ever did for me was to have a tambourine made by gypsies."

"Your first man?" I ask.

"My first husband. It looks a little tired now, but it still has a Grateful Dead ribbon," she says, dropping a flick of ash on my trousers. "Or at least it did."

"You knew the Grateful Dead?"

"I played with them on one track."

"With your first husband?"

"With my second."

About the same time that Ginsberg caught a boat to Athens, before traveling onward to India, Penny's first husband left her a widow.

"No tears, Jack," she instructs me, her bangles ringing as she traces a cross over her heart. "The Dalai Lama teaches that all is transient."

"Did he play with the Grateful Dead too?"

A wheat-brown country unfolds beyond the high-rise neighborhoods. We follow the route of the ancient road, as did Eurasian camel trains and solo hitchhikers, as does a covered woman leading her cow. A cement works sprawls along the blue edge of the Sea of Marmara, salt water washing against the plains, a freighter moored beyond the harvesters.

"Things always happen to me," Penny goes on, turning towards me, her spectacles magnifying her wildly kohled, outsized eyes. "I follow my instincts and end up in happening places: London, Tangier, San Francisco. Only sometimes does stuff go wrong, like it did in Nepal in the end."

"I want to hear about California," I say, and she tells me about Kesey and his magic bus. About the copy of *Journey to the East* on his bookshelf in La Honda. About the links to the trail and Kathmandu.

The bus wheels spin eastwards. The drivers change near a city called Adapazari. The Nike mother sleeps. Her son dances in the aisle. I put on my earphones to "Rock Around the Clock". Alexander the Great travelled this way, Hannibal took his life near here in 182 BC. Along this route marched St Paul, Crusaders and – in due course – luminous Penny.

On the outskirts of Bolu, she starts to snore. We skirt eroded mountains, climb into conifer woods, rise above them on to a spreading plateau which gives way to a second plain, more arid and broader still. A duck-egg-blue reservoir – Sakarya – flares on the horizon. A purple mountain – Sömidiken Dag – shimmers out of the heat. The deserted hills are raw and desolate, daubed by an occasional flush of purple lupins or a tight bounty of green pear trees. I lift my eye above the page to follow the stretching road across a continental vista of timeless steppe.

At the heart of the black Anatolian plateau 280 miles east of Istanbul, Ankara is a modern, planned capital of brushed-steel ministries and car dealerships grafted on to Hittite foundations. Most Intrepids paused here only long enough to visit the Iranian and Afghan embassies. The wind-swept city offered them nothing more uplifting than wide views of a dank malarial plain. We, too, plan to hurry on.

"This place still looks like a dump," yawns Penny, blinking out the window as we pull into the sweeping coach station, its wings of buses stretching out toward all parts of the country. "Last time, we got stuck here for a week waiting for visas."

We have an hour's break before our connecting service so, after settling her in the Yeni restaurant, I visit the offices of the regional coach operator to ask about services a generation ago. Twenty minutes before departure, I'm back at the restaurant. But she isn't at the Yeni. I look at the departure gate. I ask in the waiting room. I call by the tourist police. She's nowhere to be found.

Then I spot her sitting cross-legged on the floor laughing with four Western kids.

"We've got seven minutes until the bus leaves," I tell Penny, picking up her pack, feeling protective of her. "Sorry to break up the party."

"There's been a change of plan, Jack," she says, pulling free of my hand.

"Debs and I are driving to Treehouses," the first English woman tells me. Clear confident eyes. Short, uncovered hazel bob. Nose stud. "Yesterday, we picked up Jeff and Terry. Today, Penny wants to join us."

"We're heading in the other direction," I say, trying to maintain order in the chaos.

"Why don't you come along too?" says Debbie, the second woman. Shoulders tanned and freckled. Air of Coppertone. "There's always room in the back."

"I'm sitting up front," says Penny.

Behind them, I see our Metro bus drive away to the east.

Treehouses is on the Mediterranean. I intended skipping Turkey's south coast, both because it's off the original trail and because no paved roads went there until the seventies. Instead, in under ten minutes, I'm hijacked to Olympos, a popular beach stop for modern backpackers.

In a lot behind the bus station is their vehicle: a canary-yellow VW Camper. Perhaps the greatest automobile ever built. Mary bought it from a Newquay surfer, took a gap year from UCL and drove with Debbie across Europe to spend a couple of months under the sun.

"Whoa-wheee," Penny cheers again as the Camper gathers speed, breaking 45 miles per hour on the southern road. "This sure beats queuing for my pension at the post office."

The guys are from California, doing Turkey and the Holy Land. At eighteen or nineteen, they're about the same age as were the first Intrepids though, unlike them, they haven't left the "system" behind. Terry tugs at the stub of his James Taylor ponytail with long, bony fingers and sends text messages home. A simple gold cross hangs on a chain round his neck. Jeff is curly-haired and baby-faced, a cross between Nick Cave and Jerry Seinfeld. He carries a Blackberry.

South of Ankara, the steppe opens on to a wide khaki plain. Flights of plovers rise from the grasses. In the creases of low hills, tight hamlets gather like sand in folds of paper. At the edge of the new highway, villagers hold back their thin herds of cattle and wait for us to pass.

With an arm around Debbie, Jeff watches the countryside roll by the window and says, "Get a load of this view. I keep thinking of friends stuck back in San Francisco."

"Now that was a happening town," says Penny.

"Penny knew Ken Kesey," I tell them.

Terry sniffs at the air. "I can still smell the burning brain cells," he says.

"Whose?" ask the girls.

"A generation's."

As we drive towards the sea, Penny tells them about Kesey and the Merry Pranksters, who in 1964 partied across America on *Furthur*, a glowing orange, green and fluorescent pastel International Harvester school bus with no springs. Their acid-laced, media-savvy wanderings popularized for a new generation the idea of the youthful journey of self-discovery.

"Kesey's trip started with Kerouac," she adds, pulling another roll-up from her small, black rucksack, taking out a lighter, leaning back in her seat.

"How's that?" asks Mary.

I explain that Kerouac – as author of *On the Road* – was the father of the Beats and grandfather of the hippies. According to Ginsberg, "he was the first one to make a new crack in the consciousness."

"I've read *The Dharma Bums*," volunteers Jeff, Kerouac's story of the spiritual quest of a group of Californian travellers. *Dharma* is the Sanskrit word for the righteous path through life.

"After Kerouac died, Ginsberg took Bob Dylan to his graveside because to both men he was a point of origin," I say.

The playwright Sam Shephard witnessed their tombstone seance. "This life seems like a miracle. Still ongoing," Shephard wrote as he watched Dylan strum his guitar and Ginsberg play a flute, moved by the communion of men who embodied the potent force of the age. "Allen and Dylan singing on his grave. Allen, full of life, hope and resurrection. Poets of this now life. This here life. This one being lived and living."

"The Beats and hippies are ancient history," says Terry.

"History that put us on the road today," I reply, trying to ease his cynicism. "History that brought minority rights, ecology and alternative medicine into the mainstream. History that also for a few short years tied together the world."

"There's too much economic pressure on us to have those kinds of aspirations these days," he goes on.

"And Haight's now a mix of Carmel and Calcutta," adds Jeff. "Gentrified real estate, wall-to-wall beggars and way out of my price bracket."

Penny stares at them though the cigarette smoke. The light catches her rings and flashes prisms across the ceiling. A shiver crosses her lips. "Back then, we believed we were all one," she says with feeling.

"Taking acid does that to you," I point out.

The raised, arrow-straight road drifts west to skirt the Tuz Gölü salt lake. Knuckles of burnt earth reach down from supine hills, through yellow grasses, to stretch their fingers into the dirty, white water. The sweep of salty liquid blazes in the heat, promising cool relief, delivering only crusty, ankle-deep slough.

"Wicked scenery," says Jeff with a yawn.

Low clam-shell islands, flecked with feeding gulls, break the horizon. A far cloud of dust is thrown up by a tractor. The sunlight is red against wind-breaks of poplars. We stop for fuel and split the cost.

As we drive on, Penny's monologues rove across the universe, or at least most of southern California, from the ghosts of Owsley's LSD factory to Cassady, the model for Kerouac's Dean Moriarty and chauffeur of Kesey's bus. Then she sleeps again, slipping back into the sixties as day slides into night. Jeff and Debbie talk in hushed whispers, saying, "Isn't she something?" and "Yeah, a tie-dyed dinosaur."

I stare at her folded figure and see a story-spinner, stuck in a time warp, so tribal that she speaks only to those who know her language. Her juvenility fringes on the naive. Her introversion whiffs of egotism. Yet there remains an enticing purity about her, as if the ideals of her youth still guide her daily decisions and the trials of the world have not tarnished the dream of her own existence.

It's dark when we reach the coast. The azure Mediterranean is a black void which fills the windscreen. We pull off the highway after midnight and shudder down a dirt track to Kadir's Treehouses. The electricity has failed, so the only light comes from our headlights.

Along the floor of the steep, forested valley, wooden cabins rise on timber stilts. Above our heads, perilous walkways like narrow Nepalese footbridges loop between cock-eyed balconies. A year ago, the lofty shanty town won a Golden Backpack Award as the world's best hostel, but tonight its treetop love nests and rickety, cedar-bark dormitories seem deserted. No travelers do yoga on the open verandas. No sunburnt guests play backgammon in the trees.

Mary suggests that, rather than disturb her, we let Penny sleep on in the Camper, but she's wide awake as soon as the engine is switched off.

"I'm not tired," she sparks. Then she asks, "What's that noise?"

Music echoes up from the beach. I try to make out the song.

"Dear God," Penny laughs in recognition. "It's Jimmy Morrison."

6. LIGHT MY FIRE

"You know that it would be untrue..."

We're stumbling in the dark towards the music, blind but for torch-light playing off the stones. Around us rises a forest of ancient masonry within a lush grove of vines and wafer-leafed bay trees. Our light catches a bone, a pillar, a startled night bird. Its feeble beam shivers off a glass-smooth pool.

"...You know that I would be a liar..."

"Got to do something that scares you every day," says Penny, levering her cane between us and pushing ahead.

Our sandy footfalls curve into a hooked ravine, following a marble-lined stream broken by submerged Roman columns. The blackness and oleander banks close in on us. Underfoot crunch shards of terracotta pottery and fragments of roof tiles. There is no moon but I can just make out the wooded crest of Musa mountain against the night sky.

"...Come on, baby, light my fire..."

As we loop towards the sea, a lamp flashes in the ruins. Then a candle appears on the citadel. Another light glints across the quay of the ancient port. Open fires flare beyond the entrance to this pre-Christian pirates' hideout. The music grows louder, yet still we see no people. Not a soul in the dark.

"...Try to set the night on fire."

Suddenly we're on the beach, in the open, in a convergence of flames and figures. Hundreds of shadows throb and stamp in the flickering light. Chanting men carry burning torches above their heads. Half-naked women circle, whirl around a portable sound machine.

"Now *this* is a happening," yells Penny, her spirits lifting with the volume.

The noise is tremendous, a deafening wall of sound that beats like a pulse. Bodies gyrate along the goat paths, thrash over millennia of detritus.

Dreadlocked Kiwis kiss, black Canadians run into the sea, a lithe German couple rock together on the smooth, osseous pebbles. I won't be surprised if the uproar rouses Ken Kesey from his grave. In 1966, he was one of the main promoters of the seminal Trips Festival that gave birth to the dance, disco then trance scenes. But he'd find similarities between the two events superficial. Few of these reeling hedonists--the sons and daughters of rich consumer societies--share their predecessors' spiritual or social ambitions.

"Dance?" Jeff calls to Debbie, and they fall into the press of flesh, sharing a wild, ecstatic grin. Mary recognizes a face from their Istanbul hostel. Penny smoothes the wrinkles out of her skirt, lifts her arms above her head and shimmies around the rim of the circle. Terry squats on the beach and lights a cigarette. I look at the hundreds of faces and don't see a single Turk.

By the crackle of a fire I shout into an Aussie's ear.

"Mate, there's always a free bed at Treehouses," he assures me. "Or at least half of one. Kadir had four hundred people staying one night last week."

A few numbers later, the music eases off a couple of notches, maybe in deference to the sea turtles which nest along the Cıralı shore. Or maybe not. Jeff and Debbie take a break from the dancing. Mary strolls over to join us, having scored a little grass. Penny sways back into sight calling, "I'm not stoned, it's my hip."

The girls want to smoke, and we recongregate in a circle. Penny sinks cross-legged on to the beach as they ply her with questions about her decision to come to Asia.

"By '68 San Fran was falling apart," she says, wiping a sheen of perspiration from her forehead. "People wanted to escape from the cycle of karma. Sitars were all the rage. The Beatles had checked out Rishikesh. Leary was tripping through the *Tibetan Book of the Dead*."

Timothy Leary was the Harvard psychology professor who linked LSD and Tibetan Buddhism, espousing drug use as a means of altering consciousness.

"Most of all, we had Ginsberg's example of living in India. That was the big enchilada."

I add, "In his journal, Ginsberg wrote, 'It's my promised land. I'm wandering in India, it's like a new earth – I'm happy.'"

"We felt like there was a current drawing us east."

As Penny talks, the dance beat recedes further, yielding to the sound of cicadas. Laughter and murmurs of English conversation lift up from other groups gathered around the scattered fires. We could be at Big Sur or on Ko Samui. Turkey feels miles away.

"So, after Woodstock, we took off for Europe, me and Orrin, my final and best husband. He was a painter and performance artist but cut out when he started to make money. He didn't like the discipline of booking galleries."

"What was traveling like then?" asks Mary, passing the smoke.

"I remember Rome, tripping down the Spanish Steps with beach tar on my feet," says Penny with calm happiness, snapping her bangles, pulling again at strands of hair. "I remember going down tree-lined streets in Austria picking cherries, eating them there and then, the red juice dripping down my blouse. I remember stealing a chicken in Yugoslavia and spit-roasting it feathers and all." She drags long on the joint, holds it in, drifts on, "I remember wind-up gramophones, sweet cardamom ice cream, dancing in the desert, skinny-dipping in a sea like this ... with a Black Watch of Turks, as I called them, looking down at us from the cliff. But most of all I remember Nepal colored jade and silver. We arrived there at monsoon time with water on the paddy fields and the palaces like wedding cakes."

"Penny lived in Nepal for nine years," I say.

"In a haze of beauty. India blew our minds but Nepal was flipping paradise on earth. Those days were the happiest, the most magical, of my life."

Tree frogs croak in the breaks between songs. New kids join the party, returning hungry from a night trek to the Chimaera, the plume of natural gas flames on one of the foothills of nearby Mount Olympos. The smell of grilling meat and herbs melds with marijuana smoke. Beer bottles clink in a cooler. Two naked children doze on a raised, cushioned *kösk* under an orange tree.

"Then Orrin snuffed it," says Penny.

We don't respond, youth losing its voice at the mention of death.

"And I ran away from Kathmandu. I became a nobody, needing a new

hip, living with my souvenirs in sheltered housing in Battersea." She reaches into her rucksack, between the tissues, tarots and Tylenol, and extracts
a crumpled paisley handkerchief. "Life became so ... quiet. As quiet as the
grave. And much too safe."

Now I understand her tears, her protectiveness of the past. I try to
ease her distress by saying, "After this holiday you'll have new memories
to take home."

"I don't have a home any more."

"You moved out?"

"As we grew older, things started to get tough for us in Nepal; aches
and pains and disappointment. For the first time in his life Orrin got
frightened. He started hoarding stuff. He lay down everything we owned:
the LPs, the wine, even the ham in aspic. Lay them down for tomorrow,
to be opened and rolled on the palate at some later date, to be put on the
turntable in the future. The enjoyment was supposed to be heightened because of association and time. But then Orrin died and the point of saving
was lost. I found myself back in England, in an old folks' home, a tomb for
ancient Britons." She stops, allows herself a little cry, then leans back with
the end of the joint and gazes skywards, trying to make out stars. "So I let
it all go."

"All go?"

"Last week I packed this bag. Stacked all our crap in the middle of the
room. Then I walked out, leaving the door wide open, and went straight to
Heathrow; destination: Istanbul."

We stare at her in disbelief, shocked and fascinated.

"Who knows what happened to all that stuff. I hope someone made
use of it. Someone who deserved it. I certainly wasn't having any fun –
stuck inside that place, surrounded by things. Maybe right now someone is
listening to my autographed copy of the *White Album*."

After her moment of exuberance Penny sighs. Her head falls to her
chest. I see her old frame begin to shake as if by an earth tremor. In a moment she's gasping for air, unable to fill her lungs. I put an arm around her
shoulders and help her back into a sitting position. The tears flare like tiny
jewels on her cheeks. She stares at the bonfire, tries to roll a cigarette, spills
the tobacco on to the pebbles. She runs her fingers through her grey hair.

Debbie takes Jeff's hand.

"I wasn't on anything," Penny confesses to us when she catches her breath, reading my thoughts. "I just got depressed living alone in a box in London, living for *stuff*. That was never the dream."

Beyond our circle, the incomers have turned up the volume. The night's tempo lifts again as the revellers expand the dance, looping around our fire, drawing us unwittingly back into the deafening chaos. Sparks sail above the dark bay, into the high hills.

"For love is as strong as death, passion fierce as the grave," whispers Penny. "Its flashes are flashes of fire, a raging flame."

I can hardly hear her voice above the raw pulse of music. Her face is in shadow, as pale as chalk. Her hair has fallen out of its clips and over her neck.

"Ginsberg?" asks Mary.

"Song of Solomon," says Terry in recognition.

Then Penny seizes my hand and pulls me to my feet. She staggers ahead and I let her guide me into the heart of the dance, into the whirlpool of writhing, leaping, living bodies.

7. BEND ME, SHAPE ME

We are up at dawn, driving into a white sunrise, tracing a crescent above a searing sea. The coast road curves high above the shore, dropping into fishing villages skimmed by a sheen of tourism like the blue chintz on old chairs at the Restaurant Paradise. In Kemer, a lone angler throws his line over the rocks, lemon-yellow beach apartments at his back. A proud young Turkish woman, skin dove-brown, long black hair uncovered, kicks into the sea in her apricot bikini. Behind her, broad grandmothers ride out to the fields sitting two abreast in tractor hoppers. Corner shops sell donkey yokes and *Bain de soleil*. Skeletons of new holiday homes climb the scrubby hill like en suite Lycian rock tombs.

All morning Penny remains subdued, perhaps because of our early start, more probably because of her dramatic departure from England. She still believed that property is theft. We left the revellers asleep at Tree-houses and set out eastwards on our own. I was anxious to get back on the trail. By sunset, we'll reach her destination. Our last journey together in Turkey stirs my emotions, not least because I'm wary of her intentions in Cappadocia. I don't offer to play her "Anarchy in the UK".

More by luck than design--each shared taxi waiting to fill up before departing--a succession of *dolmuş* rides connects us with Antalya, the eastern Turkish heart of beach tourism. Here, Russian sun-seekers tan to leather around the pools at the vast Kremlin Palace, a confection of faux-Soviet holiday apartments with ersatz, onion-domed St Basil's Cathedral. Syrians bake fully clothed by the water, their *chadors* caked with wet sand. Iranian girls belly-dance on public beaches while in the blocks behind them Iranian boys buy Ukrainian whores by the hour.

The Turks stare out of our Toyota's tinted windows like foreigners moving through an unfamiliar landscape, most of them as detached from the new tourists as their parents were from the hippies. Then we swing inland, leaving behind immodesty and modernity. In only a few miles, unchanging upland villages rise out of dust. Children dig at patches of beans. Their back-bent mothers, in voluminous *şalvars* gathered at the ankles like baggy culottes, hoe yard-sized wheat fields. A farmer tips off his donkey, removes his knitted cap and unrolls his prayer mat. A man without a hand alights at a carpenter's shop.

"There!" Penny shouts, standing up in her seat, pointing forward.

The flat steppe, which for hours has been bleak and mournful, crumbles away from the roadside. Our *dolmuş* hurtles down a steep, rippling precipice. I crane my neck upwards as the Toyota twists between extraordinary, mushroom-capped stone towers. The sun strobes between and through them, ushering us into one of the world's strangest landscapes.

Cappadocia was once an essential stop-off on the overland trail to India, now it's the most easterly point of the Turkish backpacking circuit. One-hundred-foot layers of volcanic ash, dust and ballast have been sculpted by the elements into a moonscape of honeycombed cliffs and Gaudiesque phalluses.

In Göreme, at the center of a web of valleys, Penny doesn't stop to find a hotel. Instead, she hobbles out of the bus station, calling back to me over her shoulder, "This way. Hurry up."

I pay the driver and grab our bags, chasing after her past the "fairy chimneys". Cobbled streets wind between the salt-white pinnacles. Ochre spires sprout breakfast balconies. Over thousands of years, people hollowed living spaces out of the soft stone, which can be carved with a spoon when first exposed to the air. At the edge of town, we turn down a dry river bed into deserted "Love" Valley. Pigeons glide into fallow fields. Flocks of starlings rise up into yellow-flowered oleaster.

"I remember that tower," Penny assures me, pushing into the outlandish wilderness, thrilled by the prospect of rediscovery. Around us, the canyon walls are riddled with the dark portals of hermit cells and cave churches. "We stayed down here to the right."

We fork right and walk into a stone wall. A hot breeze exhales from the dead end. Undeterred, Penny retraces our tracks, laughing away my concerns about her age and the searing heat.

"I'll be dead for a very long time," she shouts, doing little to ease my concern for her emotional state.

Until the 1950s, Cappadocia was unexplored and undocumented by the outside world, save for the accounts of a general secretary of the Royal Geographical Society and a Frenchman, Father Guillaume de Jerphanion. Then, British travel writers – including Freya Stark and Patrick Leigh Fermo – visited the region, and their evocative reports captured the imagination of the first sixties travellers. They pitched their tents and unrolled their sleeping bags in the sun-baked ravines, sitting up all night playing guitars and watching the sensuous colors of the rock surfaces change hue in the day's shifting light. I'd read everything I could on the full-moon parties, the Malibu surfer who became a cave-dwelling troglodyte and the former B-52 airman, whose job had been to obliterate life on Vietnam's DMZ, planting a vegetable garden in the fertile Anatolian soil. I'd even heard of a Glaswegian who, driving his Messerschmidt bubble car to India, stopped here for a night and stayed for three years.

"Come on!" Penny shouts.

There is no shade along the winding footpath. The midday sun glares off the ashen sand, dazzling my eyes and softening my brain.

"It's got to be here somewhere."

We press along an even narrower ravine, deserted and silent but for the cries of birds.

"There," she rushes, like a lame horse on the home stretch. "There it is."

The cave – *her* cave – is perched thirty feet up a sheer face, overhung with a mushroom-cap awning. I see no ladder.

"The entrance is over here."

Ten feet above the ground, hidden behind a fold of rock, a dim aperture opens into the stone. Under her guidance, I scramble on to a ledge and crawl lizard-like into its cool darkness, disturbing flights of moths. The passageway curves to the right, then up inside the carved cliff. I unfold myself into a simple, cruciform cave church. On its threshold, a protective millstone stands ready – as it has done for a thousand years – to be rolled over the entrance. Penny puffs at my heels.

"Man, this is it."

Above our heads, a dome has been hewn out of the solid rock, an iron adze and chisel outlining door frames, marking false capitals and lattices.

Two stone seats and a ledge of pews mark the perimeter, enhancing the illusion of a conventional church. Around a thick horseshoe arch, which opens on to the canyon, are painted umber flames symbolizing the descent of the Holy Ghost into the nave.

Penny spins on her toes, her arms wrapped around herself and tears forgotten, wailing, "Whooee."

In caves such as this, unnumbered generations took sanctuary from wolves, Romans and the consumer society. Early Christians retreated up the steep cliffs to carve over the centuries as many as four hundred hideaways, chapels and basilicas. St Paul, born not many miles to the south, considered the environment suitable for inspiring and training missionaries. During medieval times, the valleys became one of the principal monastic centers of the Byzantine Empire. In the sixties, Cappadocia provided sanctuary for many Intrepids, also giving them a safe place to explore a utopian way of life.

"After Istanbul, we stayed here for the summer. All summer. Just hanging out. Just being."

Penny settles herself into the monk's seat, a look of deep contentment rising on her face. She gazes over the lip of the cave, down to a small spring and a clump of wild apple trees and starts talking about their stay, her loquacious self again.

"That summer, people put up their tents and banners, which in this fantasyland was amazing. There were Japanese glass chimes, little Tibetan prayer flags, cats doing Zhao Zen meditation, couples promising to love each other under the stars and under heaven." She takes a deep breath. "It was cosmic."

At the end of another short tunnel is a second square chamber, perhaps a funerary chapel, its ceiling darkened by centuries of cooking fires. A single pillar is smashed away at its base and dangling like a stalactite.

"This was our bedroom. Lit a few candles here, I can tell you."

I stare at the sooty, deconsecrated space, then out into the valley, at her demi-Eden, now abandoned and inhospitable. I feel an urge to protect her – and myself – from disappointment and say quickly, "We should head into Göreme to find a hotel."

Penny ignores me, dropping to her hands and knees to scrabble in the dust, looking for something, for anything: a Levi's button, a Day-Glo hair pin, even a roach clip. I know she'll find no memento. Too many years have passed since her heady summer of love. Too many younger travelers have stopped by her cave.

"Penny, let's go."

But she's laughing, digging in the earth, scooping away the soil. She pulls up small stones. She breaks a purple nail-extension. I put my hand on her shoulder and, after a minute or two, help her on to her feet. I pick up our bags and turn towards the tunnel.

"Stay with me, Jack," she says.

"Here? In the cave?"

She nods. I'm about to refuse her when I notice her hands trembling on her cane.

"But ... I don't have a guitar," I say.

Later, I trek back into town to buy water and food. I borrow a frying pan and a couple of blankets from the Köşe pension. By the time I crawl back up the tunnel, it's late afternoon. Penny has swept out the church, arranged her candles by the stone altar and sits on a pew gazing at the distant, rippling cones.

"I've been watching the light change with the day," she says, nodding into the distance. "Brick red to rust, ochre to salt-white."

I unpack the shopping, pass her a pack of cigarettes, uncork a bottle of wine for me. I cut up a cucumber, tomatoes and a shrub-sized bunch of co-riander to make a salad, tossing it together with lemon and oil in a carrier bag. In the pan I fry a monster omelette with red peppers, olives and salty, dry *tulum peynir* goat's cheese. I lay a couple of rolled *börek* pastry parcels around its rim. We balance on the rocky lip, eating from the pan in silence, breaking bread, watching our crumbs being carried away by bold sparrows and the evening's ants.

"We traveled throughout the world. We conquered the war-shattered world by our faith and transformed it into paradise," she says after supper. The words are familiar. "Hermann Hesse."

"You say faith? What do you – did Hesse – mean by faith?"

"The belief in something better," she answers me. "The search for en-lightenment."

To Buddhists, enlightenment means the passing into nirvana, the release from the cycles of death and rebirth. In the sixties, the word became generalized to describe an enlightened awareness of self.

Bands of golden sunlight gild the high branches of the pines. Its radiance filters through the veins of the olive leaves. The shadows of black crows fleet across stony cliffs. As the sun sets, we sit together in silence; Penny still studying our surroundings, me writing.

Last night, the candles burnt out before I could finish my notes. This morning, I left the cave and set about exploring Göreme, the isolated farming village transformed by tourism. I'm curious how the town looked in Penny's day.

Rock churches rise beyond the coach park. Veiled women buy vegetables alongside backpackers in shorts. Across from the Bedrock Travel Agency, down the hill from the Troglodyte Hotel, I find Flintstone's Bar. Its Turkish owner, "Fred, a local caveman", tells me how he settled on its name.

"A couple of years ago, two Australian girls were sleeping in one of my caves," he says, filling the quiet afternoon with conversation. "I gave them a morning call by shouting, 'Wilma, wake up!' We'd been watching *The Flintstones* on TV. The girls shouted back, 'Coming, Fred.' Dino," he yells at the dog licking my hand, "leave the customer alone."

To help me to revive the sixties, Fred invites over Abdullah Güney, owner of Zemi Tours, and Bayram Maden, a tall and flamboyant restaurateur.

"I remember the parties most of all," grins Abdullah, shaking my hand, settling himself on to a low cushion, eager to talk, "drinking wine, playing guitars, sitting together in the Turkish way."

"At first, the hippies camped in the valleys," recollects Bayram, one of the initial villagers to welcome the Intrepids to Göreme.

"Our mothers told us, 'Don't go near the *giaours*.' The infidels."

"My father ran the only café in the village," Bayram goes on. "One night after he had gone to bed, I invited some of them to sleep on the tables and floor. Next morning, when it was still dark, my father walked in and tripped over the sleeping bodies. He took his stick and beat them out into the street."

"Like wild dogs," laughs Abdullah recalling the old, insular days.

"I convinced my father to let our guests stay but he insisted on hanging a curtain across the middle of the café: locals on one side, *giaours* on the other."

"We called him '*Christian* Bayram'," Abdullah tells me, laying his arm across his friend's shoulders. "He grew long sideburns, which wasn't allowed, and fell in love with a South African girl. His mother wailed, 'What has happened to our boy?'"

"In Turkish, we say European girls are washing the eyes of the men: uncovering their legs, showing their arms, putting on lipstick."

"But the visitors' liberalism must have upset the older villagers," I say, as Fred slips off his stool to serve a customer, pulling a pint of Carlsberg by hand. "They covered traditional foods in ketchup. They insisted on you learning English. What did you think of that ... disrespect?"

"Nothing," shrugs Bayram, pragmatic and dismissive. "They were-you are--tourists. You could be from the moon."

In 1983, three German travellers helped to pour the concrete foundation of the first cafeteria. The following summer, it was joined by the first cave-house pension. Over the coming decades, the area was transformed from a derelict backwater into a labyrinth for tourists' consumption. Now a bustling town in Cappadocia, Göreme's two thousand residents run sixty hotels, fifteen tour agencies, eighteen restaurants and a bus-station shopping-complex.

"When I was growing up, I slept with my shoes under my pillow," says Abdullah. "Today, all my children drive cars. My daughter was the first village woman to go to university. Our prosperity started with the arrival of the hippies."

It's late when I hump the week's supplies back to "Love" Valley. The torchlight plays on stone walls so smooth, so eroded, that every sharp edge seems to have melted away in the day's heat.

I'm not worried that Penny might have done herself an injury. Or abandoned the cave during my absence. I'm no longer wary of her intentions. She may remember Cappadocia as both a paradise and a good place to die but I don't suspect suicide is part of her life plan.

I stand beneath the thick horseshoe arch. Above me, a single candle flickers in the darkness. I'm about to call out when I hear Penny's voice. I listen for a moment. She's moving around the cave, organizing her few possessions, singing as softly as the evening breeze. A Joan Baez lament. I don't join in because I don't want to break the spell. Her voice – as rusty as a temple bell – echoes off the darkening stones.

We eat a Flintstone pizza that evening, aubergines stuffed with lamb the next. We talk into the small hours. During the following days, I meet with Fred and the other men. I'm struck by the irony of the hippies' rejection of acquisitive selfishness stimulating their hosts' material prosperity. We also discuss the social cost of economic success. Fred remembers that, once, everyone in Cappadocia was family. "Every boy was my brother, every girl my sister" is how he expressed it. "Now, neighbors own competing restaurants and cut each other's throats." But when I voice a pang of regret for the lost communal life, he wags his index finger.

"Turks don't want to stay poor farmers in pretty villages, no matter how much some Westerners would wish our lives unchanged," he says. "We want schools and doctors. We want to buy toys for our grandchildren. We are a living part of this Flintstone world."

Penny seems content to stay in the cave, watching the changing light. She leaves me to make my own decisions, to find my own road. She certainly has no wish to travel on with me.

"There are a thousand paths to nirvana," she tells me. "Mine is not by way of Iran."

On our last night together, I tell Penny that Fred will check in on her every couple of days to restock her food and water. I make sure she has enough money. I offer her my email address. She puts her hand to my lips and tells me to shut up.

Nightbirds and bats drop out of their shelters, flying by the edge of our vision. A bulbul warbles in the branches. An owl hoots at the twilight. As the valley slips into darkness, the candles warm the old cave with their intimate light. In their shadow Penny's hair looks midnight-black not seal-grey. A full moon rises above the cones. The ancient horseshoe arch frames the stars.

I wake before dawn and, as she snores softly in her cocoon of borrowed bedding, I gather my bits and backpack and slip out of the cave. My bus is due to leave just after six.

In the valley, I pause to check for my passport. A thin, yellowed volume has been slipped between my notebooks. I pull out Penny's copy of *Siddhartha*. The edge of a page has been turned down. As I step along the path, I read Hesse's words on the shudder of awakening.

"He began to walk quickly and impatiently, no longer homewards, no longer to his father, no longer looking backwards."

I turn the corner and walk away, leaving behind a lone voice singing to the morning.

8.SYMPATHY FOR THE DEVIL

Beyond the fly-flecked windscreen spread gaunt plains, barren flat-top mountains and asphalt ribbons quivering in the hot sun. In every direction the prairie unrolls a hundred miles wide, broken only by tufts of white flowers marking family plots. Distant figures scythe with short, crescent sickles. Summer breezes push and pool wheat and barley, weaving waves of pattern across the steppe. Space stretches out, as well as time, dwarfing electricity pylons and a thread-like rail line, as if the earth itself is expanding in the heat.

I changed buses in Kayseri, my spirit lifting with the road ahead. A rose blooms beside a caged, blue-stone ossuary. On a blind corner we overtake an overloaded truck, its green chillies quivering free of their sacks like miniature elvers. I drop my pen.

"Excuse me," I apologize to the passenger sitting beside me, taking off my earphones, "I don't speak Turkish." *Türkçe bilmiyorum.* "Could you...?" I gesture at the pen rolling under his feet.

"No panic on the *Titanic*," says the stranger, brushing away my apology, offering me a delicate white hand. "You shouldn't bother to learn Turkish; it's an underdeveloped language."

"What do you mean, underdeveloped?"

"In French movies, a man need say only three words for a woman to kiss him. In Turkish, a man must talk to a woman all day just so she will touch the back of his hand."

I laugh, offer my hand, introduce myself.

"Call me Oscar," he says. "Everyone does."

Oscar, whose real name is Özcan, would never stand out in a crowd. His clean-shaven face is as smooth and ageless as a sea pebble. I write him off as a salesman or a crooked, small-town accountant with fastidious hygiene habits. Until I look into his eyes. They are colorless.

"Have you been traveling long?" I ask him as he returns my pen. I hadn't noticed him get on the bus.

"About forty years," he replies. "Forget that guidebook" – I'd been leafing through the *Blue Guide* – "it's no good beyond Konya.'"

"You know all about it," I say, with an unexpected shiver. Yet I'm pleased to find an English speaker, so I tell him about myself.

"A travel writer," he replies, lifting his interest but not his voice. "Then we're comrades-in-arms." He hands me his business card. Tourism Consultant. "But I have little time for the sixties. The flower children were as simple as their critics are unpleasant."

"In Cappadocia they seem to have opened the door to prosperity," I tell him, mentioning the stories of Abdullah and Bayram.

"The hash-and-hepatitis trail did spawn an industry that packaged the world," he admits, folding his hands in his lap. "I should know. I stand near the start of that trail."

"How so?"

"It was me who put Butterfly Valley on the map."

Butterfly Valley – Kelebek Vadısı – was once an isolated beach accessible only by sea; a divine holiday highlight for early, independent travellers.

"I worked as a guide for tour-company scouts," he explains. "I turned them on to its tourist potential. I went on to invent the *gulet* package holiday," he gloats with a flash of conceit, "enticing Club Med to Foça and convincing Airtours to build the first hotel in Ölüdeniz."

"That's..." I search for the right word "...impressive."

Each development marked a turning-point in the growth of Turkish tourism, transforming – in most cases – wild coastline into resort conurbations.

"I've been a planning officer, a copywriter of brochures. I've advised Kuoni, Thomson, Abercrombie and Kent. As soon as the holiday-makers arrive, with their sun-cream and condoms, I leave the place to them. You've heard of the Arab traveller al-Muqaddasi? In the tenth century, he wrote that cities on the sea are hotbeds of fornication and sodomy. Nothing's changed in a thousand years."

"Overdevelopment has changed Turkey."

"Tourism is the factory without a chimney," he insists, again in a unemotional tone. "It's good for the economy, and thriving economy improves lives."

"So why are you traveling east?" I ask him. As far as I know, the next mainstream tourist stop is Goa, 5,000 miles ahead in India.

"Let me tell you a story," says Oscar, "about two brothers from Bingöl."

I unfold my road map.

"It's a Kurdish town, poor of course, with red clay, lavender honey and so little work that men must look elsewhere for things to do. There are Koranic schools, soldiers on the street and wolves in the mountains. In truth, this is a story about wolves; about running from wolves, fighting with wolves, becoming a wolf."

Bingöl lies to the south of the overland route in Turkey's impoverished hard-baked south-east, where a vicious guerrilla war raged for sixteen years.

"These two brothers were brought up alone by their mother for, I'm sorry to say, they had seen their father shot dead."

"Shot?" I repeat, because there is no sorrow in his voice. He simply recounts the facts of a tragedy.

"He was a songwriter and a prominent member of the PKK."

Since the collapse of the Ottoman Empire in 1918, the Kurds have aspired to nationhood. The outlawed PKK--or Kurdistan Workers' Party-- led the insurgency throughout the 1990s.

"But these details aren't important to the story. What is important is that the brothers--so good, so calm--grew up in a kind of isolation, because their mother kept them indoors, fearful that the Nationalists would come next for her boys."

While western Turkey prospered, Oscar goes on to explain, with rapid economic growth and mass urbanization, the Kurds as a whole were cut adrift, forbidden to teach and broadcast in their own language, isolated because their aspirations threatened Turkish unity. Their guerrilla war unfolded far away from television cameras, claiming over 30,000 lives.

"The brothers dreamed the dreams that boys do, of becoming pop stars or inter-city bus drivers. But when they grew into young men, the only work available to them, apart from bee-keeping, was heroin-smuggling from Iran. Of course, if you can feed neither yourself nor your sick mother, you feel ashamed, you get angry, you look for someone to blame. Then, in your feeble fury, the wolves come after you."

Again I'm unsettled by Oscar's cold calm, by his chilling talk of revenge without a trace of emotion.

"Violence begets violence. No Kurd can sit on the fence. He must decide to run with the wolves or to run away from them."

Bingöl was a divided town, he tells me, a stronghold of both the PKK and a shadowy Sunni group called Hizbullah; same name, same mentality, but separate from the Lebanese Hezbollah. Together, the PKK and Hizbullah shared a hatred of the Nationalists.

"The first boy ran to the west, away from his beloved younger brother. He changed his family name. He sold himself, and Turkey. Every month he sent home money."

"And the other brother?" I ask.

"He fell in with the wolves, running east with them, along the same road as you are heading, as a matter of fact. Nothing was heard from him for years. Until last week. I received a call that he had come home."

The persecution of the Kurds shames Turkey's recent history. The restoration of minority rights has begun to redress the balance, but many of the country's 12 million Kurds – like some of Istanbul's inward-looking *dağlı* – remain embittered by both their exclusion from progress and by the frightening speed of it.

Oscar polishes his fingernails. "In Kurdish, we say, 'One hand clapping does not make a sound.' Kurds do all as family. When I say I love my brother, I mean I will do anything for him," he assures me in a flat tone. I notice that his pebble-smooth features are broken by the rough edges of three cracked teeth.

Five hundred miles east of Ankara, Erzincan cowers in a narrow corridor flanked by the rumpled bodies of fallen giants. Nut-brown fields reach over their long, wrinkled limbs as if to tether them to the earth. In 1939, these giants stirred and the entire city was razed by an earthquake. The sense of loss still pervades the evening air.

Oscar has a ride arranged to carry him across the mountains to Bingöl. He asks me to join him. "A favorable mention in your book will bring visitors and stimulate the local economy," he says.

I turn down his invitation, even though my bus is going no further tonight.

"Another time then, my friend." He smiles but his eyes remain empty. Then he takes my hand and adds, "Remember, if you want to be sexy, you must drink Pepsi."

In my concrete-and-cockroach hotel room I turn the lock and jam a chair under the door handle.

Along the hippie trail, beyond the ubiquitous crescent-and-star flags and assertions of ethnic integrity, Turkey unfolds as an elaborate, fluid mosaic; an Anatolian imbroglio of history and ideas over which great armies and ardent idealists have trampled and trespassed. In 334 BC, Alexander began his drive towards India from central Konya, the ancient city which the great Moroccan traveller Ibn Battutah passed through on his *haj* to Mecca in 1331. St Paul was thirty-five years old when he walked this way. Crusaders and Islam's horsemen galloped across this same lion-colored plain, though heading in opposite directions. A thousand years later, the Intrepids were propelled east by their dream of a better world. In 1999, after the cessation of the insurgency, hundreds of radical Kurds chased in their footsteps, escaping over the border into Iran and northern Iraq.

The next morning, my bus follows them too, squeezing out of the canyon, over the giants' outstretched limbs, beside the fast, frothy Euphrates. Boulders roll down gravel arms. Meltwater churns wild and white over outsized fingers. I'm dwarfed by the pathos of human endeavor and the precipitous, primeval mountains shot through with bone and iron. At Tercan, the driver spills hot tea on his lap and almost crashes into a gorge.

I spare only a day for grey, grim Erzurum. Women wash earthy wool in a public fountain, drawing veils across their faces as I pass. Policemen relax in the shade of the Citadel, singing soft songs to each other, gazing along the arrow-straight trading route as did Roman centurions, Danish freaks and all the travellers between them. In a broken backstreet a cracked old man seizes my hand and shakes it, crying out, "*Sie sind zurückgekommen.*" You've come back. Since the Iranians closed the trail in 1979, few Westerners have had cause to visit the city. Istanbul feels a continent away.

I push on across divided, diverse eastern Turkey, numbed by distance and busted springs, each bus slower, older and hotter than its predecessor. The Meteor Turizm coach has broken instruments and a cracked windscreen. The Doğubeyazit Express, a fiery metal coffin on wheels, rides low on its tail and stops every hundred meters whether passengers are waiting or not. An aged farmer hobbles down the aisle, hands reaching out to steady him. A baby is passed from passenger to passenger, held and kissed by strangers. The driver and conductor count and recount their takings, whispering in hushed tones, debating--as the bus isn't full--whether to make the journey at all. Every hundred kilometers, armed traffic *jandarma* shoulder Kalashnikovs to check my identification. The burnt-out hulk of a Kars Comet smoulders among the birches far below at the foot of a rocky valley.

Horasan is a mud-brick hamlet of motor grease and black sheep equidistant from the borders of Georgia, Armenia and Iran. Travelers waiting by its bus stop carry sacks rather than suitcases. I see no women in its tin-roof cafés, on the dirt street, at the plough-maker's shop. Along its alleyways, discs of animal dung dry for cooking fuel. At its market, a barefoot boy offers me home-made *pide*, a thin gloss of tomato on bread. When I buy him a piece instead, he wolfs it down as if he hasn't eaten all day. Beyond him, in a razor-wire BTC oil camp, men work on the world's newest export pipeline, pumping Caspian crude a thousand miles west alongside the ancient road.

In Doğubeyazit – called Doggy Biscuit by sixties overlanders – the Irish travel writer Dervla Murphy avoided rape at the hand of a six-foot, scantily clad Kurd by firing her .25 automatic at the bedroom ceiling. A decade later, and 2,305 years after Alexander, the unarmed founders of *Lonely Planet* guides, Tony and Maureen Wheeler, drove their Austin Minivan through this cheerless border town. Marco Polo paused here to look for Noah's Ark in the summer of 1270. He didn't find it but became instead the first European to witness a practical use for petroleum. Near here, he wrote, "there is a fountain of oil which discharges so great a quantity as to load a thousand camels. It is not used for food but as fuel for lamps."

Doğubeyazit is a place of transition, within the borders of secular Turkey yet infused with Islamic fervor. On its cramped main street, waiters, with coins jingling in their pockets, carry meal platters to the bustling *me-*

drese school. Outside the mosque, a cripple with brush-thick eyebrows sells paper cups of seed, sustaining the practice of feeding the pigeons which fed Solomon. At the *otogar*, I watch a public parting. A young man and woman stand an arm's length apart, shaking hands. Unexpectedly, their fingers knit together. She squeezes his thumb, then releases it. He draws his flat palm slowly, firmly, across her open hand. She places her hand on his waist, dips her head and he kisses her forehead. At that moment, a tall, white-robed *imam* emerges from the terminal, steps up to the couple and wrenches them apart. I'll not see a man and woman touch again for the next four thousand miles.

At dawn, the swallows rise up, circling the empty streets, connecting in their sweeping flights the mundane and mystical, the contiguous and the transient, the intolerant and the liberal. I walk alone beneath the flanks of soaring, wide-mouthed Mount Ararat. Here, at an earlier dawn, the Swiss traveller Nicolas Bouvier wrote movingly of time passing on the road in brewing tea, in shared cigarettes, in a journey's rare moments when intimacy borders on the divine. "I dropped this wonderful moment into the bottom of my memory, like a sheet-anchor that one day I could draw up again," he wrote in *L'Usage du Monde*. "The bedrock of existence is not made up of the family, or work, or what others say and think of you, but of moments like this when you are exalted by a transcendent power that is more serene than love."

A *dolmus* carries me across a flat, parched land like a desiccated estuary: desolate, biblical, lodged deep in the souls of men yet of no practical value. My last, treeless stretch of Turkish road is the same that carried Oscar's brother back to the west, to Erzincan and then Istanbul, where he would drive the 'car of death' into the British Consulate. He, like two other of Turkey's first four suicide bombers, came from angry, hopeless, nihilistic Bingöl.

At the Iranian border, all but on the threshold of Arabia, I cross the first great frontier of the trail, between the Turkish and Persian worlds. In the blue distance, the mountains rise up like hands clasped in prayer.

Iran

9. LOOK WHAT THEY DONE TO MY SONG, MA

"I hate my feelings," says Laleh, looking past me at the mirror. "I hate my weakness." She tilts her head, easing on the black hood of her *chador*. "Most of all, I hate my nose."

Babak turns up "Like a Virgin". Around him, young women flaunt spangly frocks and Lancôme eyes. The men sport designer jeans and long, swept-back hair. Two out of three Iranians are under thirty and at least half of them seem to be in this room.

"I'm going into the garden," Laleh says to me.

She crosses the floor, twisting away between the dancers, music in her walk. The irises of her eyes are auburn rimmed by darkest chocolate. I'm uneasy at being attracted to an Iranian woman, wary of its consequences. A German businessman has just been imprisoned for sleeping with a consenting Tehrani. Here in Tabriz, two toyshop owners were flogged for selling Barbie dolls. Any moment now, the morals police may break down the front door and take me away.

At the border, I jumped the queue. Hundreds of returning laborers mobbed the first checkpoint. I pushed through the red-eyed crowd, my passport clearing a path, and was whisked into a concrete no-man's-land. Three hundred yards ahead, two dozen returning Iranian tourists scuffled around a broad, elaborate, iron gate. Half an hour earlier, on the Turkish side, I'd watched the women transform themselves, removing make-up, donning headscarves, drawing the *hejab* curtain around their bodies. "Dear Ladies," read the only English sign in the customs house, "*hejab* is like an oyster shell with woman as pearl inside." One by one, the pearls and I elbowed through the gate into what is arguably the modern world's only theocracy.

During the sixties, Iran was the "in-between" country: drugs were illegal, torture was common and Islam was a religion too practical and grounded to appeal to most mystic-seeking hippies. No one came to Tehran to get high. "Iran is a repressive police state," wrote one early Intrepid. "Get through it fast." Then the Iranian Revolution closed the trail altogether. Only last year did the easing of restrictions and eviction of the Taliban from Afghanistan reopen the borders. But the abiding stereotype of angry crowds chanting "Death to America" had done little to revitalize the country's appeal to travellers.

At the border bus station, a detachment of money-changers, not Revolutionary Guards, besieged me. I hustled on to the departing Tabriz Express. Its bony-faced driver stared with a look akin to shock, then asked me in French, "In heaven's name, why are you in Iran?" I told him as we circled a dirt roundabout crowned by a concrete strawberry. "You stay tonight in Tabriz and we talk about Paris," proposed Babak, hitting sixty miles an hour while turning around to shake my hand.

"I hope to catch a connection to Tehran," I said.

"We talk about Paris, then we go girl-watching."

Babak, aged thirty-six, was a war veteran and bus-driving hero. He tapped his leg and it made a metallic sound. The son of a dead *imam*, he had been gassed in Abadan and shot in the trenches during the Iran–Iraq war – "the Iraq-imposed war", as he called it. His physical injuries cured him of the mania that martyrdom was a path to salvation. He had a short shock of hair and shoulders which hunched over the wheel. At the lunchtime prayer stop he shared his plate of eggy *kuku* and cardboard *lavash* bread and grilled me with questions. What was my religion? How much did I earn? When will America attack Iran? He didn't answer my questions about women's non-existent rights, rigged elections or the nuclear-weapons program in return. Instead, he told me about his love of foreign travel.

"Where have you been?" I asked him.

"Only Turkey so far," he said, making a coarse gesture with his fingers. "But one day I will see the whole world."

Beneath a scalding sky the color of thin milk, the bus hummed along the new highway, running fast, with me aboard feeling elated, unleashed, like an arrow shooting east towards India. Babak wanted to be hospitable. Understood. Accepted by me. He said he lived alone. At least only with a sister. I decided to accept his invitation. And to wash my clothes. They hadn't seen soap since Istanbul and had started to smell like salted fish.

"You want to know about Iranian women," Babak told me later in Bozorg Square, a wealthy northern suburb of Tabriz. In my starchy, sun-dried shirt and crumpled chinos I was the worst-dressed man at the ice-cream parlor. Around us, thousands of stylish, single Iranians strolled under the trees, enjoying the balmy evening air, greeting friends in English. "*Salam*. Hello hello. I love you." I saw no *mullah*'s turbans.

"Of course you do, you are a young man," Babak went on, watching the promenaders. "And I will tell you all about them." He licked a spoonful of sticky honey ice-cream. "In Tabriz, there are two types of women: the proper, religious ones who hide behind the *chador* and these enticing girls who reveal themselves, pushing their headscarves back one centimeter every year. Look at her, wearing sandals without socks." His eyes searched my face. He dropped his voice. "You also want to know about virgins."

In truth, I wanted to know the times of the Tehran bus.

"Young women must be intact when they marry," he explained. "It is a father's job to protect his daughters, not to let them walk late at night. If there is not a little blood the first time, then the marriage can be cancelled."

"And the man?"

"You cannot tell if a man is a virgin or not."

For my entertainment, he engaged three college students at the next table in conversation, pretending to be an American. The girls didn't believe him, wouldn't meet our eyes, but were pleased to practice their English. One asked me, "What you say that I never have boyfriend?"

Babak presented Tabriz as Iran's most liberal city, which it was, given its proximity to the western border. In its time the oasis had served as a capital for the Mongols, Persians and Azerbaijanis. Turkish was once the only language heard in its brick-vaulted bazaars. The city had been occupied by the Russians during two world wars. Yet, in Babak, as in the country as a whole, there was much theatre at play: in his obsession with sex, in the schizophrenic division between private and public life, in Tehran demonizing America for domestic advantage. Concealment was part of life in Iran.

"Let's go look at the prostitutes," suggested Babak, pandering to a stereotype, rising to his feet, moving without grace.

I couldn't imagine a prostitute in a *chador*. Nor could I fathom the dichotomy in him, a cocksure certainty undermined by liberal aspirations. He wanted to show me tolerant Iran yet insisted that men and women should not shake hands in public. He boasted of Persia's deep-rooted civilization yet hungered for details of celebrity culture. He was proud of his self-sufficient republic but admitted that the revolution had been a bitter, failed experiment.

"You can spot a whore by the way she chews gum and wears strong lipstick," he pointed out as we took to the street. "And how she looks at a man. Some of our reformers want to legalize Houses of Chastity – brothels – as a way of coping with our one million homeless women. I think this is not so different in Europe."

We strolled along the suburban "Champs-Elysées". We drank Coolack Cola. A girl – smooth empty face in the halogen shadows, chewing gum – turned away when he asked her a question. "And for two?" he called after her, exercising his licit superiority, a sour look on his anxious face.

In the taxi back to his house, Babak yelled in my ear the sordid dreams of a crippled life, his neck muscles straining, his hand on my thigh. "I did not tell you the truth about Turkey," he confessed. "I can't ... you know." He made a pumping motion with his fist. "Landmine."

In the morning, outside my window, a young woman moved through a walled, private garden. Babak had said only of his sister, "She teaches English and looks after our father's dying flowers." When he and I sat in the garden, surrounded by rosebushes and jasmine, she stopped her dead-heading to serve our breakfast: black tea, dates and crumbling goat's cheese.

"Your presence blesses our home," she told me in a formal expression of politeness.

"Are there no eggs?" Babak asked her. He believed eating three eggs every day would restore his strength. She shrugged – there was a cool distance between them – then sat down and asked if I would stay for dinner.

"I don't want to be any trouble."

She said that nothing would give her more pleasure. Her heart-shaped face narrowed into a pointed chin. Her uncovered, hennaed hair gleamed like spun copper thread in the sun. I complimented her on the garden.

"It is a gift," said Laleh, assigning credit for earthly beauty to the divine. "A little paradise."

"And a big headache," complained Babak.

"'Paradise' comes from an old Persian word meaning 'walled garden'," she added.

The late *imam*'s paradise was oblong in shape, surrounded by whitewashed walls and overlooked by the half-closed windows of the house. There were dwarf tulips, musk roses and a hidden alcove of pink orchids. A small fountain rose from under a persimmon tree, feeding miniature stone waterways and a turquoise tile pool shaded by mulberries. Above us, the blue sky rippled beyond its branches, as did the crude balconies of a neighboring apartment block. I thought of the first Eden, both garden and paradise, which was said to lie not far off the trail, either to the east of Palestine or near the source of the Tigris and Euphrates in Turkey.

"Would you like to watch the TV5 news?" Babak asked. "We have a satellite dish."

"I'm happy here, thanks."

"I tell Laleh she should keep up with events in the outside world."

"I'm more concerned with matters at home," she said.

"At least television would keep you indoors."

Laleh smiled at me, brushing aside an old argument, pouring fresh tea. I could see that Babak struggled to control his sister. She was a woman, fifteen years his junior, so his word took precedence, yet his moral inferiority and physical wounds emasculated him. She had been born to ageing parents who had answered Ayatollah Khomeini's call for patriotic acts of procreation during the Iran–Iraq war. With Babak embittered by his injuries, she alone perpetuated their hope and piety.

"She goes to demonstrations," Babak confided in me, as if she wasn't at the table, as if male solidarity might rein in her behavior. "Last week she stood outside the university with masking tape over her mouth."

"It was a silent protest."

"Which will change nothing in this Shia paradise," he exploded, at once angry, on his feet, pacing away from the table then turning back to speak with an undertone of fear in his voice. "If Hazbollahi take her away, who will visit her in prison?"

Ansar-e-Hazbollah, the "Helpers of the Party of God", were a small cog in Iran's vast security apparatus. Its members had been responsible for uncounted violent acts against protesters: lashing students with chains in their dormitories, throwing a dissident out of the window to his death, killing some eighty Iranian journalists and writers.

"I have a class to teach," she said, turning her watch with tapering fingers and making formal apologies to me.

"And I have a business meeting. You should go with her," he told me. "Her students never have the opportunity to listen to a native English speaker. To hear what they're missing."

Babak went out to find us a taxi, filling the role men assign to themselves to sustain the impression of superiority. Some senior clerics assert that a woman needs a man's permission even to go shopping. When the taxi arrived, Laleh appeared on the threshold in full black *chador*, draped in her public façade.

On the drive, she sat in silence, seemingly unaware of me, as though no words had ever passed between us.

Her features were clearly delineated: a pronounced nose, a strong, firm mouth, deep-set eyes that were neither happy nor defiant, beneath which lingered pale shadows. The long, smooth line of her eyebrows traced the contours of her skull, turning sharply down above the corner of the eyes like the wings of black seagulls.

"Do you wear the veil by choice?" I asked her after a couple of minutes.

"I wear it out of loyalty." To her parents, her society, her traditions.

"But you believe in change," I said, confused.

"You misunderstand. Women put on the *chador* in defiance of the Shah, to reclaim themselves from alien ideals. I protest now because the revolution promised women dignity and equality."

"And after a quarter of a century you have neither?"

"One of the great falsehoods, deployed by men, is that the Holy Koran decrees women should remain in second place," she said.

Outside the window, a billboard of martyrs – led by thirteen-year-old Hossein Fahmideh, the world's first suicide bomber – marched off to a paradise of sunflowers and roses. Beneath it, a young man tried to cut across the frantic press of traffic. His T-shirt read "Broken System".

Laleh's private language-school was above a row of electronic shops selling pirate Berlitz tapes and Holy War DVDs. The class was a waste of time, at least for me. The students, all of whom were male, only wanted to know about New York salaries and the cost of flats in London. I answered them, of course, even though the information would be useful only in gilding their fantasies.

"Those boys think Europe is a utopia" Laleh said later in the school office. "In the cybercafés they trawl sex pages. On satellite television they see couples kissing in the street. They think if they get to the West they will have a job, a house, a nice life. I tell them it is not so. I tell them that there are 22 million unemployed in Europe. But still they go, at least as far as Turkey – you probably know for what reason – and many never return."

After lunch, Laleh went to the university for a Koranic Studies lecture. She, like other modern Iranian women, was rereading the Koran, not to please the male clerics but to ease Islam away from bigots and chauvinists, to seek an interpretation for the twenty-first century.

In the evening, I did not catch sight of her. She stayed out – perhaps because she had no father to prevent her from "walking late", perhaps to avoid Babak. He let me cook him supper.

The next morning, the sound of digging woke me. We had an hour together in the garden – pruning the fig, watering the honeysuckle – before her brother returned from another business meeting. I talked to them about the sixties. I asked Laleh if she could see a parallel between Western students then and Iranians now: in the popularity of Aldous Huxley and Jamal al-Din al-Afghani, in bra- and *hejab*-burning, in Berkeley's sit-ins and Tabriz's silent protests, in the shootings at Kent State and Tehran universities.

She mocked the notion; the sixties were about individualism, promiscuity and decadence, she said, forces which undermine Islam and its brotherhood of believers. Then she considered my argument about the shared aspiration for self-knowledge and an earthly utopia.

"I think your spiritual awakening has much in common with the six-ties'," I said.

"Maybe there are similarities," she admitted. "At both times, a mass of young people try to bring about change."

"The big difference is that in America the Church never seized execu-tive power," interrupted Babak.

"My generation must either change Iran or leave Iran," Laleh said, meeting my eyes.

I spent the day with Babak, knowing that I should move on, but the prospect of seeing Laleh kept me in Tabriz. To fill my time, I hired a car and driver and headed to Kandovan, a nearby town touted as another Gar-den of Eden by the local tourist office. Along the riverbank lounged fami-lies of picnickers, the doors of their cars open like birds' wings. In a tea house I treated Babak to a bowl of *abgusht* mutton stew. On the drive back to the city, I tried to draw him about the Iran–Iraq war, which had lasted eight years and left a million dead, but he was preoccupied. He said only, "Khomeini promised us all a place in paradise. Today, most Iranians would rather check their email than die for Islam."

I waited at the house again that evening.

In Iran, life is largely a grind relieved by parties. Hence the country's greatest treasures are said to be found indoors, usually on a Friday evening. On the street, alcohol, Madonna and the mingling of the sexes are banned, but in their homes people are for the most part left to enjoy themselves.

I was as surprised as Laleh when Babak suggested holding a party. At first she refused to co-operate, distrusting his motives, but when he insisted the occasion was for my benefit, she could not refuse. He seemed deter-mined to draw together all their friends. All *her* friends. As Laleh prepared the food and we rearranged the furniture, she kept looking at him, saying hardly a word all afternoon.

Around eight, the women arrived, slipped off cloaks and veils, emerged in skimpy skirts and teetering high heels. Laleh wore a dress only slightly more modest than her friends'. She set vases of fresh flowers on the table, laid out grilled fish, herbed rice and sweets. Couples paired off, revived old conversations, made new acquaintances. Babak showed me off like a trophy, introducing me as "his" travel writer.

Over glasses of fruity, home-made wine, I enjoyed the easy banter. One student asked me what I thought of Iranians.

"Hospitable," I assured her.

"But are we beautiful?"

"Tabrizi women are said by Iranians to be the country's most beautiful," her boyfriend pointed out.

"I've seen nothing to prove otherwise," I told them.

"You'll find the road becomes less civilized as you head east," said Laleh's teacher, a tall and elegant academic wearing a heady perfume.

"Afghans consider us to be as soft as girls," the boyfriend told me, shaking his long, gelled mane. "Do you know they call us 'sandwich-eaters'?"

Guests started to dance as casually as if in Forest Hill or Windsor. The academic said, "Before 1979, we used to drink in public and pray in private. Now we pray in public and drink in private."

Babak seemed to be his usual troubled self. He lit cigarette after cigarette, took a single drag, puffed his cheeks, then stubbed out the butt. He danced once, an unbalanced, graceless stumble across the living-room floor. No one laughed, good manners preserving his dignity, for he was respected – as a hero if not as a man.

Around ten o'clock, word spread that he had an announcement to make. When Laleh heard this her mood darkened. She found a chair in the corner, smoothed back her hair, then sat on her hands in a hopeless, childish gesture.

In front of the closed door, Babak said, "This is a historic evening in our lives." At first, his voice wavered but, as he spoke, he gained confidence. "Tonight, a new life begins."

Babak announced he had resigned his bus-driving job that morning. He had decided to emigrate to France and, because money was needed for fares and to arrange the visas, he had arranged for the house to be sold. Although she would miss her many dear friends, he went on, Laleh would be coming with him. As a single woman, she could not remain alone in Tabriz, nor could she choose a fate apart from him.

"Now, friends, eat and laugh," he said. "Enjoy the music and be happy for us."

Few guests were surprised by the news. To escape the confiscated revolution, about 200,000 Iranians emigrate every year. The men shook Babak's hand. The women embraced Laleh. Only her teacher hesitated at the back of the room. All assumed Laleh had known of the plan.

"You must visit us in Paris," Babak said to me.

For her part, Laleh said nothing. Babak could act alone. I looked at her and imagined the strip of masking tape over her mouth. When he cranked up the music, the guests wheeled back on to the dance floor. Laleh stared in the mirror, reeling in shock, full of inward rage. "I hate my feelings," she said.

I followed her into the garden.

She's by the pond, her body turned away from me, sheltered in darkness.

"You said that you would never leave Iran," I say to her back.

"This is where I was born, where I grew up. How can I leave my father's garden?"

"Can you stay?"

"Without parents or relatives?" Her laughter mocks my naivety. "You, as a foreigner, will never understand." Her voice cracks in frustration at the contradictions. "I chose not to have a boyfriend. I didn't want to be trapped. Now, my own brother..."

Laleh – whose name means tulip, the symbol of martyrdom – turns to face me. Her blanched face seems to shimmer in the shadows of the trees. She is angry, desperate, bitter: at her bondage, at my freedom, at her brother.

"Who do you – in the West – turn to for moral authority?" she demands, no longer speaking in polite half-truths. "To answer your questions and to know yourself?"

I turn the question over in my mind. I realize that she has touched on my dilemma. "Mostly to ourselves," I say, choosing my words with care.

"Hence your dislocation and fragmentation," she hisses at me, her mouth so close that I feel her breath on my ear. "You lost your way, forgot your God and now belong nowhere. You wander alone in a spiritual desert. You are a cancer."

10. TURN TURN TURN

Iran has struggled for security throughout its history. The Persians built an empire stretching from the Mediterranean to India only to surrender it to Alexander the Great, the Parthians and then the Sassanians. In AD 637, five years after Mohammed's death, the country was conquered by the Arabs. Persian society flourished under the caliphs and the Seljuks, until destroyed again by the Mongols.

In modern times, Iran has continued to be a battleground for foreign and internal rivalries. The CIA helped to topple a democratically elected, nationalist prime minister in 1953. Both Washington and London had disapproved of the nationalization of the Anglo-Iranian Oil Company, forerunner of BP. But the new Shah's brutality and impatient reforms inspired anti-American Islamic fundamentalists to hijack the 1979 revolution which overthrew him.

That February, 3 million Iranians took to the streets to celebrate the Ayatollah Khomeini's return to Tehran. Many considered him to be God's envoy. All knew he was a ruthless leader. He seized real power for the clergy. He permitted the execution of the Shah's generals, praying on the spot where they were shot. He ordered the killing of "anti-Islamic" modernizers, adulterers and homosexuals. His Revolutionary Guards – an elite parallel army – stormed the American Embassy to prevent the CIA from plotting another coup, holding US diplomats hostage for 444 days. His regime exploited the Iran–Iraq war, initiated by Saddam Hussein, and the Shia ideology of martyrdom to consolidate its grip on power. Khomeini changed the balance of power in the Middle East and introduced a new ideological force into world politics. His pursuit of security even led him to incite murder beyond Iran's borders, innovating a death sentence against a foreigner – British author Salman Rushdie – for expressing contrary opinions, spreading seeds of fear into the century ahead. Today his successors build nuclear weapons to protect clerical rule.

I put down my pen, turn off the Byrds, gaze out of the window of my Partisan Black Super Saloon. "GOD'S TRUCK" flashes past me on the electric name-board above a driver's cab. "*Allah Akbar*" is painted in green lettering along the flank of a government oil-tanker. "Victory is Ours" proclaims a Shiraz Turbo bus, lying on its side among scattered suitcases, limping passengers and thick black skid marks.

Babak and Laleh are on my mind. Her unhappy, angry words ring in my ears. She's right, despite all her insecurities. Western society is dislocated and fragmented. We're dismantling the social order of civil society. Our God is all but forgotten. But it wasn't always so. The counterculture tried to reform the West in the sixties. A generation rebelled against institutional authority, espousing communality without ideology, confronting spiritual emptiness by pursuing a collective dream for self-knowledge. Youth wanted to change the world.

Which was why one of the first actions of Khomeini's Revolutionary Council in 1979 was to close the trail. The Intrepids – liberal, curious and often stoned – weren't welcomed in the Islamic Republic. Not that any of them set out to influence Iranian self-determination. The overlanders were, after all, the first movement of people in history traveling to be colonized rather than to colonize. But travel opens minds. As I had witnessed in Turkey, visitors' values and comparative wealth did – and do – change places. The irony is that the very people Khomeini locked out may have helped to kindle his revolution.

The first European tourist bus to cross Iran was probably Société Dubreuil's *La route des Indes*. In the spring of 1956, its Chausson coach left Porte d'Italie in Paris under police escort with two well-known actresses – Danielle Delorme and Micheline Presle – and fourteen passengers on board. Two engineers and a complete set of spare parts accompanied them on a second coach. The 2-month, 8,733-mile journey to Mumbai, which apparently went as per timetable and without a single mechanical incident, also took in Italy, Yugoslavia, Bulgaria, Turkey, Syria, Lebanon, Jordan, Iraq and Pakistan. After its return Dubreuil never attempted to run another trip, even though 22,000 people watched the film of the journey at the Gaumont cinema in Place Clichy.

The next year a British traveling salesman, Paddy Garrow-Fisher, established the first regular coach service to the subcontinent. For almost a decade, "The Indiaman" operated the world's longest bus route from London King's Cross and across the Middle East to Mumbai and Calcutta.

"Whoever had this brilliant idea deserves some sort of memorial," wrote the editor of *Meccano* magazine in 1959, "and I believe he finds it in the minds of those who travel with him. Anything may happen on such a long land voyage, and those who venture on it accept cheerfully any discomfort that may arise, whether caused by a dust storm in a desert or by such a misfortune as sticking in the mud of some primitive road."

"The Indiaman" and its twenty-six tourists shuddered over stony tracks and sank in loose sand. Its tyres had to be deflated to cross the Iranian deserts. In the absence of road signs – and sometimes roads themselves – navigation through Iran was often by the Safavid towers which once guided camel caravans. After forty-eight days or so, its AEC Regent rolled into Pakistan.

Dozens of cheap tour operators followed in Garrow-Fisher's rutted trail. In 1960, the first backpacker hostel – the Overseas Visitors Club – opened in London. Young Australians, the real Barry McKenzies, sailed to England on one-way tickets, served in pubs, slept with New Zealanders, then headed for home. Autotours, Exodus, Intertrek and the Beesley brothers showed them the way with inclusive camping trips via the bulls in Pamplona, the beer halls of Munich and the Asia overland trail. Ford Transit vans loaded and unloaded punters at all hours of the day and night along Earls Court Road. Penn Overland ran two new coaches to India. Swagman used dilapidated bangers acquired from nationalized companies. A young Australian vet bought a lumbering green Bristol double-decker to drive to Morocco with his mates and within a few years built up a hundred-strong fleet of converted "deckers". Top Deck and Hughes Overland then pushed the trail beyond India, across the Bay of Bengal and south-east Asia all the way to Sydney. The *caravanserais* and doss-houses of the old Silk Road echoed to the strains of "Waltzing Matilda" and "Kumbaya".

At the same time, British freaks were grooving on Hugo Williams. German kids were reading *Siddhartha*. French students were in-

spired by Nicolas Bouvier's prescient journey from Geneva to Japan. They
hitched to Istanbul to link up with other tribes of independent travellers,
following the Beatles' procession to Rishikesh. Americans tended to start
in Paris. In the late fifties, in the Latin Quarter, the Beats had sketched
out the road map for the hip generation: eastwards towards mysticism,
inwards to creative expression, out of this world with the recreational use of
drugs. At the fractured, transatlantica bookshop Shakespeare and Company, Ginsberg had slept among the stacks and Burroughs researched *Naked
Lunch*. John Lennon had dropped by the shop in October 1961. Now boys
from Queens and girls from Sarah Lawrence began their journey sitting in
Henry Miller's chair, stroking the press on which the first edition of *Ulysses*
was printed, scoring a dime bag of Paris's cheapest marijuana in dingy
Chez Popoff's before heading to the teeming bus depot at Porte d'Italie.

"Where's you guys going?" shouted hopeful travellers into the open
passenger doors of idling vehicles.

"Nirvana," came the reply.

The original Magic Bus operated from a cockroach-infested office on
Amsterdam's Dam Square, carrying students, lone voyagers and brigades of
hippies to India. Its buses were diverse and decrepit, especially after financial troubles forced the company to subcontract. Not that hard seats and
broken springs lessened the pleasure of the journey. The secret for a suc-
cessful trip was to get the passengers smoking chillum dope pipes before
breakfast. In the early days, the buses almost levitated across border posts.
On their return, so much Afghan hash was stashed in their tanks that
regular smokers in Europe became accustomed to the aftertaste of diesel.

Magic Bus spawned many copycat operators, one of whose coaches
was held to ransom for almost six months during the first Lebanese civil
war but, in the early 1980s, the original company met a prosaic, unenlightened end when forced into bankruptcy.

In the seventeen or eighteen years of the trail's existence, before the
Iranian border was closed, the land of extremes was baking in the heat of
the Shah's White Revolution. The Shah – installed by the CIA coup –
wanted his country to embrace Western values without bloodshed, to for-
sake religion for capitalism. He listened to Dolly Parton records. He drove
a Cadillac convertible and a Rolls-Royce. He drank a glass of wine on

national television. Most Iranians were unsettled by the speed of change. They mistook the Intrepids – the first Westerners that many of them had met – for ambassadors of the capitalist world. In the tense political climate, their casual morality and liberal humanism must have insulted – even enraged – traditionalists and zealots alike. These breezy unorthodox travellers, hitching across Iran on a shoestring, helped to stir the stern Islamic reawakening.

South of the highway, a scorched, stony plain unfolds toward Iraq. Power lines loop above parched squares of fields, between mud-brick settlements and distant grain silos. Distant flames of oil refineries plume on the horizon. A greenhouse catches the sun, flashing semaphore signals across the land, and the bright light sears my eyes.

Khomeini's portrait looms above a bustling chemical factory. The military guards wear white spats. At a highway checkpoint, a well-spoken young man in neat black trousers and pressed shirt studies my passport, asks the purpose of my visit and wishes me a safe stay in Tehran.

11. MAGIC CARPET RIDE

Tehran. Capital of revolution. Shrine to martyrs. Home to the Revolutionary Guard's nuclear-weapons program. An urban disease fed by anger, despair and pollution so thick it tints the air. Once the most westernized city in the Middle East, it's now a sprawling cemetery to tolerance.

I push out from the pavement in a clump of riders, calling out my destination to the trawling drivers. With four other men, I snatch a shared taxi downtown, spiralling into a coil of roundabouts, chaotic concrete flyovers and filthy squares. On the heaving streets, muscular paramilitaries hold hands, beggars intone prayers, young women promenade in tailored *rupushes*, tight on the rump, drawing attention to their figures. Flights of mopeds congest the grids between identical grey tower blocks, squeezing the wrong way up bus lanes, racing into littered bazaars. If the Americans ever try to invade Iran, goes a current joke, their tanks will get stuck in Tehran's traffic jams.

In the sixties and seventies, after the Gülhane and Doğubeyazit, travelers headed for the Amir Kabir; *the* place to stay in Tehran. "Dirty, only one sheet per bed, but at the very heart of the soulless, tinsel and glitter Coca-Cola city," according to the trail's first guidebook, published in 1971. The hotel occupied the top two floors of a concrete horseshoe of balconies and walkways. Downstairs was a tyre emporium. Sixty rials – about a dollar – bought a mattress in the dorm. The toilet was at the end of the hall.

"The Amir Kabir?" remember trail veterans. "That's where you contracted *real* dysentery."

Today the tinsel and glitter has been dulled by the search for moral purity but Amir Kabir Avenue remains, and still satisfies Tehran's huge appetite for motor parts.

On foot, I press along its length, through the roar of raised male voices and the stench of old Ford Falcons. The pavement is lined with racks of Volvo bus springs, sets of Torx wrenches and rolls of sheet metal. A shopkeeper leans against the bars of his display window as if imprisoned by pistons. A mechanic repairs mopeds under a flyover. A tinsmith makes throttle cables on his lap. Above him, behind enclosed concrete balconies, shrouded eyes watch, women's lives unfold and the songs of caged birds lift to the tall blue sky.

I climb the steep stairs to the Hotel Mashhad, ducking because of the low ceilings. Its owner thinks I want a room.

"Only Western tourists stay here," he assures me. "Last night there were twenty: Norway, Sweden, Canada."

Young Pakistanis peer over his shoulder. I see no Westerners, not here or on the streets. "And the hippies?" I ask. "Did they stay here too?"

"They date back to the period of the diseased person." The King of Kings. The American snake. The Shah. "Maybe this hotel was then called Amir Kabir," he says, trying to oblige me. "Maybe not. Everything change. You want see room?"

I don't.

Next door, the Goodyear Guest House has been driven out by Caspian Tires. Toora Wheels have run over the Youth Hostel Ferdosi. At the Hotel Arman, where the arguments of Russian traders funnel down the lift shaft, the duty manager simply shakes his head. He tells me that all the old overland hotels – the Toos, the Mehr and the Amir Kabir – have gone, their dormitories now stacked floor to ceiling with corroded batteries and inner tubes.

"Could I meet someone who worked at the Amir?" I ask the manager.

"No Tehrani can remember those days."

Of course. Too much history has passed since the last Magic Bus was hurried out of town by an adolescent guardsman waving his Kalashnikov.

I drop back down to the street. A prehistoric Oldsmobile rams an ancient Volkswagen, spilling its load of newly picked oranges. They scatter across the tarmac like fugitives, rushing for freedom until their sweet sticky juices explode beneath tyres. Swarms of flies sizzle in the pulp and under the midday sun.

"It's gone," says Rudy.

"The Amir Kabir?" I guess. What else would a sixty-year-old Englishman with a pierced ear and bandanna be looking for here? Except perhaps a Rover fuel-injection pump.

"What a drag," he sighs. Hooded eyes stare at me from under thick eyebrows. And at my notebook. "You look like someone who knows where a man could buy a beer."

"A friend in Tabriz told me that Iran Air stewards smuggle in duty-free to sell uptown."

"Then I'm out of here."

Rudy's face is thin and dry, hatched by laughter lines, thatched with sparse red hair and spiked by a majestic, bulbous nose useful for sniffing out artificial stimulants. His lanky, hard-muscled frame bespeaks a life un-hindered by moderation. As he strides back toward Khomeini Square, I tell him, "The uptown neighborhood's called Zaferanie."

"Zaferanie?" says Rudy. "The drive-in used to be there. I'd park the Bedford sideways so everyone could see the film."

"What Bedford?"

"The Silver Dart. We'd drop the windows, put up our feet and watch *Yellow Submarine*."

"When was this?"

"I started driving to India in '66."

Rudy was a bus driver. Forty years on – with kids grown up, wife en-rolled on an Open University course and his Cornish tourist coaches sold to a local entrepreneur – he, like Penny, has returned on a sentimental journey.

"My Bedford was a tatty Barnstable school bus with bad brakes," he tells me. "The idea was to drive to Pakistan and flog it for a profit. I got to the Maidstone bypass and the brakes caught fire. Bam! 'How far you going in this thing?' the fireman asked. I told him Lahore. He said, 'You won't reach Southend.'"

"So the Silver Dart didn't make it?"

"It made Istanbul," says Rudy, flourishing his hands, uttering wide-mouthed automotive sounds. Narcotics alone could not account for such frenetic energy. "I was about to leave for Pakistan when I noticed that the other buses driven by Europeans were taking passengers. I thought, just a minute, never mind selling the blinking vehicle, I'll fill it to the gunwales with freaks. $25 to Tehran. $50 to Kabul. I mean, we're talking about absolute nu'pence but when you've got thirty or forty people onboard and you're doing your backwards and forwards, you can make *beaucoup* bucks."

Beneath a "Down with foreign mercenaries" poster a small boy calls out to us, "OK USA!", novelty in his voice. We flag down a Zaferanie-bound taxi on Hafez Street. On the back seat Rudy tells me that for more than a decade he followed "that long line of loonies" between London and India, a trip taking about three weeks each way. He advertized in *Oz* and *Private Eye* ("Want to take a trip on a little £.s.d.?"), hand-printed his own tickets, collected passengers on a corner outside Victoria Coach Station.

"On my second run, there were twenty of them, all stood on the street with their huge suitcases and backpacks..."

"Don't tell me: girls in beads, guys with battered twelve-string guitars..."

"...plus a chick in a mauve boiler-suit who was going to Ceylon to surf, if you can believe it. Her board flew off – along with the roof rack – when the paved road ended outside Ankara. I'd sent everyone an itinerary, telling them to bring only essentials, plus a blanket for when we broke down. They turned up with sewing kits, St Christophers, even steak pies and Christmas puddings. Everyone's auntie had been round the night before saying, 'Ooo, you're traveling around the world, you can't go without *this*.'"

Rudy's first stop on the continent was Amsterdam. In Dam Square, he would open the old Bedford's door and shout out, "Anyone for India?" He'd call by the youth hostels in Munich and Salzburg. He'd stop at the places where the Intrepids picked up mail, cashed traveler's cheques, found themselves stranded.

"People would get off, people would get on. No one was in a hurry. They'd sleep, play the guitar, slip back together into the love bunk."

"The love bunk?"

"The *fabulous* love bunk. I'd taken some seats out at the back and made a bit of a bed, just like on Kesey's bus. The Bedford's springs and shocks were terrible and we'd go bouncing, *bouncing* across Europe. Dear God," he says, looking out at a wide hot boulevard, "this used to be Eisenhower Avenue."

At an intersection, women in long-brim *chadors* funnel between the cars. A tout taps at the window and offers us an illicit pack of playing cards. Rudy leans forward to shout directions but, as our driver speaks no English, he reverts to body language, rocking left and right on the back seat.

"Did you hear about the Sheffield City coach owned by a Bradford insurance agent named Quddus?" I ask him. "In the winter of '71 it started out for Rawalpindi, but the engine was so useless that all thirty-five passengers – barefoot Westerners in flowing dresses and Pakistanis in saris – had to push the bus over the Alps in a blizzard."

"Must have been another Bedford," sighs Rudy, turning away from a child prostrate on a traffic island, exposing his hunchback, holding aloft an alms tin in his small, outstretched fist.

In Turkey, Rudy had been a regular at the Pudding Shop. He convinced the Çoplans to paint their logo on his bus in exchange for a free fry-up every time he passed through town.

"You were some entrepreneur," I say.

"I had to keep the wheels turning. Nearly lost them once or twice. In an Istanbul traffic jam, this little fibreglass Ford started edging alongside me. I've never liked people who try to get away from the lights before me. Well, the bus's aluminium trim lipped in behind the Ford's wheel arch. When the lights changed, I pressed the gas – vroooom! – and heard a terrible tearing noise. I'd ripped the entire bodywork off the Ford. The poor Turk leapt out of his car seriously pissed off. Then – talk about Moses and the Red Sea – all the traffic cleared. I started driving for my life, with the Turk running behind and an American passenger sliding down a window, waving his fist and yelling out, "Don't fuck with the Dart, man."

"Another trip – and this is the gospel truth – I almost drove Timothy Leary to Delhi. He was on the run from the FBI here in Tehran."

"That'd be 1973."

"Could be. Dates were never my strong point. Leary phoned Indira Gandhi to ask if she would grant him political asylum. 'India is my spiritual home,' he told her. Like, give me a break. He said the bus was too dangerous and flew to Kabul, where Interpol arrested him."

Outside the window unfold endless, stifling suburbs. Distances seem huge, destinations unattainable. A decrepit taxi passes us, towing a smashed ambulance with a lash of seat-belt webbing. A Pontiac, another gas-guzzling memento of the former elite, cuts between them, snapping the belt. With its frayed, stubby end, a furious medic beats the offending car.

"Travel was easy back then. A Western passport protected you," Rudy says, watching the arguing drivers. "When you're young, you're immortal, aren't you?"

Our taxi drops us in Zaferanie, the Belgravia of Tehran on the slopes of the Alborz mountains. Here, men in ties buy NAD stereos and drive new LandCruisers, indulging themselves in the present day, while elsewhere in the city the poor embrace a populist message of heavenly promise.

We stroll between airline offices, advancing uphill, Rudy dropping broad hints about the nearest beverage bar. Caution is not a word in his vocabulary. No duty manager offers us a tumbler of Talisker in a back room. No local financier invites us to a private party in a penthouse suite. I let on that my information on illicit alcohol might have been another of Babak's distilled fantasies.

"But my thirst remains most real," says Rudy.

"How about some tea?" I suggest.

Above the noise of the city rises Sa'd Abad, a lush, lofty park surrounding the former Shah's summer residence. Parrots and woodpeckers dart in the canopy of green, sixty feet above the winding footpaths. On the tree trunks are carved the initials of male friends. Outside the White Palace are two head-high bronze boots, the only remains of a giant statue of Reza Shah Pahlavi.

Rudy and I climb to a tea house beyond the Green Palace, now a museum of ostentatious furniture not looted during the Revolution. We sit on a carpet-covered *takhts* lounger, shoes off, drinking tea and eating dates. The waiter welcomes other patrons by wiping off tabletops with a towel. We listen to their scattered laughter.

"At least the air's cool," says Rudy, thinking again of beer.

In the course of telling him about my journey, I say, "I've never been able to find a proper road map of the overland trail."

"Never was one."

"But didn't you get lost?"

"Sometimes there weren't any roads. My first trip across Iran I saw only one paved highway in the whole country. But every few months I'd come back and see the change. One time a town would get its first street lamp. The next there would be a new stretch of tarmac. The third, a round-about with a fountain and a road sign. Then everything started to look so *American*: police uniforms, Budweiser beer, the Peace Corps."

As he talks, Rudy lights a cigarette and blows the smoke straight above us toward the trees.

"Nothing changed in the desert, of course. The road was never paved and overtaking was nasty. You had to get a view several miles ahead to make absolutely sure there were no approaching sand clouds. Once you committed yourself, you couldn't see a thing. I tended to turn the music way up loud when overtaking."

"To the soundtrack of your lives?" I ask him.

"The stereo system was the first thing every driver arranged," he nods. "I played stuff with meaningful lyrics, the tapes getting stretchier and stretchier in the heat. Reeeeur reeeeur."

Aboard the Silver Dart, Rudy also played the music of the country through which he was driving: marching tunes through Austria's mountain passes, Beethoven's Ninth in Germany, *bouzouki* tapes across Greece, *arabesk* songs in Turkey and *qawwali* chants in Pakistan.

"As well as kids in Indian headbands, I carried dead-ass dentists, Essex shop-assistants, Welsh council-workers, people who'd spent all their lives in an office and had never left the UK. All of them were looking for an Adventure. I couldn't let the trip be just a bus ride. I had to knock them out with *foreign* vibes."

With its patchwork radiator and without any windows (they had fallen out on his thirteenth run along the rutted Caspian road), Rudy finally sold the Bedford in Lahore.

"I don't think there was one original part left in her," he laughs. "Praise Allah for the mechanics outside the Amir Kabir."

Pakistan International used the Bedford for another decade as an airport courtesy bus.

"And that was the end of the Silver Dart?"

"I'd always dreamed of owning a Mercedes," he recalls, shaking his head. "Every trip I'd watched them sail past me, their engine brake going buurrrp burrrrp."

In 1972, Rudy bought a Mercedes 321 with a 5.6 liter engine and a split windscreen. With its two supplementary 100-gallon fuel tanks, the Last Silver Dart ("LSD") could cover the 7,250 miles from London to Kathmandu with only two fuel stops – in Greece and Iran.

"On its first trip, six Italian lesbians got onboard. In the early seventies that was – bam! – in your face. They were proud, defiant and very hairy. They refused to shave any bodily parts."

At the next table, a customer drinks his tea in the Iranian manner, from a saucer, with a lump of sugar between his teeth. As the waiter refills our glasses, Rudy goes on, "Somewhere between Kandahar and Kabul we stopped at a blissed-out hotel. My schedule was always flexible, to say the least, so in that beautiful place I decided to let a day or six slip away. But the lesbians were on a timetable. 'Rudy,' said the pretty one, putting down her pipe, 'we have to be in Kabul tomorrow. We leave now, yes?' They stood there with their hands on their knives, cutting no slack. When I didn't respond, they said, 'Rudy, we don't want to kill you...' In a flash, half a dozen other passengers jumped up and formed a human chain around me. We left the next day."

Rudy flicks his ash on the ground. I watch him with close interest as his eyes take on a look of mystification, as he says, "Afghanistan, man, was another world. The gate opened and the light cleared. One minute, the world was dull and dusty. The next, the poppies were *luminous* red, the rivers *electric* white, the mountains balanced against the sky. The whole journey went from black-and-white to color."

"Maybe it was the dope," I say.

"The border police practically gave the stuff away. They lay on string beds on the customs shed veranda, slicing melons, calling for green tea, saying to us, 'This is for you. First quality. Welcome to Afghanistan.'" Rudy smiles, stirs his tea, doesn't drink, says, "Baggy Aladdin pants, flowery shawls as big as blankets, hubble-bubbles filled with humungous *chunks* of the finest Masr. My single best moment happened in Kabul. Someone at Friends' Hotel put on the new Steppenwolf album." He leans forward, lifts his voice and his hands to the table, sings softly about flying free on a magic carpet ride. "It doesn't sound like much now but I was blown away."

He stretches his arms out along the bench, looks up into the trees. I watch his face. He says, "I wanted to go back there this trip but the wife wouldn't wear it. All the news about the Taliban and American bombing had scared her. I told her, 'Janie, don't get your balls in an uproar. I'm a survivor.' She said to me, 'Rudy, honey, you're not immortal any longer.'"

The waiter stands by our lounger, breaking Rudy's concentration, catching my eye. Perhaps he doesn't like hard rock. Or maybe he just wants us to pay the bill.

Rudy's face is flushed, almost as if a discharge of psychic heat is racing through his veins. "We were kids, turning nineteen or twenty, questioning and rebelling just like the world itself," he says as I find my wallet. "That synchronicity gave us such a sense of sharing, of possibility."

"Can you still smell the patchouli?" I ask.

"Yeah, I can," he says without a hint of cynicism. "Like it was yesterday."

As I pay for the tea I think of Laleh again and ask him if, after all his journeys, he feels attached to any single place. He shakes his head. "I felt the world was mine and that I belonged to the whole world." He takes a long, deep breath. "I found my little piece of heaven on the road itself."

The evening light is golden, the shadows now soft. Above our heads a gentle breeze rouses the woodpeckers, stirring beating wings and rustling whispers from the interlocking branches of the poplars and plane trees.

Rudy adds, "But I lost it after the Iranian Revolution."

"Not just you," I say.

"All the guys stopped driving then: Rob and Keith with their Setra, George on Budget Bus, ugly Bob from Chattanooga who had the Volvo. It broke my heart having to stop."

We're standing now, descending towards the city. I ask, "Was driving always a big thing for you?"

"Since reading travel stories as a boy," he says.

At the age of eight, Rudy's imagination had been captured by an anthology of automobile journeys in the *Second Motor Book*. In its pages, an army Major FAC Forbes-Leith set out in 1924 in a 14 h.p. Wolseley Felix, intent on being the first man to drive from England to India.

"I carried the book on both the Bedford and the Merc, along with Heyerdahl and Vonnegut. I suppose Forbes-Leith was my inspiration. He and an amazing pedal car."

"What pedal car?"

"When I was growing up, my uncle had a toy shop in St Austell. One Christmas he gave me a pedal car. It was made by Liberty Brothers – registration LIB 1212, I remember – and had a long bonnet, pneumatic tyres, spoked wheels and little doors with knobs which opened out like this. It was painted buttercup-yellow with dark-green upholstery and silver headlights. When I was very small – about five – I could just squeeze a little girl into the seat next to me," he says.

"For a magic carpet ride?"

"It was such an item in my life. One day I came home from school and my dad had given it away. *My* bloody pedal car." He's quiet for a moment. Then he says, "Hey, did I tell you that I drove the first double-decker bus into Kathmandu?"

Rudy is determined to track down a pre-dinner drink. We agree to meet later and I leave him at the edge of the park. I'm heading back to my hotel and to reach the Metro station must cross a main road. Iranian drivers ignore traffic lights so, to survive, I've learnt to tuck myself in behind groups of pedestrians. As a body, we leave the relative safety of the pavement, striking out into the organized chaos of fast, filthy vehicles, looking straight ahead, not stopping. Horns blare, a bus hurtles down a contraflow lane piping its piercing whistle, a green and white BMW police car slices by my tail.

I duck into the station.

In the ticket hall, every sign is written in Farsi, except for an arrow on a city map reading "You Are Here". On the platform, the first two carriages are reserved for women. I am packed into the male section of the train, pushed up against a middle-aged man with rough, fawn-colored skin. He starts to talk, says, "I have been to the cemetery."

He extracts from his breast pocket a photograph of a young man, maybe twenty-one years old. In the prime of life. "My youth," he says.

"Your son," I say, attempting to correct him.

"He died 3,212 years ago."

"*Days* ago. I am sorry."

"He was an artist. A poet. A scholar. A helicopter pilot. I am unfortunate."

I repeat my regret.

"He flew for *Ghalicheye Parandeh*. Air Squadron – how you say? – Magic Carpet." He takes back the photograph as the carriage flickers into darkness. Under the flashing tunnel lights he stares at the black-and-white image of his lost boy. "I used to work in the south with the Americans on oil wells. That is where I learn my English thirty years ago. Now I forget my English. But never I forget my youth."

12. DARK SIDE OF THE MOON

"If you do not allow me to drive you I will eat sorrow," said Sahar, my lean, persuasive taxi-driver.

Ten minutes ago, he spotted me outside my hotel, advised me to avoid the central bus station, offered instead to drive me the 250 miles south to Isfahan. The price, even before negotiation, was not expensive. Now, we're barrelling out of Tehran in his shattered Paykan as I tell him about the hippie trail. He says, "I've been on it. I've been on it."

But when? Why? He's too young. He must have been born years after the Beatles broke up. Then I notice his eyes.

In the early 1990s, when he was sixteen years old, Sahar's family – itinerant fruit-farmers in the Zagros mountains – decided to send him and his younger brother to England to give them the chance of a better life. Visas were not available for unskilled Qashqa'i boys so their father, a hard-working *khan* who only wanted the best for his family, decided to pay to smuggle them to Britain. The family had contacts – a cousin in the police, relatives on the Turkish border – plus the example of a friend whose own sons had made it to London.

"His boys have good slippers and their own television," said the *khan*. "My boys have none of these things."

The fee was exorbitant, almost two years' income, but the boys' earnings would in time pay off the debt and enable the family to plant an acre of orchard.

Only half of Iranians are Persians, descendants of the Elamite and Aryan tribes who first settled the central plateau. Azaris and Kurds make up the largest minorities, followed by a sprinkling of Lors, Arabs and Turkmen. The smallest ethnic groups are proud, independent nomads: Bakhtiaris, Baluchis – whose name means "Wanderers" – and Qashqa'is.

Since displaced by a grandson of Genghis Khan in 1256, the Qashqa'is have roamed the wilds of Iran, driving vast flocks of sheep from winter pastures on the southern plains to grassy summer highlands in the Zagros.

Sahar was born in a black kilim tent, nursed on horseback, swayed and pitched up into the hills at a few weeks old. During his first, month-long, 400-mile spring migration, his father walked beside son and wife, wearing his cylindrical camel-hair cap, sweeping aside the new grass which grew to the height of a horse's girth. At night, when a hundred tents were pitched along a barren hillside, Sahar was a warm bundle dozing on thick Persian carpets. Around him, his family shared plates of rice, tore off thin leaves of flat bread, talked of the next water hole, a lame·camel, the death of a lamb. By lamplight, his mother, unveiled, wearing a bright saffron and green dress with the coins of her necklaces gently ringing, sang old lullabies to him.

His people's high pastures lay to the east of the Karun river, in the shadow of a hill named Sartog, or "roof of the world". The broad, weather-beaten plateau, 2,600 meters above sea level, was treeless, fertile and fed by springs frothing from its embrace of dusty mountains. Here, Sahar spent his summers, from the age of three collecting dung for the fire, at five minding the goats, by seven drawing water for the compact green oasis of apricots and cherries at the base of the hill. His mother produced for him a baby sister who died and a brother who lived. Sahar promised to look after the boy and taught him to watch the flocks, to twine goat-hair rope, to whistle lambs down from the hill. When he did things wrong, Sahar called him useless, saying he didn't do enough to support the family, but they were really better than the best of friends. On clear dark nights when dogs barked and voices whispered in nearby tents, Sahar and Ali lay on their backs reaching for the stars. Before sunrise, they watched for the rise of the new moon, seeing it only by the dark disc of absent stars.

In the low-lying winter lands the brothers were taught arithmetic and Islamic history in a tent schoolhouse. Their father wanted his boys to learn English, to use a pen and paper, to be respected. "I want to see them become something, to look after us when we grow old." Sahar had a good eye and hands and he excelled at drawing, skills that would later serve him well. Ali preferred playing football.

A month after Sahar's sixteenth birthday, after the brothers had helped for the last time to bring the family to Sartog, their father made the arrangements. No contract needed to be signed. The local broker was a respected elder in Aminabad – "Honest Town" – and the organization for which he worked was powerful and not to be betrayed. Neither boy slept that last night on the roof of the world, in excitement more than doubt or trepidation. Money was needed to find a better life; their role in its acquisition could not be questioned.

In the stillness before dawn, the old rooster crowed. The sheep bleated in their deep, guttural voices. A woman's bare feet padded on the earth. Then, the bellies of the clouds turned silver. The rising sun traced the tops of the tents and stirred the breeze. The shadows of sparrows flitted across the tent flaps. Flies buzzed from their crevices. It was time to go.

"*Bei salamet,*" the father wished his sons. Go honestly. Ali cried. Sahar wrapped his arms around him. Their mother had packed in their bags dried apricots, nuts, lentils and leaves of her bread. They carried a single change of clothes. Nothing else.

On horseback the brothers rode off the plateau, away from the goat herds and oases of apricots and cherries, down on to a flat plain, featureless but for the scrub bushes. Behind them, the haze distorted distances, sucking color and detail from the receding ranges until their peaks seemed to dissolve into the sky. There were no road signs, of course, no notable features for the alien eye, only sharp stone slopes and spiralling dust devils. The sand covered their clothes, settled in their hair, crunched between their teeth.

At dusk, they reached Aminabad's narrow lanes, drank tea with the broker's family, slept their first night under a solid ceiling.

"I have many friends who live there," the broker's grandmother said to them.

"Live where?" asked Sahar.

"Where you will live," replied the senile old woman. "But no one can tell me if there are any goats in paradise."

The next morning, a van carried Sahar and Ali to Tehran where, without papers but with a sense of adventure, they were hidden beneath crates of oranges on an ancient lorry. Their euphoria survived the day's drive west along the trail to Tabriz, despite the boredom and a leaking exhaust, and even lasted through the long, tedious week in a rough, alpine village, waiting for the snows to clear on the pass over the Turkish border.

Their hosts were kind enough, giving the boys a place beside the stove to sleep, but – for the first time in his wandering and rooted life – Sahar felt dislocated. He couldn't understand the Kurds when they spoke between themselves. Their food was unfamiliar. The village policeman demanded a bribe which, although expected, unnerved him. On the muddy edge of Asia Minor, Sahar realized that he and his brother had been born on the wrong side of an invisible line. In the turbid hamlet, he first understood that a passport enabled any man to cross over it. Through the cold nights, he gazed at his hosts' identity papers, studied the befriended policeman's ID card, looked at the designation of opportunity in tamper-proof typefaces, watermarks and official stamps. He saw that the right documents, in order and unquestioned, could change one's future, opening the door on to a luckier world.

The brothers went with the new moon, under a black sky, stepping into the nightmare. Their guide was Cemil, a pale boy of about Ali's age, who didn't own proper boots. He'd walked over the pass many times but never on such a bitter night. The path out of the village ran through fast, meltwater streams and their feet were sodden and icy before they even reached the border hills. They climbed quickly, wary of using a torch, losing their footing on the steep, starlit slopes. The piercing cold cut through their thin jackets. The air was still, every noise echoing for miles in the darkness. Ali looked over his shoulder and searched the sky for the dark disc of absent stars but, as yet, it was too early in the night.

With the altitude, the drifts began to thicken, closing in on them, muffling all sound except the soft crunch of their footsteps. There were no trees or scrub on the barren slope, no lights below or in front of them. Around midnight, by which time the silent snow blanketed every slope, Cemil lost the path.

With a little fall of heart, the boys pressed together against a boulder to share each other's warmth. Sahar was determined not to retrace their steps. Instead, they'd push straight uphill, toward the pass which must open somewhere above them like a nick in the rocky horizon. But, just as it had obscured the path, the snow hid foot-width fissures and blade-sharp stones. Ali started to lag behind, falling and tearing his trousers, cutting his knee. Their clothes were stiff with dirt and sweat. It took them almost an hour to scale the last few hundred meters to the pass.

Turkey spread below them, ice-black but for the lights of a far-off town. They zigzagged down the slope, trying to make up time, anxious to reach the safe house before dawn. As their legs whirred out of control, a sound rose out of them, half laughter half fear, wild relief in their moment of greatest vulnerability. Then, out of the darkness, the dogs fell on them, outrunning a patrol. Cemil panicked and turned back the way they had come. Sahar and Ali lost their footing, cartwheeled over the lip of a ledge and fell twenty feet into a snow bank. The cold was numbing but the brothers didn't dare to move, barely to breathe – their limbs wrapped around each other, snow crystals in their mouths – as the dogs cantered back and forth along the ridge, trying to pick up the scent. The Turkish guards were close enough for the brothers to hear their breathless voices. When shots were fired into the air, the boys started, nearly giving themselves away. At last, the men moved on and the night fell quiet again. With bare, frozen hands, Sahar and Ali dug out into the bitter air. They fled downhill stooped like chimpanzees, in terror and silence, to the shuttered Kurdish farm.

An hour later, with clothes still wet, they were in a van. Two hours after that, they were on a truck. At a depot in an industrial city, they changed vehicles again, this time into a big trailer, empty but for an Afghan couple and a miserable, red-eyed Iraqi. Sahar and Ali were pleased to have company, sharing out their apricots, making conversation in broken English. The couple were heading for Denmark. She was pregnant. The Iraqi told them he hated Americans. The transport drove all day and through the night. The brothers tried to sleep, tucked womb-like into a breezy corner, lulled by the engine's pulse and the numbing distance. They took turns gazing through a tear in the tarpaulin at the lights of passing towns. Despite their tiredness, they were excited again, each new destination beckoning, every new place promising them strangers to befriend, hot food to share, a place to sleep. But the driver only stopped once in twelve hours for a meal at a roadside canteen. No one had told the boys the length of each stage of the journey and soon they ran out of water.

Ten days after leaving the roof of the world, they reached sea level in Istanbul. They were given a room in a low-built concrete warehouse, not far from the ferry landing where Penny had first set foot in Asia. But the boys wouldn't have seen her light, even if it had still been burning in the Maiden's Tower. Their window was nailed shut. To pay the rent, they worked downstairs in a pencil factory until the arrival of a second truck of refugees. Only once did they venture out along the narrow asphalt alleys and post a card home, care of the broker in Honest Town, to relay their pride at having reached the Bosphorus. "The journey here took longer than expected," Sahar wrote simply.

Ali added, "I miss seeing the moon."

All week, people arrived – a Syrian, an Azerbaijani, two more Iranians – until there were ten of them snatching brief, static sanctuary behind the bare doors along the dark corridor. Without a word the Afghan woman cooked for them, preparing an evening pan of *pilau*. The frowning men stole back to their cubicles with their portions, eating in solitude like starved animals, feeling grateful and shamed. Later, the woman's husband took up a collection to buy the next day's rice. She was cooking it when a driver came to take them away.

In the van, the Syrian argued for repayment of his dinner money, the meal having been left uneaten. At the depot, the nine men and one woman were led into the trailer and locked inside a hidden steel cubicle. There was room only for them to sit down – no one could stand or stretch out – so all were thankful that Ali and the woman were quite small. Pallets of tinned fruit and house paint were loaded against the false partition. The doors were sealed by a customs officer. An hour later, a cab was coupled to the trailer. In the pitch darkness the refugees rocked, rolled and tried not to touch on the drive to the port.

Sahar never discovered how the air vent became blocked. Or how long it was until the first of them died. Those who had a watch could not read it in the darkness. The cab's engine had been switched off and their metal cell swayed with the ship's movement.

The woman's breathing was the first to quicken. Between short, shallow gasps she whispered to her husband. He soothed her in intimate, reassuring tones. Then the Iraqi started to cough. Fear rose hot and dry in the metallic air and Sahar's throat. The husband pushed at the door as the walls seemed to contract around them. Other men, it was impossible to tell which ones, also uncurled their limbs and scrabbled forwards. The Syrian started to kick at the door, calling out for help. The woman was now panting, wailing. Sahar clawed at the corner of the door, hoping to find a sliver of an opening, telling Ali to relax and conserve oxygen. Together, they turned their backs on the shouting and pushed their faces into the jamb. Behind them, the others fought for breath, pulled at their throats, died.

Forty hours after leaving Turkey, the steel door was unlocked in a Brindisi warehouse. All the refugees were dead but Sahar. He ran away from the metal tomb and the Italian industrial estate. He left behind his brother's little body. In a central café, he snatched a diner's wallet and bought a rail ticket to Paris. At Calais, he hid beneath an articulated container lorry. He stole in to Britain.

Every year, an estimated 500,000 people are smuggled into Europe in a trade more profitable than drug-trafficking. Few illegal migrants are victims at the start of their journey, apart from women and children trafficked in the sex trade. Most choose to leave home, desperate for the chance to improve their lives. No more than fifty gangs handle the bulk of the world's human trade. Most illegals reach their destination heavily in their debt. Some are forced to work as prostitutes or "soldiers" for the smuggling rings.

So it was for Sahar. His skills made him a valued forger. He paid back his dues without feeling, out of desperation, living on the frayed fringes of society. The once-gentle fruit-farmer's son grasped at whatever handfuls of life came within his reach. He financed his parents' new orchard. He never told them that his beloved brother was dead.

Rubble roads run eastwards toward Dasht-é Kavir, a wasteland of parched riverbeds and salt pans. A sweep of low scrub clings to a gorge cut by the last rain, three years ago. A shepherd in a white shirt, buttoned to the collar, waistcoat and jacket draped over his shoulders, stands at the edge of the desert, his flock far out of sight.

"Last year, I was arrested in London," Sahar complains to me, not taking his eyes off the road. "The police seized all my equipment and told me

I must go to a British prison for two years – or go home. So I came back to drive this taxi. In some months, I'll have enough money again to leave."

In the sixties, all along the trail, cash-strapped Intrepids sold their passports on the black market, knowing that their embassy would replace them. It was a practice which hadn't died out.

Sahar asks to see my passport. I reach into my money belt and hand it to him, too disturbed by his story to deny him. He turns it over, picks at the corner of my visa, studies the lamination around my photograph. I scrutinize those pale, distant eyes, living a separate life. I notice his hard-lipped mouth, high cheekbones and broad Mongol features.

"Good quality," he says. "These biometric chips are the new challenge."

"Not for sale," I say.

"$200," he smiles, showing his teeth.

Mist-blue and melon-green tulip domes bloom in the desert. Indigo mosaic monuments rise above lines of white poplars. In the soft light of late afternoon, I'm dropped off in the most splendidly proportioned city in the world. I planned to come to Isfahan to see its sublime Royal Square, but now the story of Sahar's tragic journey – and the desperate need which motivated it – casts a shadow over the city.

In 1934, Isfahan's beauty gave Robert Byron, the English aesthete and travel writer, "one of those rare moments of absolute peace, when the body is loose, the mind asks no questions, and the world is a triumph". Thirty years later, knowledgeable Intrepids came here also to wonder at "the pearl of Islam".

The immense *maidan* spreads beyond a labyrinthine, vaulted bazaar, enclosed by tiered arcades the color of pale honey. Its two great mosques – with majestic, recessed portals flanked by minarets – are positioned in near-perfect symmetry with the buff, brick Ali Qapu Palace. Byron wrote that the square's beauty lies in the contrast between a formal space and a romantic diversity of buildings. I'm reminded both of St Peter's in Rome, but with none of its bellied weightiness, and a soaring, tiled Jardin des Tuileries.

I walk its half-kilometer length among ice-cream vendors, tourist calèches and picnicking families. Fathers and sons gnaw on cobs of char-grilled corn. Mothers laze on tartan rugs, loosen cumbersome *chadors*, offer a glimpse of red hem or tight denim. Daughters release long braids of brown hair from beneath their scarves, then wade barefoot in the fountains.

Ahead of me is the Masjid-a-Shah mosque, the culmination of a thousand years of Persian architecture, virtually untouched since its completion in 1638. Almost the entire surface of the vast, airy building is covered with exquisite glazed tiles. Swallows sweep across its tranquil inner courtyard, the arc of their flight as elegant as the line of receding arches. In a sunken porch, two young school friends sketch the intricate arabesques, adding dark-blue and golden-yellow watercolor, re-rendering the inscriptions. A caretaker arrives on an old bicycle, his reflection rippling in the wide ablutions pool.

In this serene space, beneath the mountains where he spent the summers of his childhood, I can't stop thinking of Sahar.

"Hey, Mister, where are you from?" shouts a bold young man, shattering my thoughts. I ignore him, walking away from him and his friends. He calls after me again. "We are Pink Floyd fans."

This I had not expected.

"The lunatic is in my head..." he quotes, arresting my step. "You lock the door, and throw away the key. There's someone in my head but it's not me."

The four men are engineering students from Mashhad on a study visit to the Isfahan Nuclear Technology Center, part of the ring of weapon and defense industries which surrounds the city. They're all in their late teens, with pale skin from indoor lives, wearing clean white shirts and black slacks. One of them carries the latest issue of the Ferdosi University magazine – *Fanoos Khial* or *Lantern of Dreams* – which features a six-page article on Pink Floyd.

"We know all about Roger Waters."

"And Steve O'Rourke going to that great gig in the sky."

Their knowledge of the band is better than mine. They also tell me that a previous issue of the magazine was devoted to Dylan interviews and reviews.

"Hey, Mister, what is the song at the end of *Dark Side of the Moon*?" I am asked.

"The song?"

"If you listen to the very end of 'Eclipse' and turn the volume up really high, you hear faint music."

"Paul is dead?" I suggest.

"Some people do think it's a Beatles number."

"I heard it was classical music."

"You know, these songs are over thirty years old," I say to the students.

Then, in the vaulted main sanctuary, standing on a black paving-stone under the great dome, the four young men start to sing. "And if your head explodes with dark forebodings too..." Other visitors stop and stare. Old men dozing in the cool of the *madraseh* sit up on their prayer blankets. "...I'll see you on the dark side of the moon."

I'm shaken by their display, anxious of its impiety, denied my moments of both reflection and "absolute peace".

As the clear echo reverberates a dozen times around the sanctuary, a stranger pushes forward, not meeting our eyes. He puts down his mobile phone and, as if to nullify their irreverence, chants up into the dome, *"Allah Akbar."* God is Great. Now, his words ring around the dome.

The agitated caretaker is at our side, hissing at the students in Farsi, shepherding them out of the mosque.

"Mister, you know there is no dark side of the moon really," one of them calls back to me, paraphrasing Pink Floyd's lyrics. "It's all dark."

13. HOOKED ON A FEELING

Salt stains leech across the earth. Sand dunes pool around mountains, stranding mouse-brown islands in a waterless sea. A tarred road slithers between scorched fields like a black serpent searching for water.

The Simorgh Top Train – air conditioned, on time and with a flask of tea by each padded seat – slices out of the stark Salt Desert, a gritty cyclone in its wake, and east into Khorasan province, "the land of the sunrise". Ahead on the wide plain lies Mashhad, Iran's most sacred and remote city. Its name means Place of Martyrdom, for here the eighth Shi'ite *imam*, Reza, a direct descendant of Mohammed, was interred in AD 817. Here, too, in 1970, Penny ate a noxious banana pancake.

I'm sharing this leg of the trail with 15 million pilgrims who every year cross the flat and featureless plain to pray at the Holy Shrine. But this Friday morning, the city's streets are almost deserted. I walk alone from the station. Beneath leafy *chenar* trees, a grocer lays out his trays of aubergines and carrots. A baker shapes a ball of dough, pounds it flat, then tosses it in the oven. A single *mullah*, in long, collarless gown, rides past me on a motorbike.

At the reception desk of my hotel, a dozen Turkmen girls with bulging suitcases and boxes of new kitchen appliances are checking out. I assume they are religious tourists, escaping both the paucity of consumer goods and restrictions of Islam at home. Until the loud-mouthed Turjik beside me nods at them and asks the porter in Farsi, "Do they use *arz*?" Meaning foreign currency.

"Not *arz*," the porter replies, lowering his eyes, "but *darz*." Meaning slot.

Not every hotel guest uses their complimentary prayer-mat.

Shall we just bum around together?"

Mashhad's broad, baking avenues burst from the Holy Shrine like the points of a star. I'm jostled by the crowds, trying to make notes, when Nazzer Poor spots me, drives up on to the pavement and almost knocks down a white-robed Afghan in his rush to shake my hand.

"You are my guest," he says.

Which won't mean his services are free.

Nazzer is a professional tour-guide, a sweet-tongued humanist who arouses my interest at first sight. He's about sixty, devout and ebullient, with unblemished good looks. His beaming face is punctuated by jet-black eyebrows between a white goatee and groomed, silver hair.

"What can I show you of our sacred city?" he asks.

I tell Nazzer I want to see the shrine and the Martyrs' Cemetery.

"So you are writing the new Koran."

"I'm writing a travel book, not a guidebook."

"*Lonely Planet, Rough Guide, Let's Go*: they are the travellers' bibles."

"You make them sound blasphemous," I say.

"Not at all. Our government wishes foreign tourists to be our political envoys, so to speak, to show the world that life in Iran is good." He's quoting the official line, looking at the reflection in a shop window, but whether of himself or the people around us, I cannot tell. "You are most welcome here."

Nazzer manages to park his car without injuring another worshipper and we join the press of rich Bahrainis and impoverished Azerbaijanis converging on the vast, walled complex. He launches into a routine history of *ziyarah* as we push towards the golden domes of the shrine.

"*Ziyarah* or pilgrimage is probably the most important act of a Shi'ite's life ... a deeply significant expression of faith ... ensuring a place in paradise..."

On woven carpets, barefoot Kuwaiti pilgrims in voluminous robes sing, drink green tea, read the Koran. Bands of Caucasian Turkmen hustle between the airy courtyards. Three boys brandish plastic revolvers, chasing one another around a clutch of mourners and an open wooden coffin. In the low concrete crypt, the deceased are laid to rest on payment of a $10,000 fee. The air – and the devotion – are hot. The Holy Shrine has little of Isfahan's beauty, none of its peace or humility, but I am moved by the outpouring of prayer.

Constructed between 1405 and 1416, this exquisite building..." Nazzer babbles, leading me around the eight gold-tiled minarets, through grandiose arched doorways and into the Great Mosque of Gohar Shad. He rattles off historical dates and hands me a souvenir prayer disc of Meccan clay. In the Qods Courtyard with its carved drinking fountain dedicated to Palestinian martyrs, he recites the improvements made to the shrine since the Revolution. Then he moves on to criticize the Shah.

"That snake was an empty drum, the grasping puppet of America. He banned the *chador* and allowed girls to wear tight blouses that showed off their overhead lamps." He shakes his head on cue. "The idiot tried to westernize Iran."

"Westernize or modernize?" I ask him.

"This is not New York, you know," he answers, disregarding the distinction. "The Shah never understood that ours is a traditional society."

In this most reverent place, I suddenly want to tease impiety out of him. I want to shake him – and myself – out of regurgitating a complacent, unquestioning view of the world. So I tell him about Penny.

His diatribe falters.

"The word 'hippie' entered our language," he says in a different tone, "to mean an idealist who takes life easy."

"Did the hippies help to spark the Revolution?" I ask, again trying to provoke him.

Nazzer laughs in shock, holding his hand over his mouth. He searches for the correct response from the prepared text.

"The hippies who crossed Iran were ... on a kind of pilgrimage," he says.

I shake my head. Pilgrimage seems to be a means of reinforcing certainties of faith. Independent travel can be about challenging one's idea of living.

Nazzer's mouth moves but no words escape. He considers my question again. A perplexed look crosses his face. He glances around the courtyard. He presses his lips together. "Let's go somewhere else," he replies.

The air in the Hezardestan Tea House is as cool and still as the ornamental fish in its central blue-tiled pond. Its walls and pillars are decorated with scenes from Ferdosi's *Shah-namah*, the Iranian *Iliad* which harks back to an older, pre-Islamic Iran. Guests descend a discreet flight of stairs, settle themselves cross-legged on sofas, wait for tea and *qalyan* water pipes, moving as infrequently as the fish. If a guest does stir himself to talk, he – or she, for there are a handful of couples here – does so in the lightest voice.

"In 1967, I was a young conscript at Do-qaram on the Afghan border," says Nazzer, letting drop both hyperbole and facade. "One day, a group of hippies – three boys and a girl – came through in a van. They wanted to relieve themselves, but there was no toilet, only one small bush. So when the woman crouched behind it, I turned my binoculars towards her."

"What did you see?" I ask him.

"Nothing. Apart from another bush."

He smiles as if to hide his embarrassment, though I'm sure he feels none. According to the Koran, men and women should not let their pubic hair grow longer than "a grain of wheat".

"That sight was like the first bite of a forbidden fruit," he hurries on. "Next, I heard about an oasis, a little paradise fed by artesian wells near the border, where hippies often stopped to sunbathe and swim."

"And you spied on them there too?"

"Who does not love to see a naked woman? Who can ignore such perfection?" he says, pleasure in his voice. "An Iranian man may have seven or eight children, yet he will never have seen his wife unclothed. I went there often."

Again, I wonder aloud if the hippies had in some small way strengthened the traditionalists' anti-Western resolve; the vaunting of personal freedom helping to send an unsettled nation reeling back towards an antique world.

"Their revolution changed *my* life," Nazzer concedes, his eyes now shining. "After the army, I had decided to go into law. One day in Vahdat Park I met – what did you call him? – an Intrepid? In our short encounter, he taught me that one of the best subjects in the world is human science: that is, human relations, human rights, how complicated it is to be a human."

Before my eyes, Nazzer Poor is transformed from the dutiful, rote-reeling guide. His smile is no longer forced.

"That philosophy moved me," he nods in agreement. "I realized then that under the Shah our lawyers were cowards. They didn't try to protect those who were less than equal. They only wanted power and influence for themselves. A door opened and I walked through it to find – as you said – a different idea of living."

"How?" I ask.

"By moving to a commune in Yorkshire."

Now I laugh out loud. Few places on earth could be more different – and damper – than sun-struck Mashhad.

"A nudist commune," he adds.

Iranians will never cease to amaze me.

"To walk naked in the open air, to allow the body its natural allocation of sunshine."

"In Yorkshire?" I repeat.

"Not far from Wetherby," he says. "In those days, many of us – in Iran and the West – believed that a sickness hung over society, a society based on the accumulation of capital and the suppression of the underprivileged. I joined a community of equals and waited for the next revolution."

"Didn't you get cold?" I ask.

"I grew Elvis Presley sideburns."

In the late sixties, at the height of the commune movement, many hundreds of co-operatives, kibbutzes and collective squats operated around the world. In Welsh valleys, on the West Bank and in Nicaraguan jungles, dreamers, escapists, radical Shakers and naturist-socialists built earthly utopias, experimenting in post-modern survival, group marriage and "non-acquisitive contentment". Publications like *Resurgence*, *Akwasasne News* and *Country Bizarre* held the movement together, linking the isolated communities. But by the end of the seventies, the euphoria of most communards became bogged down in mud and jealousy. Some communes even found themselves in the middle of war zones.

"In 1979, I came home. Joyfully. During the Shah's years, a million Iranians – engineers, intellectuals, artists – had left the country. After the Revolution, many of us came back."

"Only to emigrate again in even greater numbers," I say.

"We thought we were putting our ideals into practice. We trusted in perfection, in equality, in *jamé tohidi* – a pure society of believers. I shared the dream of living and working in a community where everyone served a common good. At the beginning it was altogether superior to Yorkshire."

I try to imagine this devout, dutiful guide, after striding naked across the Moors in the name of one revolution, donning green battle fatigues to help to fight another. In both cases, he believed himself to be healing a sick society. I raise my glass of tea to Nazzer and to his dreams.

"That was our utopia," he smiles. "But within a year I wanted to run away into the ground like water."

The waiter brings us a plate of macaroons. Nazzer leans back on the cushions, falling silent as the sugar dissolves in the tea.

"Thousands of people were executed when Khomeini revealed the true nature of his interpretation of God's will," he says after a moment, afraid to raise his voice, unable to contain himself. "Newspapers were closed, politicians disqualified, the 'just and pious' Council of Guardians became our new masters. The Holy Shrine here in Mashhad became a $2-billion business, running farms, mines, carpet factories, in fact, most of Khorasan province. It, like the Foundation for the Oppressed and War Veterans, is among the biggest employers in the Middle East. Who controls them?" He looks around the room and whispers, "The clerics – and their lawyers."

He goes on, "Twenty-five years ago we made a choice. The people welcomed Khomeini. We championed the Islamic state. We died for it. But we never expected our choice to last for ever. Today, if every simple man and woman in Iran voted for a secular state, our wish would not be respected."

Nazzer is speaking so quietly now – and with such taut anger – that to hear I must press my head towards him.

"You ask me if the hippies caused the Iranian Revolution. I tell you no, my friend, because there was no revolution. Only betrayal. Today, we still live in a dictatorship; the only difference is, the new version hides its greed behind beards and turbans."

He falls silent. He chooses a macaroon. For a time, the only noise is of his eating.

"We were all idealists once," he adds, reaching for another sweet.

It's not just lost ideals Nazzer shares with the West. I ask him, "You no longer believe you can change the world?"

"Our high-minded leaders think they are ordained to govern until the Hidden Imam reappears, along with Jesus Christ."

In Shi'ite Islam the Twelve Imams are believed to have been sent by God as guides to mankind.

"But you told me the Hidden Imam disappeared into a cave in the ninth century," I say.

"And so we wait for his return," he replies, at once bitter, detached and defeated. "We wait." The waiter returns to refill our glasses. "Now," Nazzer announces in his energetic, official voice, "do we still need to visit the Martyrs' Cemetery?"

At the evening market on Modarres Street, bookstalls sell copies of the Koran and out-of-date L. L. Bean mail-order catalogues. A beggar leans on a broken wall, cracking sunflower seeds with his teeth. I walk back to my hotel, past a fresh, talkative Turkman girl loitering in the foyer, and return to my room. I set the chair by the window and, within sight of the gilded resting place of Imam Reza, begin to type up my notes.

After a few minutes, I realize I'm staring at the blank screen, unable to find the right words. I stand, pace up and down the room, return to my chair. Again nothing. I look at my notepad. My thoughts dwell on Nazzer, Sahar and Babak, on their disillusionment and the power of dreams. I think of the calm order of my private striving. I get out of the chair again. Look out the window. Gaze at my face in the mirror. In my weakness, I grasp for the familiar, turning on the television. *Harry Potter* is showing. In Farsi.

In the grey dawn, the Holy Shrine is swathed in ruby-red spot lamps and strings of fairy-lights. Hotel cleaners in full black *chador* and yellow Marigold rubber gloves mop marble banquet halls. A neon-lit bronze of Khomeini – cold eyes, sensuous lips, imperfect – growls at a segregated queue of locals waiting in line for thin, platter-size loaves of bread pinned to boards on line of nails.

As my coach pulls away from Mashhad, a passenger walks down the aisle offering dates to fellow travellers. A Bugs Bunny Santa Claus dances from the rear-view mirror, around quotations from the Koran. A student lawyer sits next to me. He's distracted by my tattered photocopy of the first trail guidebook.

"Hippie?" he says, leafing through its heady pages. "In my language, the word means a wastrel, a messy person who has no plan for life."

My magic bus heads towards the border.

Afghanistan

14. GET OFF OF MY CLOUD

Three days I've been here in limbo. Three times I've hired a car and driver and headed out of Herat. Each morning at the same time, I've pulled up outside the remaining walls of Maslakh camp, called out to the Pashtuns in the fields, "*Senga ye?*" – "How are you?" – then climbed back in the car and returned to my hotel. Yesterday, three white beards – *spingera* – awaited me, squatting on the ground at my usual spot, their long, loose, cotton shirts gathered over their knees. I greeted them with phrasebook in hand. My driver helped me to exchange a few pleasantries.

"Are you a journalist?" they asked me.

"I'm a seeker," I answered – borrowing from V. S. Naipaul – then drove away.

I want to speak to the Pashtuns, proud, independent and largest of Afghanistan's four ethnic groups. The Taliban, with Pakistan's contrivance, sprang from their number. I want to understand the origins of their idealistic religious fantasy, to create a perfect global caliphate on a model of Mohammed's seventh-century Arabia. I'm also curious to see what remains of Maslakh, until last year the largest refugee camp in Asia. But I need to be invited as a guest, not to force my way in like an intruder. Then, this morning, I broke through, catching a glimpse of a hidden world. I was invited to tea.

Twenty-five years of war – first against the Soviets and then amongst themselves – displaced more than five million Afghans. One-third of the population fled to Iran, Pakistan and other neighboring countries. Near the Iran–Afghanistan border, Maslakh, which means slaughterhouse, was at its peak home to 160,000 displaced men, women and children. After my experience in Turkey and Iran, I realize that I can't sail past this bleak outpost.

The driver drops me off at the gate. A hawk-nosed raisin-cleaner,

English-speaking and carrying a Kalashnikov, leads me into the mud-brick alleys. A cobbler sells single shoes for one-legged mine victims. Barefoot children play a game like marbles with the vertebrae of small animals. Boys carry scraps of firewood and greasy plastic bottles of river water past cell-like bakeries. In a bare courtyard a woman in frayed blue *burqua* blows on a cooking fire. In the last months, much of the sprawling, five-mile-square clay city has been flattened by bulldozers, the dispossessed given ploughs and money to go home, their irises scanned to prevent them from returning and making a second claim. My hosts are among those too frightened to leave the camp.

A wooden door opens in the street wall on to a plain yard. Above us hangs a grape trellis. The vine has withered and died. In a corner stands the *hujdura*, the male guest-room.

"You can call it a Pashtun drawing room," says my guide. His face is so deeply lined that I cannot guess his age. Twenty-five? Forty? "And pride for a Pashtun is to have his *hujdura* filled with guests."

The tidy room is painted sky-blue with a hip-height band of white. Colored mats cover the earth floor, and cushions run around the edge. On the wall are posters of an idyllic Swiss village, a truck on a Karakoram highway and one listing the advantages of polio vaccination. There is no furniture. An informal *jirga* – or community council meeting – has been convened to welcome me. I leave my shoes at the door. My guide stows his gun.

He gestures for me to sit. The men are at prayers and he asks if I will wait until they finish. A boy – one of a dozen looking through the deep-set, unglazed window – pours water from a tin jug over my hands into a tooled basin. A cloth is laid on the carpets and upon it an unexpected meal: goat curry, stewed okra, yoghurt and na'an.

"You Canadians have fed us many times," explains my guide. "Now we will feed you." He stretches his hand out over the food and says, "In the name of God the Merciful, the Compassionate."

I eat some vegetables and the bread, dipping it into the gravy, leaving the meat for hungrier mouths. Ten elders arrive singly and in pairs, sitting cross-legged around the room in white *shalwar kameez*, embroidered Kandahari caps or twisted turbans on their heads. Their beards are clean and combed, every hair in place. In their plastic sandals are husks of chaff. They wait in silence for me to finish my meal.

Only when tea – milky and tasting of cardamom – is poured do they start to talk, passing around a bowl of boiled sweets. Each man then rises to shake my hand. I introduce myself again, explaining that I want to carry their words and stories back to the West. "I need to understand," I say to them.

"I left my fields in 1978," says a stony-faced white beard, holding my eye. The year Afghanistan began its long slide into chaos. During the first communist revolution, thousands of villagers were executed in a Stalinist attempt to reform rural society. "I was a landlord with good land."

"What did you grow?" I ask.

"Grapes. The most delicious grapes in Zabul. I was arrested and my neighbors took my fields, forging the sale document. I escaped to Iran."

He met his wife in a camp there, my guide translates. Their children were born there, and a first grandchild. The family only moved back over the border to Maslakh when the Iranians closed their camps.

"The Russians did not kill individuals," volunteers the next man, a bicycle repairman. His tone is formal, his account dispassionate. "They bombed villages."

In 1979, the Soviets invaded Afghanistan, propping up the pro-Moscow regime. Over the next decade, more than 100,000 Red Army soldiers occupied the country. The United States seized the chance to injure its Cold War enemy by supporting the factional *jihad*, feeding $700 million a year to the *mujaheddin* in one of the largest covert operations in history. An army of 35,000 fervent fighters was trained in part by Pakistan's Inter-Services Intelligence Agency as well as by the Green Berets and US Navy Seals. A handful of *mujaheddin* were even schooled at a CIA paramilitary camp in Virginia.

"Twelve years ago, the governor called me to his office, saying that the Russians were about to attack my village and to protect my family," the bicycle repairman goes on. "That night, seventy-six people were killed, including my sister and her three children. Killed not by the Russians, but by arguing *mujaheddin*."

The dream of a pure Islamic state was used by the US to defeat the

Soviets, then channelled by Pakistan into the creation of the Taliban. In 1989, the Red Army withdrew, leaving behind 1.5 million Afghans dead. Nine months later, the Berlin Wall collapsed. In Washington, the CIA celebrated their victories with champagne, while civil war would soon reduce Kabul to rubble.

A third man, thin and grim-faced, opens his mouth to speak, revealing small, pearly teeth. "My teeth are white because I never lie," he says, "because I never eat my words, nor those of another man." His body is a skeleton covered with faded skin. "I tell you, every night I dream of smelling my soil again."

"I want to build *my* mud house on *my* land," interrupts a fourth elder, his impatience and powerful voice punching through the civility. "If you tell me I can do this in two years, I want it in one. If you say one year, I want it now."

"But why can't you go home today?" I ask them. It is eighteen months since the Taliban, the radical rural movement which emerged as the victor in the civil wars of the late 1990s, was bombed out of power by the US Air Force. Already, "remnant Taliban elements" are attacking the International Security Assistance Force and undermining the precarious national stability.

"Home?" says the white beard. "Look at us. What do you see?"

I see swan-white turbans and beards "long enough to protrude from a fist clasped under the chin". I see guns at the door. I know that their wives and daughters aren't allowed outside the house unless accompanied by a male relative. I realize that for them Islam is to be practiced as God intended: as a religion, a code of law, a political system, a way of life.

"Every good Muslim must wear a beard," he explains, "but ours make travel impossible."

"We cannot go home. We have old enemies who will say we are al-Qaeda and tell the Americans to kill us."

"But I will never swap my turban for a cap," insists the bicycle repairman, his voice terse.

"Only because a turban keeps your ears warm," interjects a round-faced elder, the joker in the pack, smiling over the tea leaves in his glass.

"The Taliban had our support because they protected us," explains the white beard. "They ended the civil war and executed criminals."

At first Islam's Warriors were welcomed by most Afghans, restoring order, making the country safe for the first time in a generation. But their narrow and chauvinistic interpretation of the Koran espoused absolute piety and unquestioning conformity. Television, music and chess were banned. Cassette tape fluttered like bunting from checkpoints. Their rigid dictatorship was based on a kind of fascist idealism, rather like that of Franco's Spain; a combination of strong, existing institutions and heavy-handed neo-traditions.

"But the Taliban restored order at the expense of tolerance," I say. "And diversity. And more lives. They closed women's hospitals, stopped girls from going to school..."

"Would your daughter be surprised if you told her to go out of doors wearing the veil?" interrupts the white beard, spreading his broad hands.

"Of course,' I say. 'Because mine is not an Islamic culture."

"You are the Raw, the unenlightened, the *Khareji*," says the thin, grim elder. *Khareji* means foreigner. "You cannot understand."

"Please clarify," the round-faced elder asks me, easing away the sudden sharp anger, "why the Americans supported us as *mujaheddin* but are now against us?"

I try to explain to them the West's long struggle against communism and how the *mujaheddin* contributed to the collapse of the USSR. And why, to this end, in 1988 Washington supported the formation of the anti-Soviet quasi-independent terrorist cells which later became al-Qaeda. But I can offer no explanation for the subsequent, myopic betrayal of Afghanistan. If, in 1989, the United States had looked beyond the short term and supported the forces working for a multiethnic government, then the radicals – the Taliban – could not have seized power in Kabul. Osama bin Laden would have been denied a base – al-Qaeda means "the base" – from which to attack America.

"What business do Americans have in our fields?" blurts the bicycle repairman. "The Americans are the terrorists. We are on our knees but where is their humility?"

"Why do you think America attacked Afghanistan?" I ask them.

"To steal our oil."

"To take our gold and diamonds."

"To destroy Islam."

No one mentions the Sunni Taliban's murder of thousands of ethnic Shia Hazara, the public executions for adultery, the destruction of the giant statues of Buddha at Bamiyan. No one mentions 9/11.

"What of bin Laden's attack on America?" I ask, the event in 2001 which reminded Washington of Afghanistan's existence.

"We have heard that some of his men bombed a five-story building," shrugs the white beard. "I do not believe it is true."

"It is true," I tell them. "Almost three thousand people were killed."

"Against the millions we have lost."

"But it is not Islamic to kill innocents," I say.

"It is the will of Allah and the word of the Prophet, peace be upon him, that we defend ourselves," says the round-faced joker, cracking his fingers. He speaks slowly, softly, now without a smile. "The Soviets bombed our land so hard that I don't know if anything will grow ever again." As he speaks he touches his heart. "Then America promised to bring us peace, promised to rebuild our country. Tell me one place where they have built a factory? Tell me one place where I can find work?" His voice breaks with emotion. "I went to Kabul last month, in secret, just to look. I could not rent a shop there with Afghan money. Some taxis accepted only dollars. How can I not now fight for my country, my faith? Do God's work?" He bites his lip, falls silent, shakes with such violence that he cannot unwrap a foil-wrapped sweet.

"We are injured – both our souls and bodies are injured – and now America is pouring salt in the wounds."

I try to assure them that the West does not want to "destroy Islam", that many Americans – and most Europeans – were against the war.

"We have been lectured that Western countries are democratic. We consider your people to be behind their governments. If they weren't, they would have stopped the invasion."

"If any occupier comes to our country, it is our right to kill him. We do not differentiate any more between Americans and Russians."

"Americans have the watches," says the joker, not looking up from his glass, "but the Taliban have the time."

The arrival of more tea eases the tension. The white beard asks how many children I have. Conversation turns to marriages and the distribution of food aid. The bicycle repairman twirls his turquoise-blue prayer beads. We pass around the boiled sweets. I ask if – after a generation of war – the men can imagine their country at peace.

"When the invaders forget about us again," says the white beard, "then we will rebuild our Afghanistan."

"As a fundamental Islamic state?" I ask. "Without the possibility of diversity?"

"*Inshallah.*" If God wills it.

The raisin-cleaner indicates that it is time for me to leave. I thank the elders for the privilege of the meeting. I promise to relay their stories. The white beard recites a short prayer, his palms turned upward to heaven, then rubs his hand down his face as if to wipe away sin. Each man shakes my hand. The joker pauses beside me, closing both his hands around mine, touching his heart again.

"Stay for dinner, my brother," he says to me. "We will split open a lamb."

I doubt any of them own livestock.

"Mountains do not come to other mountains but man can come to man."

On the walk back to the road, the raisin-cleaner, Kalashnikov hoisted again on his shoulder, says, "Those men have led a difficult, holy life." After a few steps, he adds, "When I was a child we had a sheep. Life was good."

A sweltering heat shimmers over the broken earth. In the distance, a bulldozer flattens another clay wall. Reams of torn plastic sheeting – printed with the words "Gift of People of the United Kingdom" and "USAID" – drift in the breeze.

15. TAKE IT EASY

In the 1960s, the Family of Man – in flowing turbans, gaily striped *chapans* and embroidered dresses – streamed through Afghanistan's crossroads. School girls in white scarves swept by sweet-smelling *mullahs* and pony-tailed Cockneys in stinking Afghan coats. Donkey caravans and camper vans wound between carts of apricots and wads of money-changers. Hand-made kites soared above the haze of hash shops. Travellers thickened the air with rollie smoke and road news. French couples lingered over onion omelettes in crammed, cupboard-sized Chicken Street eateries. Americans sidestepped the lean boys waiting outside the Kabul AmEx office. "Hotel, my friend?" they asked, taking hold of a hand. "Tourist's hotel?" A Dutch-man – no one knew his name – lived on an abandoned bus teaching him-self medical Dari. His dream was to become a doctor, to build a mobile hospital and to distribute free health care. Sandals, Hush Puppies and bare, hardened soles stepped out of the desert and towards the Himalayas. The proud, medieval, easygoing country got under everyone's skin.

Forty years on, the US State Department advises Americans that "travel in all areas is unsafe due to military operations, landmines, banditry, armed rivalry among political and tribal groups, and the possibility of ter-rorist attacks." In recent months, there have been rocket killings, a suicide car bombing of ISAF peacekeepers and the murders of a dozen aid work-ers. The British FCO warns that "the security situation remains serious and the threat to Westerners is high." Australians are told to hire "permanent armed protection". Canada's Department of Foreign Affairs states plainly that "Canadians should not travel to Afghanistan. Canadians in Afghani-stan should leave." At the lower end of the Richter Scale, it points out that homosexuality is illegal and that "traffic laws are non-existent or not enforced." It also advises against traveling after dark.

I never expected Herat to be as safe as Ottawa because Afghanistan's history is one of invasion, subversion and bloody pipe-dreams. Its geography has made it the battlefield and graveyard of empires. Persians, Greeks, Arabs, Mongols and the British tramped through this place in-between. In 1898, Lord Curzon, Viceroy of India, wrote that Afghanistan, Transcaspia and Persia were "the pieces on a chessboard upon which is being played out a game for the domination of the world". The country buffered British India from Russian expansion. The Soviets invaded to tighten their grip on the region. Pakistan, pursuing its own agenda, worked throughout the 1980s to make Afghanistan its client state. The first salvos of the "war on terror" were fired from the Hindu Kush where al-Qaeda hijackers began training to attack New York's World Trade Center and the Pentagon. Now, America is in town.

At first, *Pax Americana* promised to bring stability to the region. In the *Economist* and *New Republic*, political analysts wrote of a turning-point – much like the fall of the Berlin Wall – in the battle of ideas, in defence of the open and tolerant against totalitarian ideologies, both religious and secular. A month ago in Turkey, I had met two Belgian travellers following the overland trail from east to west. They'd crossed Afghanistan by bus, drunk tea with former *mujaheddin* gunmen and slept in villagers' houses. Along the road they met only kindness, as I did with the Pashtun white beards. But not long after the Belgians had crossed into Iran, the reclusive Taliban leader, Mullah Omar, dressing up his political ambition in religious garments, called for attacks on Westerners and charities.

"Oh Muslims, know the enemies of your religion – the Jews and Christians, America, Britain, the UN and all Western aid groups are the greatest enemies of Islam and humanity."

Black-turbanned guerrillas then started attacking UN mine-clearers. An Italian journalist was ambushed and shot dead near Kandahar. Local administrators were dismembered "for collaborating with the US military and Hamid Karzai's puppet regime". According to some (including the late travel writer Bruce Chatwin), Afghanistan's long slide into anarchy had begun not with the Soviet invasion, or even the communist coup, but with the pony-tailed, peace-loving hippies who drove "educated Afghans into the arms of the Marxists".

I'm thinking these thoughts whilst standing at the roadside outside the camp. My driver has vanished, so I'm on my own in the land of leg-

endary hospitality and ten million landmines. I'm counting on a passing
Toyota HiAce taking me back to Herat. Then, something small and hard
strikes me on the back. I think the worst. Hit the dirt. Roll into a ditch.
Look up at the towering silhouette of a man – carrying a golf club on his
shoulder.

"Aren't you supposed to shout 'Fore!'" I say.

"Surprise attack," he replies.

He's about thirty-five years old, with Atlantic-blue eyes, a solid
Mount Rushmore nose and a taste for unorthodox spots to practice his
golf swing.

"You look like you need a ride," he says, picking up the offending ball
and gesturing at the white LandCruiser pulling up on the opposite side of
the road. "Just shove my stuff out of the way."

The softly spoken American has a firm handshake, broad shoulders
and Callaway clubs. His Cobra shades are pushed up his high, almost precipitous, forehead. His driver – hard-eyed, hazel-skinned and cleanshaven
– turns around and introduces himself. "Hi, I'm Rashid."

"Jim," says the American. "Sunny Jim."

I make room on the back seat. Jim's "stuff", scattered like so many
road-trip burger boxes, includes two laptops, a satellite phone and dozens
of rolled Russian charts. I wonder who's more out of place here? I try to
guess what *they're* doing. Mine-clearance? Surveys? Golf enthusiasts ready
to call in an USAF air strike?

"I'm a geologist," says Jim.

"Looking for...?"

"Oil, man. Welcome to the Wild East."

Rashid hits the gas. Maslakh is left behind in a dust cloud. I'm learning that Afghanistan lends itself to coincidences.

I'd read about the Caspian energy reserves, the last, great untapped
fossil-fuel resource, second only to Saudi Arabia's in size. Between 1880
and 1910, the Rockefeller, Rothschild and Nobel families made fortunes
there. In the Second World War, Caspian oil fuelled the Red Army, and
Baku, the Azerbaijani capital, was the decisive prize that Hitler failed to
capture. As OPEC extends its dominance of the market, America is racing to diversify its sources of energy. The new BTC pipeline, which I drove

alongside in eastern Turkey, will ease its reliance on the Gulf. A million barrels of crude will be pumped from the Caspian each day, into tankers on the Mediterranean and then US gas-guzzlers. A second pipeline has been proposed by Union Oil of California – along with the Japanese and Argentinians – to run across Afghanistan to Pakistan and the sea. In this last oil-rush, government geologists like Jim are picking over the ancient steppe, backed up by US Special Forces in Kyrgyzstan, Green Berets in Georgia and the 2nd Battalion, Royal Anglian Regiment in Jowzjan province.

"I cannot think of a time when we have had a region emerge as suddenly to become as strategically significant as the Caspian," said Dick Cheney in 1998, then CEO of the oil-supply corporation Halliburton. Two years later, he became America's vice-president. A year after that, the US Army drove into Kabul.

"Striking oil is more fun than hitting a birdie into a minefield," volunteers Jim.

The LandCruiser rushes past an Iranian truck pitching and yawing under a top-heavy load of Japanese televisions. Beside us, the old road, built by USAID in the late sixties, is cratered and ruined, its ragged concrete surface twisted like a scattered shuffle of playing cards. The ends of bridges have been blown out by precision missiles. The new UNOPS road, built by the Germans in the last months, is smooth, straight and black. Beyond rusting shells of Russian tanks, a barren landscape rises towards northern, purple mountains.

The Eagles are on the CD player and the quiet American is in a talkative mood. He tells me he was conceived on China Beach in the Bay of Danang in December 1967. His father had been a US Marine on R&R. His mother was a nurse with politics and legs like Jane Fonda. On the morning she found that she was pregnant, Jim's mother ran the half-mile from the cafeteria to the chopper pad. Ten minutes earlier, a Chinook, forty feet long with rotors front and rear, had carried her lover back to the Khe Sanh Combat Base. The next day, on a routine Search-and-Destroy operation, he was pinned down and killed by "friendly fire".

Not long afterwards, Jim's mother – broken-hearted and big-bellied – returned to the States. She raised Jim in the redwoods of La Honda, just over the hill, in fact, from Ken Kesey's Merry Prankster Nest. At eighteen, he won a scholarship to Northern Arizona University and then MIT, studying geology because it had prospects. After graduation, he joined Unocal, then the US Geological Survey. His life was as straight as a bore hole. Like many post-sixties babies, Jim reached out for the security of wealth and, in a meteoric career, he set up his instruments on the Alaskan slope, on rigs off the Mozambican coast and in Central Asia. He was grounded, patriotic and got a buzz from playing golf in war zones.

"I saw the start of the Afghan project," he tells me, turning around in his seat. "I was in Texas in '97 when Unocal flew in a Taliban delegation. I met Hamid Karzai – you know he's the Afghan president now – when he worked as a company adviser."

"Unocal went into business with the Taliban?" I ask.

"Tried to."

To corporate America, Afghanistan's significance was as a potential transit route. The Caspian oil was worthless unless it could reach the market. Unocal hatched the plan to build the 900-mile line from Turkmenistan to Gwadar, the Pakistani ocean terminal east of the Persian Gulf. The Taliban would have collected millions of dollars in fees.

"The company sent a guy named Boardman to Kandahar to win them over. He dressed in traditional robes, grew the prescribed beard, handed out gifts: fax machines, generators, Frisbees."

"You gave Frisbees to the Taliban?" I'm thinking about their banning of kites and music.

"Nobody was going to tell the *mullahs* to stop beating their wives, but the pipeline wasn't built."

"Because of human rights abuses?"

"Because al-Qaeda started blowing up our embassies in Africa," says Jim. "Now who knows what will happen?"

"Well, I'm running down the road, trying to loosen my load, got a world of trouble on my mind..."

"Take It Easy" fills the cab as the minarets of Herat rise beyond the windscreen. Or at least what remains of them. Herat was once the most civilized city in the Islamic world, an oasis on the Middle Silk Road between ancient Merv and Neishabur. Here is Asia, Robert Byron wrote in 1934, "without an inferiority complex". As late as 1962, Chatwin saw here "men in mountainous turbans, strolling hand in hand, with roses in their mouths and rifles wrapped in flowered chintz". Then, earthquakes and Soviet carpet-bombing flattened the city. Today, it's both a shattered Timurid jewel and an Iranian shanty town; a city as much Persian as it is Afghan. Broken glazed tiling – jade-green, grape-blue and turquoise – glints in the dust. The ringing of bells, from horse-drawn traps and unanswered telephones, rises into the pine trees.

"Where are you staying?" Jim asks me.

"At the Marco Polo," I say.

"Come join us first for a bowl of turkey fricassee."

Rashid swings the LandCruiser through a blue wave of women in *burquas* rolling down a narrow dirt street like fresh water released by flood gates. They wash past us, on the way home from school, parasols and spirits carried on the froth. A guard wearing a black-and-white Palestinian *keffiyeh* scarf steps down from his sentry box, wades through the swell and swings back the sheet-metal gate.

Jim's residence is a squat, walled guest-house on the slope next to the provincial governor's palace. Behind its barbed wire is a putting green and a well-tended, irrigated garden. Five or six turkeys gobble beneath the bougainvillaea. Rows of organic American vegetables – scallions, yams, eggplants and snow peas – grow beyond the staff compound. I think back to Maslakh camp. This is not an Afghanistan I expected to find.

"We'll eat in an hour," says Jim.

His guest room has an en suite power shower. Green bottles of Aveda cleanser are set in a neat row above the sink. Michael Herr's *Dispatches* and copies of *Sports Illustrated* are on the reading table.

Later, in the kitchen, Rashid slices fresh carrots and celery, dices turkey pieces, shapes the dumplings. He moves with economy and agility. No motion is overstated or spare. *The Joy of Cooking* is open on the counter.

Jim strides into the lounge wearing a long white *shalwar kameez*. His sneakers are decorated with silver stars and purple butterfly-winged skulls.

"Tell me about the golf," I say.

"I try to play a round every evening," he says, uncorking a Napa Valley Zinfandel and pouring two glasses.

"There's a course in Herat?"

"More a dirt-and-scrub fairway. The problem is with shell casings and craters. And that the hazards might explode."

"That could ruin your game," I say.

Rashid lays out olives and rolled asparagus canapés on the coffee table. Jim drops down into the sofa and asks me about my writing. I could be in Tucson or Seattle discussing books and careers, looking forward to an evening on the green after dinner, except that outside the barred window rises Alexander the Great's Citadel. I gesture towards it and say, "That's probably the only thing in town that hasn't changed since the sixties."

"The whole world has changed since then," says Jim.

"Bruce Chatwin – an English travel writer – wrote that Western kids nudged Afghanistan along the road to ruin."

"How's that?"

"By propagating the idea of ideal society," I say. "The hippies believed in Afghans' right to self-determination. Maybe that's why in the seventies there was a sign at their consulate in Mashhad which read, 'Visas will not be issued to people with hair like beetle.'"

"The dream of new political ideas changing the world has died," says Jim, spitting away a decade's – a century's – idealism along with an olive stone. "Have a serviette."

"Died with Vietnam?" I ask.

"Died with the Wall. Died with the Muslim Brotherhood. The only viable, enduring philosophy now is wealth creation. Everyone wants to make money."

"Do they?" I ask.

"You tell me what else holds us together?" he says, sipping his Zinfandel. "Afghanistan isn't like anywhere else in the world. Anyone who claims to understand the country is missing something crucial: it's a complex, diverse place. But the Afghans are pragmatic. They tolerate us clumping around in big boots and Humvees because we've promised them so much."

"Dollars," smiles Rashid while laying out dinner.

"Come on, let's eat," says Jim, and we make our way to the table.

I sit between them. The glasses and cutlery are matching sets. A candle floats in a water bowl of pebbles.

"Everyone wants a comfortable life with home electronics," Jim says, spooning out the carrots. "Look at Rashid. He was one of the Afghans trained by Unocal to construct and operate a pipeline. That gave him a start. Now, he never stops running."

"I never turn down work," he says, passing me a plate of home-baked cornbread.

"I always tell Rashid to take it easy, that he's stretching himself too thin."

"At school I was the dunce," admits Rashid. "I sat at the back of the class, and all the clever students were killed, by the communists or the Taliban." The smile never fades from his lips. "So now there is no one in front of me. I have to stretch myself."

Sunny Jim picks up his knife and fork and says, "Enjoy."

16, AQUARIUS

I spend a couple of days in Herat, exploring the old city, losing a golf ball in a *real* bunker. At sunset, I stand on top of the Citadel and watch Jim practice his drive toward the distant ridges of the Safed Koh and the old trail to China. Then I turn away from him to stare south-east to Kandahar and the Indian subcontinent.

Like many Intrepids, I planned to catch the bus along that road to Kabul. But on my second morning, a UN employee, twenty-nine-year-old Bettina Goislard, is shot dead while driving through a bazaar in nearby Ghazni. She is the fourteenth aid-worker murdered in the last months. A hand-grenade attack follows in Kandahar. Then, a bicycle bomb explodes in a market. *Médicin Sans Frontières* blames the killings on heavy-handed and naive American policy. UN staff are ordered off the streets and into their compounds.

"Six weeks ago, that road was safe," says Jim over breakfast. "Now, even Afghans think twice before traveling it."

I consider the alternatives.

The northern route is a hard, four-day slog through steppe and desert by way of Maimana and Mazar-e Sharif. But recent disagreements between rival warlords – using tanks and artillery to settle the argument – reduce its attraction.

The central route isn't really a road at all, rather a succession of broken paths and animal tracks. To cross its half-dozen 3,000-meter passes, survive lawless Chaghcheran and reach the lakes of Band-e Amir can take a week. Along the way are landmines, unexploded US bombs, and wolves, both the two- and four-leg variety.

"I'm a local," Rashid tells me while passing another English muffin, "and I wouldn't drive to Kabul."

His advice is convincing. I've already seen enough to know that, even if I make it to Kandahar, no one alive there will remember the Intrepids. Any echo of the sixties will have been drowned out by the howl of intervening years. I also don't want to get shot. Or to lose testicles to a venerable Soviet butterfly mine, designed to spring to hip-height before exploding.

Ariana Afghan operates a daily service to Kabul. Usually. The two-room office on Bagh-e Azadi appears to be shut but, after five minutes hammering on the door, a yawning employee with a mangled hand opens up and sells me a ticket. Rashid runs me out to the airport, a barrack-like building with splintered walls and windows boarded with planks. I check in, take a seat in the so-called departure lounge and, through a shell-hole, watch our 727 take off. My fellow passengers – traders in mud-pie *pakoul* hats, a congenial Tajik family, a pair of Chinese businessmen – and I wait for its return. One hour. Two hours. No surprise that Ariana is known as the *Inshallah* airline. At the end of the third hour, word filters through to us that a government minister borrowed the aircraft to visit his father in a distant town. The minister intended only a short stay but his father has invited him to stay for lunch. In the lounge, the Tajiks resign themselves to the delay, setting up a gas brazier to cook their own midday meal. I, on the other hand, run out of patience after five hours' waiting.

At exactly that moment, a white UNHAS Fokker F-28 touches down on the tarmac. The United Nations Humanitarian Air Service ferries UN and NGO personnel, medicine, anti-locust pesticides and de-mining dogs around the country. Its three twin-prop Beechcraft and single Fokker hold the cities together while gunmen block the roads. At the UNHAS desk I discover that the incoming Fokker is due to return to Kabul. There are seats available. I explain my predicament to the Afghan behind the desk. I hand over my Ariana ticket. I weep.

"What is your agency?" he asks me.

"No agency."

"What is your country?"

"Canada."

"Then we will say you are with CIDA," he replies, noting down the aid agency's name. Canadian International Development Agency. "This is how we help our friends in Herat," he goes on, giving me a photocopied ticket. I hand him $100. "Welcome to *my* Afghanistan."

On board, a *Médicin Sans Frontières* doctor opens a week-old copy of *Libération*. A Nigerian working for the Aga Khan Development Network reads the collected sayings of Mohammed. An Irish vet explains Edward Thomas's poetry to a CARE officer from Virginia. In the back row, a Danish politician chats to her minders. The Fokker is leased by the UN from a South African charter airline called AirQuarius, but the Kiwi stewardess doesn't break into a medley of songs about universal harmony. Instead, she asks me, "Are you willing to help us when something goes wrong?" She points belatedly at the over-wing emergency exit. "In the unlikely event something goes wrong."

"Have a safe journey," says the Kuwaiti in the row behind me.

The take-off is fast and steep to avoid – according to the Frenchman – any Stinger ground-to-air missiles. I laugh, but he doesn't.

We rise above the apricot earth, scattering a flock of fat-tailed sheep. Behind me in the lounge, the Ariana passengers brew another pot of black tea. Ahead, the purple Paropamisus – named by the Greeks from the Persian "peaks over which eagles cannot fly" – slip beneath the port wing.

"*My* Afghanistan," the UNHAS agent had said; proud, independent and defiant. His ravaged land unfolds beneath me. Deserted Tajik hamlets crumble into banks of shale. Cultivatable fields lie barren after four years of drought. The plain gathers into the hill country of Ghowr, its high pastures impoverished since the last caravans used the Silk Road. The province of an estimated 300,000 people does not have a single doctor.

I gaze in wonder at the earth's beauty, so rich and varied even in this war-torn land. I catch a flash of incredible deep blue; the Band-e Amir lakes glittering on a distant plateau. Below, I see no electricity pylons, no paved roads, no windscreen flash of a moving vehicle. The stewardess serves plastic tumblers of bottled Pakistani water as the Koh-e Baba range melts into the vast deserts of Wardak. I press my cheek against the window to catch sight of the cedar-forested slopes of the Hindu Kush. Then the intercom crackles to life.

"Folks, I've just been informed of a little incident at Kabul," says the captain. "We can't land until the pieces have been ... uh ... picked off the runway."

The Frenchman lowers his newspaper.

We're told that an Ariana Airbus on a return flight from Islamabad made a heavy landing. Its starboard wing tip dug into the earth and the undercarriage disintegrated. No passengers were injured but the German ISAF contingent needed a couple of hours to tow the aircraft on to the apron.

"Why so long?" I ask.

"Because there are still minefields alongside the runway."

The AirQuarius pilot's fuel and options are limited. He can return to Herat or fly on to Peshawar in Pakistan. No nearby airfield is long enough for a Fokker. Except for one.

"Listen up," he then announces, with a relief which doesn't resonate along the cabin, "we've been given permission to land ... uh ... at Bagram."

Forty miles north of Kabul, Bagram is a central hub in the US military's five global commands. At the sprawling former Soviet air base are stationed 15,000 of the one million Americans maintained at arms in 137 countries on four continents. From here, round-the-clock missions are launched against al-Qaeda and the Taliban by the 82nd Airborne Division, the Task Force Panther Light Infantry Brigade and the 3rd Special Forces Group. The 354th Fighter Squadron, the Army XVIII Airborne Corps' 18th Air Support Operations Group and the Nevada National Guard also fly from the base, as well as the Coalition's Task Force Sword, "tasked with pursuing high-value targets". In addition, Bagram houses about 500 Afghan "detainees", two of whom will die from "blunt force injuries" while in US custody only a few months after my visit. Later will come Abu Ghraib. It's not just the hippies who would hate this presence.

Our white Fokker circles the Shamali plain. Earth dams and high wire fences delineate the mile-wide "security zone". Within it spreads an enormous green tent city. Lines of identical, low barrack blocks are under construction. Graders and bulldozers work extending the 10,000-foot runway. Along its apron gather Abrams tanks and Black Hawk battle helicopters. Ahead of us, a USAF A-10 Thunderbolt is on short final approach, back from providing close air support for ground forces.

We put down, and a Bradley fighting vehicle shoos us away to a far corner of the field. The captain is told not to open the doors. Alongside us, a shaven-headed maintenance team replaces an engine on a Combat Talon

Hercules. Beyond them, F-16 and F-18 fighters painted with white fangs take off in pairs. Marines jog around the seven-mile perimeter fence.

"I hope they don't drive us to Kabul," worries the Nigerian. "It wouldn't be a good idea to leave here on a bus full of foreigners."

Thirty minutes later, an UNHAS Beechcraft joins us on the slipway. Kabul's runway clearly isn't yet open.

After an hour, we are allowed out to stretch our legs under the supervision of a Reservist lieutenant. "Do *not* step off the hard surface," he instructs us. "Do *not* approach any American personnel." Underfoot is new concrete. Bullet casings flash on the gritty earth. On the other side of the runway, the shell of a huge Antonov cargo plane lies where it was downed by a rocket, now spray-painted with American graffiti. "Welcome to Armor Geddon ... Ali Baba was here ... call me Terminator." Beyond it, ruined cinder-block houses are daubed with red paint to warn of UXOs – unexploded ordnance.

The aid workers greet associates from the Beechcraft, gathering in the shade under its wings. Their mobile phone calls bring conflicting news: that a bus has been sent from town, that the *Médicin Sans Frontières* Land-Cruiser has been stopped at the outer "Afghan" gate, that Kabul airport will be closed for a week. Only one fact is certain. Kabul is a daylight-only operation. No landings can take place after dark. We have to get away from Bagram before dusk. Above a sandbagged look-out, the stars-and-stripes flutters against the Hindu Kush.

"It's an awesome sight when the sun sets over those mountains," volunteers the lieutenant, following my eye-line. "I'm a sucker for sunsets."

A wiry, wide-mouthed FAA air-traffic controller, he's as bored as the aid workers are agitated. He is from Washington state, mid-thirties, divorced, still unused to the heat after two tours of duty. Sweat dries on his forehead, in his dark curly hair. He had just sat down to dinner when the order came for him to supervise us. In jest, I apologize for interrupting his meal, suggesting that we could eat together if we remain stranded at Bagram. The Coalition could lay on an international barbecue – Texan prime rib, Yorkshire pudding, Belgian *frites*, jalapeno peppers – to celebrate, say, common Western values.

"Sir, let me assure you that the CO wants you gone. He swears he'll stick his butt in the middle of that runway next time the UN asks to land."

The others passengers don't relish the idea of a Free World knees-up either.

"We, too, would prefer to be on our way," says the doctor.

The Irishman is late for a conference. The Danish politician has missed her flight back to Europe. The Kuwaiti was due to host a birthday party. Our disrupted journey spreads gloom over the passengers.

In order to "win over Afghan hearts and minds", the US Army recently started drilling wells and building schools, blurring the distinction between soldiers and aid workers. As a result, aid agencies are now targets. Most are pulling out of the south, leaving some provinces deprived of humanitarian assistance. Still the military juggernaut thunders on, distributing Pop Tarts after Search-and-Destroy missions, opening health clinics while lobbing 1,000-lb Joint Direct Attack Munitions hither and thither. Yet without it, without the helicopter gunships, Humvees and the 82nd Airborne bulked up in body armor, the whole country would still be a feudal state, and many more of its women would be shackled, its minorities persecuted.

"You American?" the lieutenant asks me.

I shake my head.

"What's Kabul like?"

"I don't know yet," I say to him. "Haven't you been into town?"

"Never been outside the wire. We're spoilt with facilities. But I'm kinda curious. The countryside looks amazing from the air."

As we talk, the light seeps out of the day, drawing our options with it. The Frenchman stubs out his last cigarette. The stewardess runs out of bottled water. The pilot looks at his watch and says, "I could have been sipping a beer in ... uh ... Dubai now." A C-17 transport casts long evening shadows over the hills. Kabul's runway remains closed.

The lieutenant's walkie-talkie comes to life. "The CO is laying on a bus," he tells us.

"I am never riding in an American bus," says the doctor, starting the mutiny.

"Nor me," adds the Nigerian. "It's not safe."

"I won't sleep in my seat," argues the Danish politician.

We can't be left in the aircraft. We refuse to be sent away. No suitable civilian airfield is open in Afghanistan.

"Anyone ready for a drink?" asks the Kuwaiti, pulling a bottle of Uzbek vodka from his bag and leaning back against the Fokker's tyre. "If it causes no offense, *akhi*?" he says to an Arab Aid employee.

"I'll join you," says the Irish poet-cum-vet.

"Did you say there's a Burger King on the base?" the CARE worker asks the lieutenant.

There are two, in fact, as well as a Pizza Hut, an Outback Steakhouse and half a dozen convenience stores. Also a sports center, a prayer-book full of chaplains and a thousand computer terminals linked by eighty miles of blue Cat 5 cable. Over the radio, the CO points out that Bagram isn't a Holiday Inn. Alcohol is forbidden on the base and there is no *fucking* room service. But concessions are made. Four tents are vacated for us in the North Engineer Camp. A female maintenance officer is detailed to chaperone the women. Half-a-dozen turbo-charged Gator golf carts collect us but not our luggage. Bags are to remain under guard in the aircraft hold. We'll be issued toothbrushes, compliments of the US military.

I sit in the lead Gator with the lieutenant, the Kuwaiti and the Irish vet. "I suppose our arrival is the most exciting thing that's happened here today," he shouts to the lieutenant.

"Well, sir, one of the towers volleyed some shots this morning. That was pretty interesting," he says, refusing the offer of a drink. "And last night an RPG hit the AirCom Camp. I wasn't too happy to have to sit in a shelter without air conditioning. At least the view of the mountains was nice."

We drive into the metropolis of green tents, turning at the crossroads of "Exxon Boulevard" and "Chevron Street". Beyond a rank of double trailer units, off-duty soldiers play softball, hang out their laundry, zero their M-16s at the rifle range. Under bleached tarpaulins, an army bus unloads new recruits, their clean boots and duffels dropping into the red dirt. In a single, unpainted wooden office block is the headquarters of the Afghan Air Force which, unfortunately, no longer has any aircraft.

The lieutenant suggests the Kuwaiti hide his vodka under his *jellaba*. We are given ten minutes to wash, then directed to the food-services compound, edging our trays along the stainless-steel tubing. After Whoppers and Personal Pan Pizzas, the lieutenant shepherds us like school children to the AAFES base exchange to collect our toothbrushes. My two months on the road leaves me in awe of the bounty of consumable Americana: Reeces' Peanut Butter Cups, Hostess Twinkies, flash-frozen Omaha T-bone steaks, Pearl Jam compilation CDs. A fortysomething volunteer behind the cash desk notices my wide-eyed look. "I can see from your face how much your favorite soda means to you, too," she says. Her Kevlar flak jacket is draped over the back of the chair.

"What's a sports drink?" the Nigerian asks her.

We aren't in the US, but we sure as hell are nowhere near Afghanistan.

Next the lieutenant tries to pack us off to bed. All that's missing are mugs of hot chocolate and leg irons. It isn't even 8 p.m., aircraft are thundering off the runway, and no one is ready for sleep.

"Do you not have a café?" asks the Frenchman.

"There's the Cat's Meow MWR tent," reveals the lieutenant with reluctance. "But the beer's non-alcoholic."

"How respectful," I say, yet the irony was missed.

Another walkie-talkie discussion, another pissed-off dressing-down from the CO, and we are given permission to sample Bagram's night life.

Under escort, two dozen aid workers and I troop across the North Camp to the Cat's Meow. We open a screen door and step into *Cheers*. Stools surround the central bar. Guys shoot pool and drink giant cups of malted milk. In a private booth, a detail of female engineers discusses *I, Lucifer*, their book of the week. Clouds of cigarette smoke hover over the laminated tables. There is a Wurlitzer, a dance floor, a glowing Michelob sign and the acrid smell of spilt beer and dank fries. The bartender's T-shirt reads "(There is no) Hard Rock Café, Kabul." A poster announces Robin Williams' upcoming USO show. Only three elements would be out of place in Boston: the general sobriety, the weary Special Forces commandos watching *Star Trek* and the terrarium full of scorpions.

"I keep goldfish myself," says the stewardess.

"Can I offer you all a drink?" asks the lieutenant.

He produces jugs of non-alcoholic beer, which the Kuwaiti spikes with vodka. Our pilot opts for a Coke. "I'm ... uh ... driving," he explains. The Frenchman sits apart with the Dane.

"When I first arrived, there was hope and optimism," I overhear the CARE worker tell the Nigerian. She is sincere, passionate and from Charleston. "People would open the doors of our cars just to shake our hands."

"In our education program, we had former Taliban fighters studying Grade 3 maths alongside eight-year-olds," he replies.

I lean over the back of the bench and tell them of my visit to Maslakh.

"A month back, we organized a focus group in Lowgar," says the woman. Her area of expertise is family planning. "The average rural couple have ten children: men gain status with each new birth; women know that after their seventh child their chance of survival drops to 50:50. A week later, the Marines flew in a couple of medics for the day, the insurgents tar us with the same brush and 'off' the policemen who'd been our guards."

"More pretzels?" offers the lieutenant.

"The lieutenant here does his job and we end up hiding behind barbed wire, unable to do ours."

"Ma'am, I joined the National Guard after 9/11 to protect America," he replies, "and I banked on my duty amounting to little more than two weeks a year." He has been stationed at Bagram for eighteen months.

Soldiers play cards, drop quarters into the jukebox, look at each other and smile when they think we aren't looking. Their civility brings to mind blue-collar shift-workers more than fighting men and women. None of them seems scarred by war, except for the commandos in their beards and Afghan *patou* scarves. Their eyes, dim with exhaustion, never flicker from the widescreen television.

I'm jotting in my notebook when the lieutenant asks me, "You aren't an aid worker, are you?"

I tell him what I do and, around me, the conversation stops.

"You're a what?" asks the Danish politician.

"A travel writer," I repeat.

I half-expect to be asked to leave by the back gate. Or to be marched away by a dozen angry humanitarians for misuse of the UNHAS. But, instead, the vet says, "Where have you been?"

"Most of Europe and America," I reply. It's the usual question. "Australia and the Pacific, south-east Asia, Burma..." I tend to mention the places which will interest an audience.

"Burma," gushes the politician.

"I bet Burma was amazing," says the vet.

"It's a military dictatorship," I remind him.

"What a perfect job," says the CARE worker. "Any room for me in your suitcase?"

Serious discussions about appeasing hatred, "frag" wounds and the balancing of US military power with European altruism are forgotten. All the politician wants to know about is cruises on the Irrawaddy River. The vet asks me to recommend a bargain Manhattan hotel. The Nigerian has a dozen questions about air miles. I tell them what I'm writing about.

"The hippie trail?" laughs the politician, moving to our table. "I wouldn't be here now if I hadn't hitched to India in 1967."

"My older brother did it too," cuts in the captain. "I was so jealous of him."

Even the Frenchman takes an interest. "The sixties was *the* journey from innocence to experience."

"Another beer?" asks the lieutenant, a great grin spreading across his face.

Then someone selects the 5th Dimension on the Wurlitzer.

"We had a sixties evening last month," one of the book-club engineers calls above the music.

"The junk's still back here," says the bartender.

The vet stands up to take the cardboard box and unfolds a tangled web of beads, bells and Beatles wigs. He puts on a pair of John Lennon granny glasses. The politician joins him, talking of Big Dreams and a broken-down Peace bus, stretching a plastic flower headband over her coiffed head. Then an engineer pulls a leopard-spot mini-skirt up over her work overalls. I can't imagine how all this stuff reached Afghanistan again, except aboard a USAF C-130, but suddenly everyone is at the bar wearing buckskin, paisley shirts and brocade Carnaby Street waistcoats. Even the commandos look towards us, though they keep themselves apart. But like burnt-out rock 'n' roll veterans, they fit right in too, especially in their Afghan *chapans*.

"When the moon is in the Seventh House, and Jupiter aligns with Mars, then peace will guide the planets..."

In the box, the vet finds two volumes of poetry by Richard Brautigan – that joyous and skewed American original – and, sitting Buddha-like on a tabletop, starts reading from "The Galilee Hitch-Hiker" and "Karma Repair Kit: Items 1–4". He skips to "Our Beautiful West Coast Thing" "...listening to The Mamas and the Papas ... singing a song about breaking somebody's heart ... I think I'll get up and dance around the room. Here I go!"

And he does. The vet gets up and starts to dance. The CARE worker and Kiwi stewardess join him, as do a couple of the engineers. The Dane takes the Frenchman's hand and swings him on to the floor. The Kuwaiti boogies into the throng. I start strumming an air guitar. It all happens in a second. The pilot claims he's having an acid flashback. The Nigerian leans over to shout at me, only half in jest, "Good vibes, man."

Suddenly, we are intoxicated. Because of our anxiety, because of the day's frustrations and, especially, because of Uzbek vodka, the group relaxes, lets down their hair – at least those who still have hair – and allows wide-eyed, youthful exuberance to sweep aside our suspicions.

"...No more falsehoods or derisions..."

Do-gooders and door gunners spin on tiptoes. Aid managers and Sergeants First Class sing along to "Aquarius". Our gestures become animated, our conversations flow. A commando holds a single plastic flower in his fist. A PsychOps corporal with cinnamon-brown skin tells me, "Actually, I'm a Capricorn." The poems, lyrics and gracious ideals are seductive and hypnotic, deluded and naive. The words move our hearts and for an exquisite moment keep at bay our rational scepticism.

"...Golden living dreams of visions..."

"I have this recurring dream," the Nigerian yells at me, as he drums on the Formica bar. "I'm in the mountains, caught in an avalanche. I touch a warm body. I grab it, then see I'm balanced on a precipice, holding a Taliban fighter. If I let go of him, he'll tumble to his death. If I keep hold of him, he might kill me."

"What do you do?"

"I hold on to him, of course. I hold on."

Then, four minutes and forty-eight seconds after it began, the song ends. The music stops. We stand self-consciously at the center of the tent, arms raised to the canvas roof or held out at our sides. We slip off the wigs and rose-tinted glasses and retreat to our tables. I hang up my imaginary Stratocaster. Beyond the screen door, the 455th Air Expeditionary Group launches an A-10 Thunderbolt II patrol into the dusk.

Not much later, the party breaks up. The lieutenant asks if I want to walk with him out to the perimeter. "It's truly amazing how many stars you can see even when the moon is out," he says. "I counted four comets yesterday alone."

The handmaiden of the stars sends me a single comet that night. At first light, our white UNHAS Fokker lifts off the scorched runway for the five-minute flight to Kabul.

17. WHAT A DAY FOR A DAYDREAM

The white Fokker circles a sprawling, ruined world. Rolling streets of shattered tarmac skirt cruise-missile craters fifty feet deep. UNHCR plastic sacking wraps khaki compounds which have "eaten a rocket". Skeletons of civil aircraft serve as temporary shelters for refugees. Early in the twentieth century, King Amanullah instructed his architects to create a "monumental" new capital. Italian villas, formal gardens, a narrow-gauge railroad and the vast white Dar-ul Aman Palace were built. When the first Intrepids reached Kabul, pausing at Siggi's for a puff on a hookah and a glass of his *amazing* mint tea, they wondered if they'd found paradise. Of those buildings and days nothing remains now save a monumental sense of loss. Our wheels touch the tarmac and I realize with a shiver that I want the security of a guidebook.

In the translucent, powdered morning light, I blag a ride into town with three others from the flight.

"They were executed on the Kandahar road," says the tall Norwegian, turning around to tell me and the other passengers. CARIAS's Kabul chief has an exaggerated facial tic, his mouth puckering as if to make a lonely, one-sided kiss. His news of yesterday's killing of two Afghan aid workers didn't reach us at Bagram. "The Taliban made them kneel on the road and shot them."

Around us, every tenth vehicle seems to be another NGO Land-Cruiser. UN Toyotas jostle with Shelter for Life pick-ups. Arab Aid trucks negotiate pot-holes the size of garden ponds. A six- wheeled ISAF armed personnel carrier pulls out of a side road and pushes into the traffic behind us. The front gunner smokes a Gauloise beneath the French *tricouleur*.

"Let him pass," the Norwegian orders our driver. "He's the target, not us."

Pedestrians – in battle fatigues, in lilac *burquas*, shouldering Kalashnikovs – cover their mouths against the dust. Bicycles clatter between *kara-*

atchiwaan handcarts. Savvy, Mister-One-Dollar beggars circle us waving smoking tin cans of incense. Peddlers sell petrol at the kerbside, decanting it by hand into one-liter cans. Behind them, metal shipping containers have been turned into barber shops and greengrocers. An old man washes his face in the drain outside the Hospital for War-Wounded. A legless veteran levers his crude cart forward, propelling himself with a stone in each hand to save his knuckles.

"I hear you're writing a travel book," the Norwegian says to me, his mouth puckering at the irony. "Do you want to ruin Kabul?"

"Tourism is the future of Afghanistan," the driver, a local man, interrupts. "And Afghans are the most hospitable people in the world. *Chans-e khub.*" Good luck to you.

"Just don't write about the beaches," advises the Norwegian, deadpan again. "The surfing here is rubbish."

The LandCruiser drops me at the Mustapha. A US soldier in full battle kit strolls by its iron-grill entrance. Around the corner is the Chelsea Supermarket where bin Laden used to shop. Above me rises the country's single billboard: "Enjoy the Taste of America – Pine Cigarettes". I step inside Afghanistan's only surviving Intrepid hotel.

In 1970, Penny stayed here. Two years later, the Mustapha was Tony and Maureen Wheeler's favorite place in town, "new and built around a central courtyard, more like a college residence than a hotel". Rudy was a frequent guest, his busloads unrolling their sleeping bags on its roof. The Mustapha caught the first wave of independent travelers, was closed during the Soviet occupation and for most of the Taliban years, then reopened when the owner's son returned from twenty-one years' exile in New Jersey.

"Where the hell's the security guard?" an AP stringer complains on the stairs. He and a fellow journalist wear identical flak jackets and rimless peaked *karakul* caps. Both are off to find a Pulitzer-winning story before lunch. "There's supposed to be a security guard at the door."

In the sixties, there were no guidebooks to Asia, at least none that suited young shoestring travelers. No one on the hippie highway carried a copy of Fodor's *Islamic Asia*. The route to spiritual enlightenment wasn't revealed in the pages of the latest Baedeker. Intrepids were on a journey of spontaneity and reinvention. Kids simply arrived in a town, dropped by the freak hotel, hit on other Westerners for advice and checked out the travelers' noticeboards. Don't pay more than twenty Afghanis for the ride to Jalalabad. The Crown Hotel in Delhi smells of roses. Bhagwan Rajneesh has moved his ashram from Mumbai to Pune. If the best bus didn't run for another day or three it didn't matter; the Intrepids just hung out, went with the flow, absorbed the moment – and were absorbed in it. Few were ever in a hurry. Most spent months, even years, on the road.

Come the seventies, travelers had less time but more money. They were less inclined to leave arrangements to the vagaries of chance. They weren't as trusting either, and with reason. The Vietnam war and the commercialization of the East hadn't only disillusioned them. The promise of fast money had drawn rip-off artists and passport thieves to the fringes of the trail. People were robbed and raped. Curries were made with dog meat. Hashish was cut with horse manure. The seventies overlander needed guidance.

Let's Go was first published in the early sixties as a pamphlet for Harvard students heading for Europe. Almost a decade passed before it reached over the Bosphorus. Likewise, *Europe on $5 a Day* and the *Hitchhiker's Guide to Europe* (subtitled *How to see Europe by the skin of your teeth*) didn't raise a thumb towards the east either.

The first travelers' guidebook to step into Asia was printed on a Gestetner in a derelict squat in London's Notting Hill. BIT – from Binary Information Transfer, the smallest unit of computer data – was an information charity on Westbourne Park Road co-founded by the irreverent social inventor Nicholas Albery. Freaks and runaways dropped by his – energy center of the Alternative Society – for free advice on crash pads, legal aid and cheap food (when available, the girls who did the cooking were often out bringing kids down from bad trips). Its precarious, hand-to-mouth existence was sustained by donations from Paul McCartney, The Who and the Gulbenkian Foundation, as well as by sales of fake student-cards (issued in the name of the imaginary "London Institute of Structural Anthropology: Department for External Studies", Albery being a follower of the French social anthropologist Lévi-Strauss).

The charity's idiosyncratic magazine *BITman* – "a survival manual for activists and deviants" – disseminated do-it-yourself information on matters ranging from rebirthing and plumbing a squat to independent travel. In keeping with the ideals of an alternative lifestyle, many Intrepids wrote to the magazine on their return home from India, sharing their anecdotes and advice. One of BIT's volunteers – a Yorkshireman named Geoff Crowther who had done the trail himself – collated this material with his own experiences and in 1970 printed the BIT travel newsletter. Its first edition, printed in purple ink in a dingy room smelling of meths and running to a dozen mimeographed pages, sold out as soon as it hit the street.

That same year, less than a mile away across London, another Englishman, Tony Wheeler, met Irish-born, would-be stewardess Maureen on a park bench. Wheeler had been bitten by the travel bug during his time as an engineer at Rootes Cars in the Midlands. Rootes had modified a Hillman Hunter for the *Daily Express* London-to-Sydney marathon. On its front seat lay an open map of Iran. Wheeler had seen it and was captivated by the unfamiliar place names and swathes of desert. Maureen had caught her first glimpse of the greater world through the Indian peddlers who called at her Belfast front door.

The young couple fell in love and decided to go traveling together. They bought a 1964 Minivan for £65 and drove it across Asia, reaching Sydney penniless the day after Christmas 1972. Wheeler pawned his camera to buy food. Maureen refused to sell her typewriter. "I bet we could do a book," he said and, in a month, he wrote *Across Asia on the Cheap*.

Lonely Planet's first guidebook had a print run of 1,500 copies. Wheeler flogged them to Sydney book shops and, like the BIT newsletter, it sold out in a week. He then did two more print runs, flying some of them in suitcases to Melbourne. He caught the airline bus into town and peddled the lot in a day, writing out invoices while eating his sandwiches in a park. The ninety-six-page pamphlet provided basic and practical travel advice in an enduring and chatty style. Wonder whether to buy supper from a certain Asian street-hawker? "If he looks like he's about to drop dead, eat elsewhere." Thinking of smuggling dope into Iran? "Forget it; Mashhad has a large, new and unpleasant jail especially for foreigners." Considering soliciting locals for spare cash? "The Indian spiritualism drug freaks begging in Delhi from people who know about *real* poverty do enormous damage to the overland scene."

The overland guides were not exclusively an English or Australian phenomenon. In the same month that the Wheelers left London, a French student, Philippe Gloaguen, began to hitchhike to India. His *Guide du routard* was printed within days of American Bill Dalton's first Moon Publication handbook. Stefan Loose returned home from Kathmandu determined to encourage fellow Germans to question their values by writing the *Südostasien Handbuch*. Mik Schultz's *Asia for the Hitchhiker* came out in Copenhagen just as Douglas Brown's *Overland to India* appeared in Canada. In his introduction Brown wrote of – and for – his readers:

> There's two or three of them sitting on the platform of the railway station in Istanbul, calmly waiting for a train, wearing Moroccan *jellabas*, carrying cooking pots, playing flutes. If the crowd goes away they'll probably smoke some dope in a chillum. Maybe they come from a communal house in Copenhagen; or from the caves in Matala on Crete; or from Essaouira near Marrakech; or from Berkeley or Toronto or Paris. They're going to India. It'll probably cost about thirty dollars or so. If you sat with them, you'd find out how to make it too; how to cop in Afghanistan, where to stay in Tehran, how to say thank you in Pushtu. This book is a result of lots of days of traveling and talking and smoking with these people.

Each guide was distinct, and their authors were on individual quests, yet the synchronicity of their vision was extraordinary, as if a single ideal had been plucked out of the air.

"*Lorsque vous êtes à l'étranger, l'étranger, c'est vous*," wrote Gloaguen in his first *Guide du routard*. Speaking for a generation of travelers, he went on, "Sartre said, 'One changes the world by revolution.' But *le Routard*" – the archetypal, open-minded Intrepid – "tries instead to better understand the world by reaching out to its people, their customs, and understanding their right to be different."

No established publisher had foreseen the importance of the alternative, budget-travel movement. It was kids themselves – Crowther, the

Wheelers, Gloaguen, Brown, Dalton and, in 1982, Mark Ellingham of Rough Guides – who recognized the potential, because they lived it, they defined it, they sold it.

"All you've got to do is decide to go and the hardest part is over," enthused Wheeler. "So go."

I take a room at the Mustapha. The owner's son – Wais, the fast-talking "Fonz of Kabul" – doesn't want to be my guide. He doesn't even want to speak to me. He has a stomach ache-cum-peptic ulcer, as well as a tendency to toy with the pistol on his desk. His minder tells me that Wais never met Wheeler, Gloaguen or the Dutchman who wanted to be a doctor. His concerns are now those of day-to-day survival. The Mustapha is an obvious target, full of shady carpetbaggers and fixers and serving alcohol. Stetson-wearing British builders and big-boned farm boys in combat fatigues clutter the foyer. The hotel is also the unofficial residence of the Afghan president's bodyguards, stocky ex-US Marines who wear two shoulder holsters and prop up the marble bar. Their Operation Enduring Freedom tankards hang from hooks on the glitter-mirror wall.

My single room is basic, divided from its neighbors by painted glass panels, but it gives me a chance to organize my thoughts. No Afghanistan handbook has been written in a generation, apart from Bradt's slender *Kabul Mini Guide*, which was conceived as a primer for NGO workers. I skim it, draft a list of highlights and book a driver at the desk. I want to travel into the heart of Kabul. But I resign myself to follow in Crowther, Wheeler and Hilary Bradt's well-worn footsteps, at least until I find my own compass bearing.

Alone, I step back out into the heat. Narrow lanes climb away from the road between a dense mass of baked-brick, flat-roofed houses, mounting the flanks of denuded hills. To the north rise mountains where the snow never melts, to the south spread deserts where snow never falls. I duck into the hand-painted Datsun and spread out my notebooks on the backseat. No passing motorcyclist takes a pot-shot at me. No crazed Islamist throws a grenade into the new Zalmai Weeding Cake Center.

"Chicken Street," I say to Ashaf, my driver.

Chicken Street has been a magnet for Afghanistan's visitors since the days of the hippie trail. Back then, "the scene" revolved around hash shops, dimly lit haunts and Siggi's eating place, with its outside chessboard and outsized schnitzel. As we cruise past the souvenir shops, I ask Ashaf, "Did you ever hear of a German named Siggi who lived here in the sixties?" Ashaf has just returned to Kabul after ten years' exile in Pakistan. "He had some connection with the royal family."

"Everyone who knew the hippies either left the country or was killed," he replies, looking at me in the rear-view mirror. "*Everyone* with money, an education, a guest house. The Taliban years were an unimaginable hell."

Outside the window, the pavement undulates without warning or purpose, its edges snapped off like dry biscuit. Every metal street lamp is scarred by bullet holes, bent by shell fire or cropped into stubby posts. "The mine museum, please," I say to him, shuffling through my papers.

I visit the OMAR – Organization for Mine Clearance and Afghan Rehabilitation – Landmine Museum (with Russian butterfly mines designed to be mistaken by children for plastic toys). We stop by the walled Garden of Babur, created in the sixteenth century by the first Moghul emperor and restored by the Aga Khan Foundation. I see the Ariana graveyard. As I fleet between the guide's "must sees", a strange unrest creeps into my blood. I'm both unsettled and frustrated with myself for narrowing possibility.

In their search for answers, the original Intrepids took the time to plunge off the beaten track. Their ambition was to be transformed by the journey. Most tried to learn a smattering of Hindi, to live in a Nepalese community, to become a Buddhist. Then, guidebooks began to spoon-feed itineraries to time-poor travelers who could afford neither doubt or a year away. More and more, travel became entertainment not *travail*, a change of scene not a life change.

Rather than inspirational, the travel market is now aspirational, meaning readers aspire to do as the writer; to walk alone in the Hindu Kush, to find a forgotten house in Provence, to discover that secret, deserted Thai beach. No writer dares to point out that there are no more undiscovered beaches. That the world has been mapped. That every country on the planet is described in one or other book.

Over the next days, as Ashaf drives me around Kabul, I begin to question if guidebooks, written to a formula, still open doors for travelers, or just direct them between holiday ghettos along a beaten track. We may go further, faster, but have Lonely Planet and *Guide du routard* in fact limited our horizon by describing one road towards it? Fewer kids now take the risk of staying in an unknown flea-pit or accepting the hospitality of strangers. We still move through an alien society against which our identity can be cast into relief, but often we talk only to other Westerners at safe, familiar spots. Of course, hazards remain – bags get lost, bungee cords snap, the vulnerable are abused – but at the first whiff of danger, most modern "global nomads" (myself included) whip out their gold card or Rough Guide travel-insurance policy.

Back in 1964 when the first wave of Intrepids hit town, the Afghans didn't have the facilities. But the surfeit of hospitality and the nights when the moon spilt silver over the city's hills far outshone the absence of creature comforts. Visitors felt at home and extended their stay, not only because they contracted amoebic dysentery. Then, a Year of Tourism was declared in 1967. The promotional posters trumpeted tourism as a "Passport to Peace". When the second wave of backpackers washed across their land between 1970 to 1979, Afghan resourcefulness had filled the gap. You like pancakes for breakfast? No problem, we give you pancakes. You want music while you eat? Then we smuggle in the latest pop cassettes. You like muesli? We make it for you, whatever it is. It was an honest exchange. A golden era. But it transformed culture into a tourist experience. By the mid-seventies, an astonishing 90,000 visitors a year came to the country.

In the same spirit of hospitality, Ashaf now takes me to the Deutscher Hof, which offers Afghanistan's only Oktoberfest, to sing "Es gibt kein Bier auf Hawaii" with former Taliban officers. He shows me the Four Horsemen of the Apocalypse riding across the wall of the Lai Thai, a restaurant which also has branches in Kosovo and East Timor. He points out Ching Ching, one of the sleazy Chinese eateries-cum-brothels serving Westerners. We even stop at Zarnegar Park to buy stolen US Army "Meals Ready to Eat" from the market traders.

As I'd heard in Turkey, the overland trail spawned an industry which packaged the globe. The commercial benefits of tourism can't be disputed. Worldwide, the travel industry churns over $500 billion and employs 195 million people. But, in such a world, can independent, intrepid travel even exist any more? Perhaps the only way to experience real wonder and freshness today is to travel without a guidebook. But, then, if you do that in Afghanistan, you'll probably end up dead.

To discuss the trials of modernity, I call by the Afghanistan Tourist Organization on my fifth morning in Kabul. I am welcomed as a lost son. I don't think another foreigner has stopped by the office in months. I want to ask the kindly staff about the seduction of foreign ideals. About the poisoning of tradition. About the banality of the material life. But they seem to have run out of those particular brochures.

In fact, the only printed material available is a personally signed pamphlet from the government's new Minister of Tourism. It assures me that many parts of the country are safe for visitors. Unfortunately, the minister is unavailable for interview. He was recently assassinated. As was his predecessor last year.

"The Kabul Museum," I say to Ashaf on my last morning in town.

18. EVE OF DESTRUCTION

The women crouched around the spring, their veils cast back, their men in the fields. Plum and wild apple trees grew around the shallow pool. The winter's fodder, dew-green and freshly scythed, dried between the mud houses. Fariba, first wife of Said, was teasing her aunt.

"Tell me again why your teeth are so white?" Fariba asked her.

"Praise to Allah, because my soul makes them clear," the old woman replied.

A little part of God was said to dwell in every man and woman.

"Then I do not understand, Aunt," she went on, "why Uncle's teeth are so yellow?"

The women bubbled as they filled their pitchers. They were in high spirits. The rush of water – unusual at this time of year – meant there was no need to walk the twenty minutes to the well.

Fariba was next at the spout. She held her pitcher under the stream and, as it filled, heard the clink of a pebble against clay. Once. Twice. Three times. She complained out loud, yet when she looked into the vessel she saw not pebbles but silver flashing in the dusty blue sunlight. The other women pushed forward, holding their pitchers under the spout, too, until each of them held more metal than water. Within minutes, the bottom of the pool glittered with coins.

"Praise God's protection and blessing." Fariba's aunt was the first among them to speak. "But now we will have to walk to the well after all."

"No, Aunt, now we will ride there on a mule."

That year, over 10,000 ancient coins were recovered from the spring. But the Mir Zakah discovery paled in comparison with the massive hoard uncovered in a nearby waterhole in 1993. Then, three *tons* of silver coins and fifty kilos of ancient gold jewelry were unearthed by Khoriuri Mangal tribesmen. The second largest treasure trove ever found included gold earrings as thick as tablespoons, silver Buddhist statues, classical Greek tableware, Scythian necklaces and Turkic bangles. The antiquities ranged in age from the fourth century BC to the first century AD. Several local people were murdered during the excavation. And because the nineties were a time of factional fighting – in 1994, 25,000 people were killed in Kabul alone – the entire find was smuggled over the border to Pakistan.

In Peshawar, the gold was sold off to American and Japanese collectors. Then, the dealers, embarrassed by the sheer quantity of coins – around twenty times the size of all the known collections of early Afghan coins in the world put together – melted down the ancient silver to make tourist trinkets.

In Kabul, I have one contact; an American who lived around the Muslim world and for thirty-five years considered Afghanistan to be her home. She is in a way a Grandmother Intrepid, an independent traveler whose wanderlust predates the Beatles and Beats. As Gertrude Stein and Paul Bowles – who, like Penny, she knew in Tangier – the defining purpose in her life has been to experience new peoples and lands. Her example – and her *Dinner of Herbs*, a compassionate portrait of an isolated Anatolian hamlet in the late sixties – had a formative influence on me. Her book's title comes from Proverbs 15:17: "Better is a dinner of herbs where love is than a stalled ox and hatred therewith."

A friend in Bath gave me her number. But her phone isn't working – Kabul's three telephone systems tend not to talk to one another – and the city's power has been switched off until December. So I decide to take a chance and turn up at her door.

Ashaf drives through Jad-e Maiwand toward the western quarter. Along Kote Sinki, old trolley-buses are stacked like battered Corgi toys, one on top of the other, shot through and burnt out. The Mirwais Cinema is a façade with bearded men playing volleyball in its open auditorium. An office building, its concrete floors like a *mille-feuille* pastry, lies where it collapsed a decade ago. The Soviet Cultural Center is abandoned, lop-sided and pock-marked with shell holes.

"This area was green," Ashaf says as we cross the remains of a destroyed university. "Here was a fountain. That was a cafeteria. There was the women's dormitory."

But as extensive as is the destruction in Jad-e Maiwand, I'm not prepared for the absolute devastation, the sinister emptiness, of Dar-ul Aman – City of Peace.

In 1937, Robert Byron wrote that Dar-ul Aman was "one of the most beautiful avenues in the world, four miles long, dead straight, as broad as the Great West Road and lined with tall white-stemmed poplars". In 1976, Nancy Hatch Dupree's breezy Kabul guidebook described the neighborhood as one of "picturesque walled castles, cultivated fields and poplar groves". Dar-ul Aman survived the Soviet occupation. But, in 1992, after the *mujaheddin* took the capital, four years of vicious in-fighting reduced the area to rubble.

"We lived on the other side of TV Mountain," says Ashaf, gesturing beyond a tangled transmission tower. "There was so much shooting here that rockets, with their flat trajectory, often overshot the hill and hit our neighborhood." Like most Kabulis, he is imbued with a basic sense of ballistics and can tell a Stinger from a Blowpipe. "That's when my family moved to Pakistan."

Not one building lines the avenue. The "walled castles", villas, carpet bazaar and match factory are gone. Only a few isolated, mustard-colored walls and smashed rubble-heaps remain. Beneath them, wild dogs pant in the shade. Behind them, for miles, is nothing. Nothing. Dar-ul Aman brings to mind Dresden or Hiroshima after the Second World War.

Ahead rises the skeleton of the palace, its formal gardens long lost, and beside it the Kabul Museum. Ashaf stops in front of the low official structure, with its collapsed west wing and caved-in upper story. The museum wasn't destroyed by the Soviets either. Until three years ago, it housed the finest collection of antiquities in Central Asia. Its Indian ivories, foot of Zeus, Roman bronzes, Alexandrian glass and Hindu Vishnu spanned fifteen millennia of history, with every item having been found on Afghan soil. "A Nation Stays Alive when its Culture Stays Alive" is painted on a bedsheet suspended above the main door. "Is your weapon unloaded?" asks the smaller sign beside it.

Dunes of grey dust drift across the forecourt. I step over them and out of the scorching daylight. A guard motions me along a gloomy hallway with the battered barrel of his gun. Its magazine is wrapped in duct tape.

At the end of the passage, under a single, sallow light bulb, a solitary figure bends over a bench.

"*Selaam aleikkum*," I say.

Carla Grissmann looks up from her work. Her mouth is tight, her haircut severe. She wears a neat, dark-blue *shalwar kameez* over her compact and fine-boned body.

"I've been hoping to meet you for a long time," I add.

"I don't know you, but *khasta habasheed?*" she replies. Considerate. Confident. "You may be tired. Have some tea." She offers me a stool, pours hot liquid from a slender Thermos into a pair of chipped cups, then sits down and looks at me. The thinness of her aged face magnifies her grave, guileless eyes.

We chat for a moment, mentioning names and finding the strands which connect us, but her attention quickly shifts back to the shards of broken pottery on the worktop. She is impatient of small talk. To hold her attention, I tell her, "I've come to ask why you've spent your whole life traveling."

Carla responds with a thrust of her chin. Her eyebrows rise, as accentuated as a circumflex. "Your timing is immaculate," she says. "Tomorrow I leave Kabul for the last time."

Carla was born in America, but America was never her home. From her youngest days, Carla longed for the wider world. Her life-long rush toward it began with her parents' divorce. In 1932, Carla moved with her mother to Berlin and then – when the Nazis invaded Breslau – to Norway and Switzerland. After the war and Columbia, she returned to Europe to live in Paris. Her mother married the French consul in Tétouan and she moved to Tangier. Her ten years there and later in Tunisia gave her a deep affinity for Muslim society, and the value placed on family unity.

In 1968, she visited Turkey and, hungry to experience village life, she found – or was found by – Uzak Köy, her Anatolian hamlet "held in the cupped palm of a rise of high land, overlooking a broad dry riverbed crawling out of sight around the feet of retreating hills". Its forty families lived in and out of each other's homes, praying, fasting, even sleeping together. Among them she found a generosity of heart, a welcoming community based on integration and camaraderie, as she did two years later when she happened on Afghanistan.

"Kabul was always an ugly city," Carla tells me in her museum workshop. "On a trip to India, I stopped here and thought what a hideous place. Then I went for a walk. Along the walls of the palace, I saw a soldier sitting on his guard box. He had a geranium on his epaulette. When I got close, he shouted, '*Selaam aleikkum, Hanim!*' He made a sweeping gesture towards the teapot and said, '*Chai!*' There were tomatoes ripening in the sun and his supper boiling in a Russian pressure-cooker. He looked me – everyone looked me – in the eye. I thought, 'Oh, this is wonderful, I want to stay here for ever.'"

"This was 1970," I ask.

"Or thereabouts," she says.

Carla found a teaching job at the university. On her first day, a student asked her, "Madame, how many children do you have?"

"None," she answered him.

"How many brothers and sisters?"

"None."

"Mother and father?"

Carla shook her head. By then, her parents were dead.

"Madame, this is a great tragedy."

Carla turned the conversation, asking the young man, "How many people in your family?"

"Too many, praise God," he laughed.

Carla uncorks the Thermos. I raise the tea to my lips and, over the rim of the cup, watch her face. Her complexion is porcelain white, her neck long and slender. She wears no make-up.

Carla tells me she lost her heart to the country and its good-looking, independent people. She divided her time between two worlds, dining one night on caviar at the French Embassy, then, the next morning, heading into the hills with her grocer's family. They'd chase wood for a fire, butcher a chicken, never be home by midnight.

"I remember laughter, music, tablecloths spread under the trees, the *phht-phht* of the pressure-cooker," she says, her quick laugh like a string being plucked. "Once I rode on the roof of a bus (inside which were two sheep and a bag of rice for another picnic) high into the Hindu Kush, winding through an indescribable landscape, thinking, 'If I have to go, let me go now. Let me breathe in this beauty and *go*.'"

"I don't think it's possible to travel like that any longer," I say, sensing the losses beyond the ruined building.

"I was lucky," she tells me. "I was the right age at the right time."

When student unrest closed the university, she came here to the museum. The Peace Corps conjured up a salary and Carla chose to start at the bottom, in the toilets which hadn't been cleaned for twenty-eight years, armed with her Swiss Army knife, a hammer and boiling water. Every few hours, she reported to the director on her progress, digging back – as she put it – through the Islamic Age, into the Bactrian century, toward the Bronze Age. When she completed the work, he proposed mounting a plaque on the wall. "This site excavated by Miss Carla Grissmann."

Her days at the museum were the happiest of her life. But her paradise became a war zone with the bloody, 1978 pro-Moscow coup. She refused to leave Kabul, even though battles rocked the country, and had to be tricked away to India.

For the next twenty-five years, Carla divided her time between London, Pakistan and Sri Lanka, returning to Afghanistan whenever a visa could be obtained. She saw the museum building laid to waste during the civil war. She watched its staff scattered by savage misfortune. She witnessed the destruction and looting of 70 per cent of the collection. When, in 1996, the Taliban took control of Kabul, they recognized the value of her experience. Carla was permitted to continue compiling an inventory of the remains of the collection, working amongst the rubble with neither electricity nor running water.

Then, in August 2000, the moderate Mullah Hotaki proposed mounting an exhibition to mark the museum's rudimentary reorganization. He invited fifty rural *mullahs* to the opening. The centerpiece of the show was a partially draped figure, an exquisite fourth-century painted clay Bodhisattva. Without warning, one of the *mullahs* spat at the Buddha. Then, like poison spreading from a wound, the other men started to beat the brittle clay with their bare hands.

"That was where it started," Carla tells me, unable to keep the emotion out of her voice, "and we didn't get the message. These semi-literate, provincial *mullahs* were only doing what they had been taught to do."

The Taliban believed that the depiction of living creatures promoted idolatry and was "un-Islamic". The rural *mullahs* were hurried away to the next room but, six months after the incident, a high-ranking delegation led by Qadratullah Jamal, the Minister of Culture, arrived at the door with sledgehammers, axes and armed guards. Day after day for two months, they broke into tin trunks, opened packing cases, removed the carefully wrapped objects and smashed them. When they finished, they drove to Bamiyan to blow up the massive Buddhas. The world's greatest collection of Central Asian artefacts became one of the great cultural tragedies.

A sharp, shallow cough cuts short her story. In the half-light, she closes her hands around the shards of pottery in a protective reflex.

"I can see the loss," I say. "I can try to describe it. I know the past is gone for ever. But to feel it...? The absence is almost too painful."

Carla does not hesitate to respond. "You must feel it," she says. "You must take it into your heart."

She lifts herself from the chair. I follow her sure step back down the forlorn hallway. The light from a broken window catches a fringe of fine silver hair beneath her headscarf.

Around us work carpenters and plasterers, financed by the British Museum and UNESCO. The building can be restored but little can be done to rebuild the collection. Like the memories of earlier times, that which has been lost is gone for ever.

In the foyer is a fifteenth-century black marble basin from Kandahar. On the wall hangs a twelfth-century calligraphic frieze from Laskhar Gah. Opposite it is a reconstructed mosque. "These were only left because of their Islamic phrases," says Carla, pointing at the script.

Above a dozen empty stone plinths are pinned photographs clipped from a 1974 guidebook: the lost Kushan king, the pulverized Bodhisattva, the shattered Bagram ivories which had depicted swirling naked courtesans.

"The delegation laughed like children as they smashed the statues," says Carla. She looks away and touches the corner of her eye. "The museum employees could do nothing but watch."

The loss didn't end then. Not so long ago the museum's main corridor was still lined with steel filing cabinets containing its collection of 40,000 coins, including some of the Mir Zakah hoard. All the coins, including many dating from the time of Alexander the Great, had now been looted.

I should ask Carla about the staff members killed when a rocket blew away the museum's top floor. Or the security guard shot dead by a looting warlord. Instead I see only the waste wielded by the men with axes, smashing millennia of history.

"What happened to all the fragments?"

Carla nods toward a double metal door. I push through it and into Basement Store No. 4. To my left, a wall of barred windows looks out over a wasteland, the former museum garden. To the right is a sight of equal devastation. The storeroom is filled with carved rubble on boxes, in crates, stacked up to the ceiling. Here is a broken stone finger, there a blinded eye, everywhere lie countless jagged stones.

"They look for matching color," she tells me, smiling sadly, holding two reunited pieces temporarily cemented together.

"How many work here?" I ask.

"Four or five men," says Carla. "If they each find two matches a day they are happy."

There must be more than 100,000 shards of carved stone in Basement Store No. 4.

"This room is Afghanistan's history now."

Behind us, a French archaeologist picks through the pieces, sweeps back his hair, and says nothing. Nothing.

Carla asks me for a drive back into town. She folds the veil around her head, as fastidious about her appearance as she was with the broken shards, and says goodbye to two old men in suits in an empty office. Ashaf opens the Datsun's rear door for her. She perches on the seat beside me.

"You said this is your last trip," I remind her as we drive away from the City of Peace.

"I know that I could stay," she answers me. "I could get a grant and be useful at the museum. The younger staff have only ever known a ruined building without electricity. That's why I gave them all copies of the museum guidebook. But..." Another cough leaves the sentence unfinished. She sits in silence for a moment. Then she says, "I weep for the Kabul I knew and loved."

On the pavement, a veteran in a wheelchair combs a cowlick of black hair out of his eyes. A scrawny boy yanks on the lever of a hand-pump. A woman's *burqua* balloons in the breeze of a passing truck.

As we near the martyr's shrine on Char-i-Shahid, Carla asks to stop at the "English" cemetery, established in the 1880s for the British dead of the second Anglo-Afghan war. A heavy wooden door opens through its high wall. In the wide, cloistered space are about two hundred graves to adventurers, soldiers and diplomats. Here lies Zou Xing Zhi of the Chinese Embassy and the Henley family who died in a road accident on the Salang Pass in 1969. On the west wall are recent memorials to British, German and Italian ISAF casualties. The flowers are still fresh on the grave of aid worker Bettina Goislard.

"We used to eat wild rhubarb boiled with chunks of potatoes, served with salt and pepper," says Carla, walking along a path of white marble chips lined by pines. "And fresh radishes, sold braided like a string of garlic. And melons, dear God, the melons. Babur wrote about them, deep and heavy and spilling their juice. I used to sit on my rooftop in the evening and hear flutes playing." The intensity of memory animates her and sets off the cough again. When she catches her breath, she looks at me, at once sad and accepting, and says, "Then, last month on the UN flight, I realized I didn't recognize a soul. It's another world now."

It is the time of afternoon prayers, and the light has taken on an unexpected, golden beauty. Carla moves along a line of graves, her fingers lightly tapping each stone. Mark Aurel Stein. Frederick Mewgard. 1st Battalion, Royal Anglian Regiment. She gestures for me to follow her to a long row of wooden crosses, some of them without names, along the back wall of the cemetery.

"In 1971, coming home from a picnic, I met a young Englishman on the bus," she remembers, stopping by a forlorn grave. "He was very ill and I took him to the hospital. He died and the doctors asked me to call his parents. They said, 'You've been to England. You must know where they live.' But the hospital didn't even know his surname. They knew only that his name was John. He had sold his passport. His identity." She turns to look at me. "Why did he come here to die at the end of the road in anonymity?"

"To catch a glimpse of his paradise?" I say.

"Lost souls," she says, looking over the sixties graves toward those of the murdered aid workers. "Like the lost souls of the terrorist movement today."

At nightfall I walk along broken streets back to the hotel. The only light comes from passing cars, kicking up dust, illuminating the pot-holes, and from the hissing glow of gas lamps burning above fruit stalls. In bakeries hunched men slap long rafts of na'an into pit ovens. A teenage trader sits at his roadside desk, empty but for stacks of mobile-phone cards at his right hand and US dollars on his left.

At nine o'clock, the city, which resonated all day with the sound of bicycle bells and grinding gears, falls silent. The streets become deserted. Even though the Taliban's nightly curfew has been lifted, old habits die hard.

I climb up to the roof of the Mustapha, balancing a tea glass on my notebook, to write under the stars. Around me Kabul appears enchanted; silhouetted houses stepping above the black fastness of the rock, free of dirt, flies, death. I will the clocks to stand still for a minute, to be frozen in time, to let me capture the moment. Of course the vision is a fancy, an evasion of all that wounds and defeats us in daily life. I reach for my pen to put the thought into words when a trembling seizes me, thinking of the real darkness that will descend again on Kabul in the light of morning.

19. I CAN HEAR MUSIC

I need to see the Buddhas, or at least the space filled by their absence. The HiAce minibus heads north from Kabul through the Ghorband valley – which Dervla Murphy likened to the Garden of Eden – towards Nuristan, the land of light, then hangs a left over the Shebar pass. Eight dusty, bone-crunching hours grind away covering the 140 miles, rising on fantastic corkscrew roads from the fertile plateau into the frozen splendor of the mountains.

We reach Bamiyan at sunset, flaxen light spilling down its long, lentil-red valley, glancing the sheer sandstone cliffs. A steppe eagle soars above the one-street town. Beyond the lines of silver-barked *sinjit* trees, the cliff face is pitted with myriad caves, once the cells of monks, and my eyes are drawn toward the gigantic gaping alcoves.

Bamiyan was a waystation and pilgrimage site on the Silk Road as well as on the hippie trail. For centuries, Hellenic, Persian, Hindu and Chinese culture were woven together here like an intricate Afghan rug. Buddhism had swept west from India along the same road that the Intrepids trekked east. The two Buddhas, the tallest standing statues ever made of him, were carved from the rock face around the sixth century AD. In 632, the visiting Chinese monk Hsuen Tsung noted the town's ten convents, its one thousand priests and the statues with "golden hues which sparkle on every side, their precious ornaments dazzling the eye by their brightness".

A couple of centuries passed before Islam sent the monks packing from the valley. The great carved figures, their faces covered with gold masks and their niches painted with symbolism borrowed from Greek, Indian and Sassanid art, went largely unmolested for 1,500 years. In the sixties, the Intrepids recognized Bamiyan as the sanctuary it once had been, sleeping in tents and yurts, swimming in the blue lakes of Band-e Amir, at ease in a meeting point of East and West.

But in March 2001, the "un-Islamic" statues were shelled with tank fire and blasted by dynamite on the order of the Taliban leader Mullah Omar. Afghan soldiers are said to have refused to undertake the demolition and a special contingent of Sudanese, Chechens and Arabs had to be sent from Kabul. But the story has a ring of untruth to me. It will always be difficult for Afghans to accept that the greatest damage to the country was inflicted by themselves.

Robert Byron would not have missed the statues. "Neither has any artistic value," he wrote in *The Road to Oxiana*. "A lot of monastic navvies were given picks and told to copy some frightful semi-Hellenistic image from India or China. The result has not even the dignity of labor." Bruce Chatwin likened the larger Buddha to an upright whale in a dry dock. Carla called them stocky, large-footed and clumsy.

But at dusk, when the shadows are deepest, a trick of the light now seems to trace in their place a refined outline, ethereal and freed of what Byron called their "monstrous, flaccid bulk". The immense *trompe-l'oeil* illustrates the enduring ethos of the valley; the glories that men can create – and destroy – through faith. The Buddhas seem most poignant in their absence.

I wander towards the rubble. A path skirts a ruined tank, crosses a stream, then rises to the gaping holes. A boy soldier takes my hand and leads me by torchlight into a warren of chambers linked by passages and stairways. I'm astonished by the number of caves, as if the mountain's face had been peppered by gunshot, which of course it was. Above the plastered walls and ruined arches no painted ceiling remains intact. The fragments of golden-hued fresco are blackened by smoke.

I climb on to a shale ledge near the top of the niche and remember that Rudy, driver of the Last Silver Dart, often stopped in Bamiyan. Once, he jumped on to the large Buddha's head. In one of the highest cells, Penny indulged in the Bam-bam-bamiyan, read *Siddhartha* and gazed out from the sheer rockface cut like the end of a loaf of bread towards the spectral peaks.

Now I sit on the edge, my feet dangling two hundred feet above the ground, thinking not of what I've seen but what I couldn't see on my trip: Penny's imaginary candles, the stars behind the new moon, the museum's pulverized Bodhisattva, the vanished Buddhas.

In my shoulder bag is Penny's *Siddhartha*. In my hand it falls open to a marked paragraph. "When someone is seeking," I read as she read, "it happens quite easily that he sees only the thing that he is seeking; that he is unable to find anything, unable to absorb anything, because he is only thinking of the thing he is seeking, because he has a goal, because he is obsessed with his goal. Seeking means: to have a goal; but finding means: to be free, to be receptive, to have no goal."

As the sun sets behind the Hindu Kush, an Apache helicopter flies overhead and I hear singing.

Only now do I notice that the cliff's lower flanks are not deserted. A dozen families are living in the caves, poor refugees scraping out an existence on half-measures of rice and a couple of chickens. Boys scavenge firewood on the plain to feed glowing cooking fires. A girl lays out her father's prayer mat by a mud doorway. A grey-moustached elder exudes an aura of dignified old age as he scoops trickles of water for his ablutions.

I step toward them, beating a path along the hillside with the soldier, not wishing to intrude but anxious to find the source of the singing. I've heard no live music since leaving Turkey.

Over an arm of scree I see the boy. He is sitting quite alone in the dirt, drawing stones toward him. I watch as he gathers them into a square of walls. When he finishes, he places a threadbare toy figure inside his building. Then he knocks it down with sudden violence, scattering the stones across the rough slope.

I crouch beside the boy, who is no more than five or six years old, as he begins again to collect the stones. For a moment he ignores me.

"What do the words mean?" I ask the soldier. The song has a curious ring of familiarity.

"Words are English," the soldier replies. "You not speak English?"

The singing is phonetic, a feat of memory, and I don't recognize a single word.

"But what is he building?" I ask the soldier.

"Hose," the boy answers me. "Cookie hose."

"Cookie house?" I say.

In Kabul I heard a story about a child who became terrified of aircraft after the Coalition bombardment. Every time a plane passed overhead he raised an imaginary gun and pretended to shoot at it. To ease his fear his mother told him that aircraft now dropped sweets instead of bombs. But cookies?

"Cookie hose on TV," the boy adds unexpectedly.

An hour later, at my one-room hotel-restaurant the owner braises kebabs, dropping an egg and meat pieces into a sizzling metal platter set on the coals. With blackened fingers he serves the oily *kadai* to my table-cum-bed. A bullet round has pierced its frame, leaving a flower of torn metal at my elbow.

"TV?" he says when I relate the story of the singing, house-building child. "You talk to Sanjar. He make TV. You want more chips?"

In the morning I search out Sanjar, which doesn't take long. His electronic shop lies across the road. Behind the dusty window are stacks of televisions, both new and prehistoric, as well as tinny transistors and a rental library of Bollywood epics. On the wall are Sony schematic diagrams and fading pictures of Ahamd Zahir, the Afghan Elvis. Beyond a curtain is the studio.

Sanjar is Hazara, a tall and stringy young man without an ounce of fat on him. His light-brown hair is curly and, behind his dark glasses, his hazel eyes are optimistic. He never stops moving, yet he radiates a calmness, a kind of peace that can't be touched. In the shop – while upgrading a CD machine into a DVD player – he tells me that he is a trained engineer, which means he worked one winter in a relative's shop in Peshawar. He is probably all of twenty years old. Survival in Afghanistan depends on resourcefulness, on rising to the occasion and on the occasional lie.

A couple of months ago, an aid worker stopped by the shop with a small, broken video camera, he tells me. Sanjar hadn't been able to repair it – at least he said he couldn't do it – and, as the model was outdated, the foreigner gave it to him. Over the next few evenings, he managed to fix the camera, checking it out by recording Bamiyan's street life: his fellow shopkeepers, the rheumy-eyed beggars, kids playing in the ruins of the bazaar.

The repair was fortuitous, but even more rewarding for Sanjar was the excitement of neighbors seeing themselves on screen. The valley, with a population of 50,000 souls, has no local TV station. There is a radio operator – the upstart Radio Bamyaan – but Sanjar decided the town needed community television. So he set to work to build it.

"Just like in *ET*," he tells me. "I collected stuff together and start to send messages."

With two cycle rims, a discarded satellite receiver, a pair of VCR recorders and twenty-five transistors, Sanjar launched his backroom station. Behind his shop curtain he set up a table with a world map as background and two 250-watt bulbs for lighting. He updated a vintage Soviet military transmitter, which had been discarded by the state broadcaster, then carried a battery-powered TV set around town to test its reception. Additional condensers and diodes increased its range from a hundred meters to almost three kilometers.

Every evening, Sanjar broadcasts two hours of programming, except on the occasions when his generator breaks down. Local traders are given free air-time, as is the town's doctor, to disseminate information on physiotherapy and iodine deficiency. Village *maliks* air public announcements. Spare air-time is filled by popping any convenient DVD into the player. *Friends*, *Rambo* and all of Sanjay Khan's films are perennial favorites. Plans for a phone-in program, offering viewers somewhere to turn to for advice outside the family or mosque, are on hold until more people have telephones.

He tells me the most popular spot by far is *We Are Bamiyan*. With his hand-me-down Panasonic, Sanjar wanders the valley's lanes and orchards, filming the harvest and first day of school, quizzing locals about their hopes and demands. In his hurried yet calm manner he draws out men – and women – by asking them how, if they were the mayor or a government minister, they would solve this or that problem. Back at the shop he edits the tapes, adding titles and background music. His aim is both to make television a friend of the viewer and, borrowing a phrase, to encourage truth and reconciliation.

"For twenty-seven years, people were just surviving," he tells me. "Now they see the newest DVD movies and want to have a kind of Western life. This brings new pressures and problems."

Sanjar also includes children in his program. Most young Afghans have only ever known war. By one calculation, two-thirds of children have witnessed the killing of a relative, friend or neighbor. The legacy of loss, compounded by displacement and poverty, has scared millions of vulnerable hearts and minds.

To encourage young people to talk about their experiences, Sanjar arranged and recorded a *kishranu jirga*, or junior assembly. He brought ten boys together and asked one of them to lie on the floor on a large piece of paper. Sanjar drew a line around the body, then instructed the boys to decorate that outline with crayons and chalk.

When they finished, Sanjar – his running camera mounted on a recycled machine-gun tripod – pointed at the drawing's eyes and asked each of them in turn, "What do you like to see?" and "What don't you like to see?" He wrote down their responses on the sheet of paper.

Next he pointed at the ears, then the nose, asking again what the boys liked and didn't like to hear and smell. He carried on with other parts of the body; the mouth for eating and speaking, the hands for doing, the feet for going, the head for thinking, the heart for feeling.

"I don't like tasting bad water," said one boy. "I like the smell of the mosque on Friday," reported another. "I cried seeing my father die," responded the smallest boy.

"Where do you feel pain?" he then asked, and each child told a story about their fears and the family or friends who helped them to cope. All the children's ideas were recorded on the sheet around the life-size drawn figure.

The next morning, he hung the drawing in the town office to stress its importance. Only one neighbor thought the *kishranu jirga* was a waste of time. "If we beat children with a stick," he said, "it helps them to understand everything." The next day, Sanjar repeated the exercise with ten girls.

"This is what I do," he tells me simply, humbly, not pausing while he drafts the day's news. "A good Muslim should help his community. God chose me to bring television to Bamiyan."

He has no operating licence, which irritates the state broadcaster RTA. Twice, Sanjar went to Kabul to try to reassure them that his little station benefits the community. The local warlord also threatened to shut him down, arriving in person at the shop with half a dozen armed bodyguards.

"Of course I must modify my content from time to time," he admits. "Afghanistan was ruined by Pakistan, by Russia, but most of all by ourselves. We are left with only one set of clothes, one mouthful of food, one last chance. Islam says that everyone carries their own burden. You can't be damned by Adam and you can't be saved by Isa – your Jesus. We each must make our own life now." Sanjar smiles, then looks at the clock. "Now, if you'll excuse me, I have work to do."

That day I take in the town. The Hazara, who claim descent from the Mongols, are Afghanistan's largest Shia community. The Taliban, as Sunni rulers, considered them to be heretics. "Hazaras are not Muslim," the governor of Mazar-e Sharif once claimed. "They are infidels." During the civil war, Taliban forces blockaded the poor, drought-stricken province for a year and, when Bamiyan surrendered in August 1998, they killed 6,000 residents. Houses were burnt and fields sprayed with chemicals. Men were beheaded or shot in the testicles. Women and children were loaded into metal shipping-containers without food or water and driven around the country until they died. The bazaar was put to the torch and smoke had enveloped the whole valley, blocking out the sun.

I climb in the cool sunshine past the salt and wheat shops, back toward the Buddhas' niches, thinking about Sanjar and his ambition to rise above the bitter betrayals. Near the Bamiyan Hotel, a band of Korean tourists snap photographs of the rubble.

On a hill flank beneath the sandstone cliff, the singing child sits cross-legged in the dirt, building then destroying his "cookie" house. I listen to him for a moment and then, like a window of light opening in the sky, I recognize the words.

"Sunny day, sweepin' the clouds away..."

"Cookie?" I say to him. "Cookie Monster?"

His flat Asiatic features crease into an alarmed smile and he laughs, delighted to be understood at last.

"On my way to where the air is sweet," he sings on.

I join him for the next line. After all, I grew up with the program. "Can you tell me how to get..."

And I saw the pirated DVD copy in Sanjar's shop.

"...how to get to Sesame Street."

Pakistan

20. GAMES PEOPLE PLAY.

I'm at the frontier, swept up in a Koranic scene, pressed between praying refugees, tired-eyed traders and half-starved dogs, herded by soldiers through a propitious gate.

I slipped out of Kabul this morning, leaving behind a bit of my heart, carrying my small rucksack of nascent ideas, driving towards Jalalabad and the dirty white Safed Koh mountains. As if to reflect my mood, the taxi outran the hard-skinned and reptilian landscape. Rough ranges of lizard hills, with scaly flanks and scalloped backs, rose shoulder to shoulder above the burnt-ochre plateau. The mountains seemed ready to shake their snow-capped heads, to lift their foothill tails and lash out at the car. But like the Intrepids before me, I sprinted ahead to find a new way forward.

Ten minutes ago, I emerged from that primeval terrain into this crush of men, animals and machines. A mother pulled her headscarf over her reddened lips and a pale baby. A high-sided truck hauled home a whole village and its single buffalo. A detachment of Khyber Rifles paused in their search of an aid convoy to drop to their knees and pray. The Torkham checkpoint marks the second great historical border of the trail. Behind me lay the Turkish and Persian empires, ahead spreads the Indian world. On the subcontinent live one-fifth of humanity. Here, four of the world's great religions – Buddhism, Jainism, Sikhism and, oldest of them all, Hinduism – were born. Here, too, the twentieth-century Islamic revival first took root. I'm on the threshold of a uniquely spiritual land, waiting beneath stony grey-brown mountains in the midday heat for my ride into Pakistan.

"Homeland of Muslims?" roars Iqbal, finding me in a tea shop bent over my notes, writing with new confidence. "By the grace of God, you are a dreamer, sir. I am obliged to inform you that Pakistan is no Kingdom Come." He drops his voice in sudden melodrama to hiss, "It is a heavenly nightmare."

Canadian friends in Islamabad have sent their driver to collect me. Big-bellied and jocular, Iqbal is not what I expected. With good humor and stale breath, he sweeps me into the LandCruiser. He tucks the dashboard's CD plate beneath an embroidery of the Prophet's teachings, unleashes the horn and accelerates away from the Durand Line. I feel as if I've stepped into the jovial pages of an eighties travel romp.

"I will go further," he ventures, cutting in front of an oncoming Afghan bus. "My Pakistan, which was born with such high hopes, has become a whore."

Iqbal is lucid and charming, a frank fiftysomething with piercing brown eyes and an air of urgency that suggests any delay might cause an explosion. His crisp clothes and remarkable colonial English are immaculate. Only his corpulence seems to weigh on him, as does his back, the consequence, he claims, of too often "lifting the legs".

"I will relate a story for you," he says. "When your good friends were posted to Islamabad, their house was a bordello. Shocking but true. Big Fat Tony, their driver, also secured by the High Commission, had run it under the noses of the previous incumbents. I felt it my duty to tell your friends about the taxi girls."

"Taxi girls?"

"Ladies of chancy virtue," he informs me, "who arrived every day in taxis – bold as brass – and proceeded directly to the basement."

"To do what, Iqbal?" I ask.

"Sir, to do. To *do*. The next morning, armed with brooms, your friends and I greeted the girls and whisked them off the doorstep, along with Big Fat Tony. The pretty things had diamonds in their noses and rings on their fingers and they wailed at the injustice of it all. How would they feed their babies? Who would care for their parents? I realized then how very much I love my holy, shameless country." As we barrel headlong towards a crash barrier, Iqbal stops laughing long enough to add, "Forgive me if my illustration is inexact. I do fall short of due expression at times."

"You're saying Pakistan is a whore?" I ask him, gripping the seatbelt's shoulder strap and remembering with fondness the relatively sedate journeys in Turkey. "America's whore?"

"Glorious is God," he replies. "Not just America's."

Since 9/11, Pakistan has become the United States' greatest ally in the war against terrorism. Even though the Pakistani army's backing of the Taliban helped ruin Afghanistan. And its intelligence service sanctioned armed militants' attacks on India. And its global mail-order business in nuclear-bomb technology endangers the whole world. In spite of this, the US State Department pours $700 million of assistance into Islamabad's coffers every year.

"My dear sir, people may be Christian or Muslim or no matter, but every mortal soul prays to the one and only great god of money. Like those pretty ladies, my Pakistan will sleep with *jihadis*, Koreans, even Texans, anyone who butters their bottom."

"Butters their bread," I say, unsure myself of the suitability of the expression.

"I am beholden for that apt correction," he replies.

The Grand Trunk Road veers into the Khyber Pass. Through it marched armies of Greeks, Buddhists and Mughals, carrying their banners high. The British followed them, building a new road around the side of the arid mountain, leaving behind milestones and sad little graveyards. Now, old men cool their feet in dull, roadside streams. Boys in rags play cricket on dusty pitches with stone wickets. The monsoon is weeks overdue and dirt-poor villagers have moved out of their earth houses and on to string beds under dusty neem trees. We wind around them and deep limestone gorges in a convulsion of terrifying twists, as Iqbal mops his neck with a handkerchief and turns up the air conditioning. "I beg you to excuse the woefully backward scenes before you," he says. "Ours is a country of great inequality."

I'm hungry to discover what has befallen the "Homeland of the Muslims" and say, "Pakistan was born of a flawed dream, wasn't it?"

"Not a flawed dream, sir, but a dream flawed by man."

In 1930, "the Poet of the East" – Mohammed Iqbal – called for the creation of a single Muslim state in north-west India. The compelling idea couldn't be resisted, especially in the face of escalating violence between Hindus and Muslims. In 1947, when the British left India, Pakistan was partitioned off at the cost of millions of lives and livelihoods.

In the early days, the new country was liberal and tolerant. Christians and Shias worshipped alongside Sunnis without fear of persecution. Wine and *bawas* – quarter bottles – of gin were sold in the cantonments. But, in gaining independence, the nation's founders lost their only cause and, unsure of their new role, they decided not to jeopardize their futures by risking fair elections.

With political life throttled, the army – Pakistan's only organized group – flourished. Its growing frustration with weak civil authority sparked a series of military coups. Army, government and populace became estranged. Prime ministers were deposed or executed. The population was allowed to grow unchecked. A gifted people were crippled by corruption and mismanagement. Poverty fed anger. Each dictator left behind him – according to Iqbal – "filth, stink and very ugly scars on the society". The state began to fail.

But those failings couldn't be blamed on the dream of a faith-based nation – such candor would have undermined Pakistan's very existence. Instead, its shortcomings came to be attributed to men failing the faith. The country recast itself as the first Islamic state since the days of the Prophet. Multi-dimensional Islam was narrowed into a state ideology. Opportunistic democrats bolstered their position by building up a small and passionate following of radical Islamists. National insecurity – disguised as the assertion of faith – prolonged animosity with India and propelled the building of the "Islamic" nuclear bomb. Today, poor, failing Pakistan, seventh largest nation in the world, has an annual GDP of less than $540 per head.

"Hats off to the creators of Pakistan," says Iqbal. "They changed the map. They dreamt of building a society that was – we can say now in hindsight – utopian. But to answer your question: how did Pakistan get this way? By believing that God wished to be a politician." He smiles to himself. "Now, we sit in the bazaar in our wooden cubicles, winking at strangers, offering up our rubies..."

Iqbal's big hands never leave the wheel nor the horn, driving bullock carts and taxis out of our way. He travels at a tremendous speed, past hand-painted lorries adorned with F-16 fighter jets, not pausing for breath, losing neither his narrative nor his good humor. As we drop out of the tribal lands on to the burning plain, he tells me that in his time he has been a tailor, a seaman, an actor and a cook. He says he has driven cars for the Aga Khan and the former director of BOAC in Karachi. He confesses that for a couple of years he fell on hard times.

"Gambling," he admits, "with the wrong sort of people. Just like my beloved, unequal country."

Peshawar is 35 miles from the Afghanistan border. On its outskirts spread the now-flattened Kacha Garhi camp, once home to 100,000 Afghan refugees. Across the highway from the wasteland of broken earth walls laze the manicured lawns and new condominiums of retired military men. "City of Flowers" to the Kushans, "Frontier Town" to the Mughals, "the city which comes first after the wilderness" to the Persians, Peshawar remains a thriving, rough-edged trading town. Caravans paused under its shady trees, put their animals to grass on its lush acres, bartered weapons and favors in the Storytellers' Bazaar – activities which haven't changed in a thousand years.

Iqbal jumps my first red light on the subcontinent and pulls into a sunless alleyway between the Asia Arm Store and Tip Top Cleaners. Beneath a billboard for City University ("Get studying! Get out of Pakistan!"), he tells me, "My dear, I am bushed to the bone." He has been on the road since before dawn, and we still have a four-hour drive to reach Islamabad.

"Do you want to take a nap?" I ask him.

"Not exactly a nap, sir, but perhaps you'd enjoy exploring the town?" he suggests, conjuring up his own story. "While I take a little R&R. My cousin lives in Peshawar."

"Your cousin?" I ask, both bewildered and delighted by the sudden suggestion.

"A friend of my cousin," he says with a theatrical wink. "Please forgive my lack of hospitality. I must attend to her by myself on a pressing matter. See you back here in an hour?"

I leave him to meander around the Old City, weaving between buzzing bee-yellow Qingqi rickshaws and horse-drawn tongas, into a warren of crude concrete shops, pavement barbers and cycle-repair stalls. I open my notebook and write. "Black flags, sugar-cane juice stalls, mule drivers, overstuffed fleece shops. A cyclist pushes through the crowds with a bed frame balanced on his head. Braying donkeys, broom-closet sweet stalls, *qawali* music playing on transistor radios. A dirty green kite rises on thermals of exhaust fumes over the proud new offices of the Pakistan Atomic Energy Commission."

My snatched glimpses heighten the sense of flux, both of a world rapidly changing and of myself changing within it. I find a chair in a smoky samovar house to gather my thoughts. As I gulp the black tea, I catch my reflection in the shop's mirror.

"Large, down-turned green eyes. Pale cheeks burnt by the day's journey. Translucent skin, silver beneath eyelids. Receding red hair. My father's long ears. My mother's mouth. A hungry travel writer with pen poised, trying to replace cliché with something more human and variable."

I decide to send home my notes, so make for the City Net Café. A policeman stops me at the door.

"What is your intention here, sir?" he asks me.

"I need to send an email," I explain.

"Please ask permission from my superior."

I didn't expect to need official approval to go online. But I hadn't noticed the bullet holes in the plate-glass window.

That morning, a young Pashtun named Habib had come to City Net. He logged on at one of the twenty terminals and sent a message, "I am waiting for you in net cafe. I have mother with me and will go to the village." A few minutes later, a bearded Arab entered the shop. When he greeted Habib, half a dozen plainclothes intelligence agents jumped up from the other terminals and seized the men. Habib drew and fired a pistol before he was overpowered. A dozen anti-terrorist commandos then bundled the pair into waiting jeeps.

I don't hang around to meet the senior officer but retrace my steps to the vehicle. Iqbal is waiting in the driver's seat, complaining about his back.

"I have been reflecting most deeply," he says once we are back on the GT Road. "I do not wish you to have a negative snapshot of my land."

I don't mention the incident at the café.

"It is true that in the early days there was an intense hope for improving ourselves overnight."

"And now most Pakistanis worry about their need for food and shelter?"

"Perhaps, but we've always cherished the promotion of peace," he insists. "Not only that, we've been dedicated agents of those forces who project these ideas."

"Like the CIA and the Taliban?"

"I think Pakistan can be a bridge between Islamic countries and the Western world, just as we played a role in bringing America and China together in 1972. Geographically speaking, Pakistan is at the very heart of Asia. You shout loud enough and you hear the echo from Tashkent to Tibet."

"I'll remember that," I tell him.

East of Peshawar, the colossal mountains loop away to the north and the land levels into green fields dotted with goat herds and army camps. Children cut fodder from the central reservation, darting between the buses with armfuls of grass, helping their elders stack busby-like hay ricks. In Nowshera, a camouflaged battle tank rises on a concrete plinth next to the School of Mechanized Warfare and a Military Dairy Farm. The broad Kabul River ripples on our left-hand side, its banks high, sandy and flanked by small-holdings of cauliflower and corn. At Attock, its sanguine, brown waters sweep into the swift, blue Indus – which sources high in the Himalayas – the contrasting colored currents flowing side by side for over a mile downstream.

Iqbal accelerates into the Punjab, passing on the inside lane and once on the gravel shoulder. As the shadows lengthen, the roadside grows even more crowded, pedestrians and creaking carts moving home from the fields alongside the thundering traffic. The country's only overpass, being constructed by hand, curves above our heads toward the Karakoram Highway and the Silk Road link to China.

"You know, I'm baked in this culture," volunteers Iqbal. "When I go across seas, I am mighty delighted the moment the aircraft touches back down in Pakistan. I like to listen to the language, to see the casual mannerisms of the people, to experience the hospitality."

A gauze of high, wispy cloud spreads with the night but neither dissipates the relentless heat.

"No nation is without failings of course," he goes on, the darkness unleashing a loquacious intimacy. "But in the Koran, Lord God Allah says, 'I don't give good rulers to bad societies,' so I blame myself for what has befallen Pakistan."

"In what sense?"

"In the sense that I am part of this society. Few citizens have played their role, have stood up and defied the untruth loudly and clearly. Loudly and clearly. That is where we're lacking. We shrink from risks at times. We don't call a shovel a shovel."

"A spade a spade," I say. "But if you had spoken out, wouldn't you have been shot?"

"Not shot, my romantic friend. Perhaps beaten and imprisoned for an unspecified period of time, but never shot. We are a civilized clan," he says, laughing himself back into good humor. "Forgive me this one last time, but it is never easy being a divided man of torn loyalties."

"Loyal to what?" I ask him.

"Loyal to Islam and money. Loyal to the old British ways and the modern world. Most of all, loyal to my holy but shameless brown whore."

Lime-colored neon tubes burn in scrawny, bandy-legged eucalyptus trees, drawing drivers into busy roadside canteens with earthen forecourts stained sticky-black by motor oil. Our headlights catch them and the hand-painted road signs for "I Love Allah a/c Centers". I drop my notebook and scrabble in the shadows at my feet to find it. Iqbal races on until the lights of the capital flash before us.

Islamabad reveals itself as a planned city of leafy enclaves, broad avenues and white-walled villas protected by armed guards, like the hideaways of Latin American dictators. Even in my exhaustion, the place feels artificial, divorced from intrinsic culture, its grid system and shopping malls part of the homogenized post-modern suburb. Along Constitution Avenue – which locals call Suspended Constitution Avenue – stretches the sterile diplomatic quarter: ranks of embassies, the French School, the Canadian Club, and the Secretariat, Benezir Bhutto's folly, which looms out of the dark like a moghul's palace. As in Washington and Canberra, not a soul walks on the deserted streets.

We wheel into my friends' driveway and Iqbal hides the Prophet's teachings behind the red CD plate. I realize the muscles of my forearm have seized around the passenger's hand strap.

"Welcome to the fool's paradise," he says.

21. GATES OF EDEN

I rise up out of darkness, out of sleep, into a soft, cool dawn. Light floods my room, washing away its edges, smoothing out the corners. I blink at the brightness, in my glaring disorientation, feeling all but disconnected from the earth. Around me, the high, wide windows are draped in thin white cotton. Beyond them a faint breeze stirs into dance a silhouette of leafy branches. The shadows of pigeons sweep across the translucent veil. A pale lily stands in a stone vase. In the distance I hear the soft pad of footsteps and the click of a gardener's shears. I lift back the bed sheet, slip across the white marble floor and vomit in the toilet.

I feel bad, not from Afghan pilau or a roadside tikka but from a single unwashed lettuce leaf which garnished my late-night peanut butter sandwich. I scoffed it without thinking, on arrival at my Canadian friends' villa, overwhelmed by their larder-full of Wonderbread and taco kits. Now a boulder squats in my stomach, and in the light white room I want to surrender under its weight, but I have an appointment.

To many Intrepids, Pakistan was another "passing through" country. "You may end up blasting through West Pakistan in about forty-eight hours," wrote Douglas Brown in *Overland to India*. Mik Schultz advised his readers to "take the morning bus from Kabul to Peshawar, then continue with the night train to Lahore and India." Geoff Crowther described the country as a "heavy trip" for women. "If you're the slightest bit underdressed in their terms, you'll be mauled and touched up constantly." Only three pages were devoted to Pakistan in Wheeler's *Across Asia on the Cheap*.

In the sixties and seventies, travelers tended to overstay their time in Afghanistan, then, emerging from the blue fug of hash smoke, remember India and want to get there in a hurry. Most overlooked the Sufi shrines at Uch Sharif, the spectacular Vale of Swat and the Graeco-Buddhist ruins at Taxila. Those who did dawdle in the republic may have wished that they'd hurried on. After his twenty-two-day bus ride from Bradford in 1971, Allan MacDougall, a Canadian traveler, reached the Indus, dived in and contracted typhoid. An Encounter Overland driver was shot in the leg near Taftan trying to outrun bandits in a Toyota pick-up. A German backpacker was machine-gunned to death in her tent in a bungled robbery. Even the authors of the current Lonely Planet guide admit, "Pakistan *is* a wild and woolly place." Few kids ever considered the "volatile" nation of "drugs, guns and military coups" as a place for spiritual enlightenment.

"I don't think I'd be a Muslim today if it wasn't for Mr Zimmerman," admits the *imam*.

"Bob Dylan?" I say.

"Trust yourself to do the things that only you know best," he sings out loud. "Trust yourself to do what's right and not be second-guessed." Then, with a smile, he adds, "Allah works in mysterious ways."

John Butt, a tall and passionate man with a lean, weathered face and white spade beard, was a dope-smoking, rock 'n' roll-loving Intrepid. In the late sixties, en route to India, he ran out of money and converted to Islam. He became a *talib* and scholar, rising in time to the position of Muslim chaplain at Cambridge University. Every few months he returns to Pakistan, his beloved North-West Frontier province, and Afghanistan.

Now he sits with me on the scorched earth beneath a date palm in Shakarparian Park, a low green ridge between planned Islamabad and chaotic, sprawling Rawalpindi. To the east, the Margalla hills rise above the pines and jacaranda trees. To the west stands a vast, unsubtle sculpture of a star and crescent.

"There is a saying in the East that experience can be bitter," Butt says, holding his open palms together. His short neat hair is trimmed beneath a four-peak, green velvet Uzbek cap. "But if you can learn the same experience from another, then you can grow from it without the pain."

Butt was born in Trinidad, a son of one of the island's oldest European families. At the age of nine, he was sent away to a Jesuit boarding school in England. The experience was so traumatic and dislocating that, when he left Stonyhurst in 1969, he needed to return to his roots.

"But I didn't think of going back to Trinidad," he tells me, "even though

I'd been torn away from that country which I loved. I felt a greater need. For us in the sixties, our deeper roots were in the East. The hippie trail was my escape route from Western civilization."

Butt's journey was emotional from the outset, not simply a youthful adventure of the self but also a pilgrimage. He had been introduced to the Koran at school, and the holy book's directness moved him. Yet he never considered converting to Islam. He – like so many others then and now – simply felt a gnawing absence in his life, as well as a sense of being at odds with himself.

"I went down to Morocco, stuck around in Paris for a while, then spent the winter on Crete. There were caves in Matala, and it was like a big hippie commune. Next, I stopped in Rhodes and met a Norwegian girl who I really liked. With my Catholic upbringing, I was a bit shy with girls but she was leaving the following day. We had a sort of one-night stand and I had to smuggle her back to her parents' hotel."

"She didn't entice you to stay in Europe?"

"I wasn't into the sexual thing. I looked at my journey as a spiritual path. I felt the need to control desire. Uncontrolled self-gratification seemed to be part of what I had to relinquish." His sage-colored eyes soften and his long mouth stirs into a smile. "But that Norwegian was a very nice memory."

"After she left, I spent two weeks in Rhodes just *looking* at Asia. Just *thinking* about Asia. It's quite important, you know, coming to Asia for the first time. Asia meant so much."

As well as hedonism, Butt also renounced materialism. He wanted his life to be enriched by greater works than a new car or luxurious house.

"When I was ready, I took a fishing boat to Turkey. What hit me right away was the Muslim hospitality. The Turks brought us this huge fish and no one wanted us to pay. On the train heading east, I said to everyone, with a lot of warmth, '*Merhaba*'. Greetings! There was so much love. I felt at home."

As he speaks, the morning heat ripples up from the twin cities like the wash of a tide, bringing with it the smell of roses and drains.

"I was set on going to Afghanistan and India. I reached Kandahar sitting on top of hay bales in the boot of an Afghan post bus. I liked Kandahar, and not only because of the fabled dope. Everything was so different: shepherd boys playing their flutes, old men smoking hash chillums in the tea shops, bells tinkling in the morning."

But, in Kandahar, Butt contracted dysentery. He tried to stick to his macrobiotic diet by eating onion sandwiches – the only *yang* food he could find – and became seriously ill. He ran out of money. In Kabul, he sold his cassette recorder – on which he had recorded Dylan's *Come Back* Isle of Wight concert – and nursed himself back to health. Then he overstayed his visa and was ordered to leave the country. He hitched to the Pakistan border.

"My first night outside Peshawar there was a full moon," Butt remembers. "I was with two friends in the tribal territory. I wasn't under the influence of anything so I wasn't hallucinating. Suddenly, celestial lights started flashing around the sky, landing close to the spot where we were sitting. I was spellbound."

The experience was to mark the beginning of Butt's conversion to Islam. He later learnt of the "Night of Power", when celestial lights fill the skies and sins are forgiven. The phenomenon is described in the surah *Laylat'al-Qadar*. "Verily, We revealed the Koran during the Night of Power. And how can you realize what the Night of Power is? The Night of Power is better than a thousand nights. During it, the angels descend, along with the Spirit, with the permission of their Lord, imparting peace to everything: peace, until the breaking of the dawn (Koran, 97:1–5)."

Butt traveled deep into northern Pakistan, crossing the Malakand Pass into a land "like something out of Middle Earth: a tapestry of meadows and rolling hills". He fell in love with the patterns of the fields and the juxtaposition of scooped ravines and jutting mountains in the Swat Valley. He realized he felt at home amongst the people. On a bus a tribal policeman tried to collect from him a foreign-traveler tax. A local man sitting next to Butt took issue with the policeman, saying, "He shouldn't pay. He belongs here."

Above all, Butt felt he belonged in the religion. In Kalam, three curious Punjabi men broke into his room, just to have a look at a long-haired, disreputable European. "Oh, believers, do not enter homes other than your own," Butt snapped at them, quoting the surah *An-Nur*, "until you have asked for permission and invoked peace upon those who live there." The wide-eyed intruders apologized and withdrew.

Finally, Butt took a long bus ride during Ramadan.

"One evening, my bus stopped and everyone broke their fast and ate a date and said a prayer. I felt so bad, so left out. I decided then and there never again to deny myself the experience. To deny that affinity.

"The next morning I got up at the right time. I fasted properly. I started rereading the Holy Koran. There I found the clues for my own journey: from the darkness comes light, from the light comes darkness, the ambience of the opposites. I also learnt that the acceptance of Islam did not mean the renunciation of other faiths but rather the acceptance of them in their true meaning. The Koran teaches that prophets have passed in every nation, and every community has been blessed with a guiding light. The only difference is the Koran has preserved what other scriptures have distorted over the ages."

He goes on, "You know, for a hippie, Islam was not particularly fashionable. Hippies became Buddhists or Hindus."

Most Westerners find it easier to relate to Hinduism and Buddhism. The two older faiths are mystical, flexible and hold out the promise of contentment, whereas Muslims accept lives of struggle, sacrifice and sometimes even suffering in the path of God. Earthly happiness is not the aim of the Islamic life, and praying six times a day sat uneasily with the sixties aversion to discipline.

"My conversion just happened. People said to me, 'When will you become Muslim?' I answered, 'It says in the Koran that Islam is the submission to almighty Allah. I have already submitted, so I am a Muslim.'"

His ardent, transforming story lightens my heart. In Islam, he found a way to end his disorientation, to make sense of the pains and mysteries of life, to touch his inner nature. Its rituals linked him with tradition and gave him a sense of belonging. In the shade, even my concrete stomach begins to feel less heavy.

Butt is silent for a moment, then says, "I think, on accepting Islam, I learnt to express myself with the certainties, the doctrines, which Islam teaches – that God is One, the prophets communicate His Word to mankind, Allah will judge men according to the way they acted on earth. It is still one of the great attractions of Islam to me that it seems to deal with everything."

"Everything?" I ask, struggling to accept that any religion could rationalize all of life.

"As the Koran says, 'We have not left anything out of the Book (Koran, 6:38).'"

"But the sixties were all about seeking self-knowledge. Are you saying that enlightenment can be achieved only through an intimate knowledge of Islam?"

"Enlightenment is an airy-fairy, wishy-washy concept associated more with Buddhism and Hinduism," says Butt, lowering his head to look at me under his white eyebrows. "Enlightened – 'roshan-fikr' in Persian – refers to those who are guided more by modern philosophical thought. Islam is about aligning oneself to the forces of nature. The Koran is a formal exposition of man's place in the natural order of things."

To find his place, Butt became a farmer, living by the natural rhythms of the seasons, studying the Koran on both sides of the NWFP tribal border. He moved for a time to Darul Uloom Deoband madrassa in India, Asia's greatest Islamic university. But when he returned to Pakistan, he couldn't find his niche. In his absence, the faith had been politicized, transformed into a vehicle for worldly power instead of eternal salvation, and no foreigner could be recognized as an Islamic scholar. To remain part of the society, Butt joined the BBC, producing – among other programs – a Pashto version of *The Archers*, a radio soap designed to offer practical solutions and ideas to people trying to rebuild their lives after the years of conflict. Over the next decade, his voice became one of the best known in the region.

"In Islam, you have the rite of Allah, that He should be worshipped, and you have the rite of human beings, that we should help one another. I feel that those two rites are being fulfilled through my journalism."

My stomach rumbles, interrupting our conversation. Butt takes sympathy on me, asking what I've eaten, suggesting the local remedy of yoghurt and banana and then, later in the day, *yakhni*, a light, clear chicken broth. I must be on the mend for the suggestion doesn't nauseate me.

We catch a three-wheel autorickshaw – "The Muslim Ricky" – away from Lotus Lake and down the hill to Aabpara market. In the sun the temperature hovers around 100°F, and the breeze feels like a blast from hell. Above the scream of the two-stroke engine, I ask Butt about his other passions.

"Do you mean Dylan?" he calls out. "Or Man United?"

"Manchester United."

"Football is life in a pure and vivid format," he shouts with a smile. "It's about teamwork, fair play. If you break the rules you're going to suffer. I took to Man United after the Munich air disaster. I loved Bobby Charlton because he survived. I loved Duncan Edwards because he fought for life. Their strength and talents caught my imagination. They went on to conquer Europe."

Much as Islam has captured Butt's imagination, I think. Faith inspires him, and I admire his attainment of calm, humble self-knowledge.

"As for Dylan, my passion for him began with 'The Times They are a-Changin','" Butt goes on. "That clear voice and guitar rang out through the corridors of my school. Resonant. Spiritual. True. I can remember listening to that song and thinking, 'This is it. This guy is crying out, shouting out, you are *not* alone.'"

In the back of the belching "ricky", the Jesuit-educated *imam* sings to me, "Come mothers and fathers throughout the land, and don't criticize what you can't understand, your sons and your daughters are beyond your command, your old road is rapidly ageing..."

In the bright sunlight, the skin on his high forehead seems so sheer, and his sinuous veins so shallow, that I can almost see his blood throbbing below the surface. The years spent out-of-doors have bleached his eyelashes and burnished his cheeks. Yet, for all its life, his body – fine, fragile and diaphanous – seems to exist simply to shelter his soul.

"I sometimes joke that Dylan's my guide, even though he's a Jew. You know, wisdom is every man's domain. We can get a word of wisdom from any source. And from wherever we get it, it belongs to us."

At the tea shop, Butt drinks a glass of water. I risk a small bowl of yoghurt. After our noisy ride, his tolerant voice sounds quiet, almost unheard, and I have to lean across the table to catch his words.

"Islam tells us that we should read the Koran and not interpret it according to our individual opinion. Dylan expressed that too. Do you know the song 'Gates of Eden'?" he asks me. I can only just hear him above other conversations and the crash of crockery. " 'At dawn my lover comes to me and tells me of her dreams, with no attempt to shovel the glimpse into the ditch of what each one means.' He's saying that things are more beautiful as they are, rather than interpreted." Butt lowers his head and looks at me under his eyebrows again. "In the sixties I came east with nothing, believing that I had everything to learn. Today, most Westerners, with their money and their technology, come here to teach. Not me. I'm still doing what I was thirty-five years ago; learning from people." Butt's long mouth stirs again into laughter. "In all these years, my life hasn't really changed," he says. "I'm still a hippie."

And I laugh with the *imam*.

In the late afternoon heat, I walk back to the house. I slip indoors to lie down, think better of it and start to do my back exercises.

I kneel down and stretch my arms forward across the floor. At that moment, I hear the evening call to prayer. The voice of an *imam* rises through the white cotton drapes. Another joins him, then a third, the invocations gathering in number and strength. With my head and eyes cast down, I feel a sudden sense of both intimacy and community, knowing that all around me at that moment millions of other men and women are praying, prostrate and alone like me on the earth, reaching out together.

But celestial lights don't fill the skies. No angels descend toward the villa. This is not my moment of revelation. The faithful are reaching out to understand life through what has already been written down. I search for something which isn't yet put into words. Which I haven't yet put into words.

Beyond the white room, banks of storm clouds gather, great grey hammerheads casting wispy tendrils across the indigo sky. The air is heavy with the promise of rain but none falls on the capital that night.

22. SPIRIT IN THE SKY

I'm on Platform No. 1 at Rawalpindi railway station. There's an hour to wait before my train. Pigeons coo under the Victorian eaves. A cat's cradle of power cables sways and crackles above the rails. Outside the broad entrance hall, the old Grand Trunk Road, Kipling's "river of life", runs on, spanning the subcontinent. A milestone reads, on one side, "Kabul 393 km", and on the other, "Delhi 785 km". It's not yet six and there are few passengers about, apart from the stranger who's walking toward me.

"Going far?" he asks in English.

"Lahore," I say. And the Indian border.

"I'm heading the other way."

His dress is Pakistani and his accent is Midlands. He's about twenty-five, talkative and good-humored with a broad smile and neatly parted hair.

"My name is Ahmed," he says, offering me his hand. "At least that's what it says on my pilot's licence."

"Sorry?"

"Did you hear about the Osama bin Laden musical in Amman? In the opening scene, bin Laden tells the audience that he's ready to travel to America and give himself up. On one condition. 'You come with me and I fly the plane!'" Ahmed laughs, satisfied with his effect on me. "I can't help it," he says, snapping his fingers. "Allah made me funny."

Ahmed is a British comedian, visiting Pakistan for I don't know what reason ... other than to wind me up.

"Travel has become so difficult for Muslims these days," he says, slipping into a slick routine and on to the bench beside me. "When I checked in at Heathrow, the lady behind the counter asked me if I'd packed my bags myself. I said yes, so they arrested me."

He smiles, stringing one joke after another, going on, "Last night in Islamabad, I played at the American Club. At the end of my gig, a belly-dancer swept me off the stage. She had a halo-like glow around her head. I thought, 'My show's so wicked this is the fire of Shaytan.' The devil. *'Khalaqtani min'narin wa khalaqtahu min teen.'* Then I saw that she *really* was in flames. As I'd swung her around the room, her lacquered hair had touched a candle. A parachute was hanging from the ceiling and I thought, if that ignites too, then the whole place will go up and I'll be on a C-15 with a one-way ticket for Guantanamo Bay."

He laughs again and adds, "Comedy is about our fears. You don't have to make it up because the edge, the truth, is inside you."

Ahmed speaks in the same deadpan manner as he delivers his lines, making it impossible to distinguish his jokes from anger, leaving me feeling uneasy. For a moment, I wonder if our conversation will turn up on *America's Funniest Videos*. Especially after he lists the pleasures of Fundamentalist Islamist Paradise (seventy-two dark-eyed maidens, eternal erections, daily Shoot-the-Buddha tournaments).

I could back off. Instead, I force myself to stay. To engage with him. To ask, "Why are you here?"

"Two reasons: first because Islam sustains and advances my identity. Second, because, like all good Muslims, I have terrible halitosis."

Ahmed tells me that his father emigrated to the UK in the sixties, worked as a night-shift spinner at a textile mill, brought up his children along the "straight path" – and marched them to cultural schizophrenia. While his sister read the Koran, Ahmed watched *The Young Ones*. As Ahmed attended *Eid* prayers, his school friends bragged about their first blow-jobs. Ahmed submitted to his parents' wishes, enrolled in biochemistry at Manchester University, then dropped out feeling alienated both from "stuffy" customs of the old country and fragmented suburban values. His uncertain identity and sexual frustration fermented into resentment, which he channeled into drink, then humor. After 9/11, Ahmed – like many others – became troubled by the portrayal of Muslims in the press and on television. To try to defuse the stereotypes, he enrolled in a stand-up-comedy-writing course at the City Lit. He played the Edinburgh fringe. He wanted to "put the fun into fundamentalism".

"I killed them at the Assembly Rooms. No pun intended. 'I don't look at you as an audience,' I told them. 'I consider you potential hostages.'" He goes on, "I'm not willing to be a second-class citizen like my old man. I'm fed up with the abuse."

"What abuse?" I ask.

"Do you know how often a brick or stone is thrown through our mosque windows? About once a week. Hey," he adds with a smile, "why do so many Muslims students study chemistry? Because we've got to make the bombs."

I put down my notebook. I look at the station clock. My train hasn't yet arrived at the platform. In the ticket hall, a barber straight-shaves his first customer, lifting his chin, exposing the throat, flicking lather on to his wrist. A railway superintendent in *topi* and tie saunters on to the platform, sipping sugary tea from a chipped Father Christmas cup. I say to Ahmed, "As a British Muslim, you can bridge the gap with humor."

"That's what I say to the Palestinian who watched Israelis chop down his family olive grove. To the Afghan whose village was levelled by American daisy-cutter bombs. To the Chechen mother raped by Russian soldiers," he replies, as if slipping back into his routine. "The West is arrogant. Muslims have to take up arms to defend their way of life." He stands and holds his hands under his stomach, miming the bulky weight of an explosive belt. "Hey, does my bomb look big in this? Boom!"

There is nothing new about suicide terrorism. In the first century AD, the Zealots and the Sicarii, two Jewish sects, sacrificed themselves to kill the Roman occupiers of Judaea. In Iran, I passed near the Castle of the Assassins, training base of the eleventh-century Ismaili cult. The enemies of colonialism in eighteenth-century India and the *kamikaze* pilots of 1940s Japan died likewise alongside their victims. After the Iranian Revolution, influential Shias adopted a strident view of martyrdom, perverting the precedents set by the Prophet and overlooking Koranic injunctions against the killing of innocents. The extraordinary power of modern suicide terrorism was unleashed by the 1983 Hizbullah bombing which killed 241 US Marines and drove the Americans out of Beirut. The practice was adopted by the Kurdish PKK and the Tamil Tigers, who killed two heads of state, but militant Islamists promoted and perfected it, dressing up their political ambitions in green religious garments. Aircraft, skyscrapers, trains and thousands of lives are being destroyed in the name of *jihad*.

In times past, volunteers for death were usually desperate, destitute and stateless. Today, bombers are as likely to be educated, affluent and Western. A Briton named Niaz Khan trained for the World Trade Center attack. The "shoe bomber" Richard Reid, who tried to bring down a Paris to Miami flight, was born and bred in suburban Bromley. Asif Mohammed Hanif, a twenty-one-year-old student from west London, killed himself and three others with a nail-filled bomb in a Tel Aviv bar. Muriel Degauque, a thirty-eight-year-old Belgian, blew herself up attacking an American convoy south of Baghdad. All the London Underground bombers were British nationals.

Although not set on self-immolation, the Taliban's *jihadis* have included the Californian John Walker Lindh, Yaser Esam Hamdi from Louisiana and David Hicks, a twenty-eight-year-old Australian. A Canadian, Mohammed Jabarah, was party to the planning of al-Qaeda's first Bali bombing. Ahmed Omar Saeed Sheikh, an Englishman and graduate of the London School of Economics, is alleged to have masterminded the kidnapping and murder in Pakistan of the WSJ journalist Daniel Pearl.

"Once at a show, I was asked if all Middle Eastern Muslims lived in tents. I said they do, but only after the Americans have bombed their houses."

I wonder if, with his quick-fire provocation, he is trying to make me spout idiocies and to demonize him, to exploit the gulf between us. I ask again why he's come to Pakistan. Instead of answering me, he slips back into his routine.

"America has tried for a century to end racism. Blacks say they can never get a fair trial. Muslims can't even get a trial. Hey, man, if you don't laugh, I'll have you stoned."

The carriages are shunted into the station, scattering goats off the tracks. Our trains are announced. Again, he offers me his hand. "Here we must part," Ahmed says. He seems about to tell me a last joke, then thinks better of it. Instead, he walks away toward the Khyber Mail and the North-West Frontier. I watch him vanish into the crowd, our conversation incomplete.

The Lahore Express shudders through early morning Pindi, the rising sun touching the tops of fruit trees and the white caps of men waiting at crossings. Children step off to school, books under arm, scarves over heads. Along a riverbank, women wash breakfast plates, the cheap tin flashing a Morse code message in the sunlight. A signalman droops a green flag out of his control box.

Every year, thousands of Brits of Pakistani origin come "home" for family matters and to attend religious schools. During their stay a very few, lost and insecure in a complex world, embrace a simple, stentorian version of Islam and are misled by zealots who blur the line between theology and ideology. I think of Ahmed and remember Carla Grissmann's "lost souls of the terrorist movement".

Both Islam and Christianity preach compassion and empathy. Mohammed brought peace to Arabia by adopting a policy of non-violence. Jesus told his followers to love their enemies. But the scriptures were scarred by the violent times from which they emerged. So, modern extremists are selective in their use of holy books, in their search for divine approval of hatred. The Christian Right ignores the Sermon on the Mount in their support of the death penalty. The radical Islamists disregard the Koran's exhortations to reconciliation.

Yet, at the end of the Islamic stage of my journey, I don't feel downhearted. I think of the generosity of the Iranians and their impatience for change. I remember Sanjar's optimism. I am inspired by John Butt's faithful, constructive equilibrium. I know that Christians and Muslims share a common value system with Jews. Mary, the Jewish mother of Christ, is the most honored woman in Islam. Abraham is the father of the Arab nations through Ishmael, his first son. His second son, Isaac, is the father of the Jews. To Christians, he is the father of all who are faithful to God, according to the Bible. Islam believes in the prophets, including Christ; whether he is God incarnate, who experienced death and rose again, or an immortal man untouched by Satan who ascended to heaven, is a matter on which friends can surely agree to differ.

Beyond the sooty carriage window, station porters balance battered suitcases on their turbans. A buffalo dozes in its mud hole. An American wrestling movie is playing on the video screen in my carriage. I reopen my notebook.

India

23. JOY TO THE WORLD

The heavens open at the Indian border. The whipping tail of the monsoon catches me there, dropping out of the sky and washing away monkeys and dead wood as well as twenty-eight people and hundreds of houses. As the summer heat hisses out of the earth, I cross the length of Uttar Pradesh, which sickles across northern India from Himalaya to Bangladesh, in a single twenty-four-hour train ride. Along the rail line, hundreds of trees are down, their red trunks revealing rotten cores. Rivers swell into flood. A jeep lies on its side, its passengers crouching blank and numb in the protection of the wreckage. The rain pounds on the roof of the carriages and I lean out of the window to feel it on my face, to fill my lungs with cool, fresh air.

I'm making first for Varanasi on the River Ganges, the most sacred city to all Hindus and home for two years to Allen Ginsberg. Here, in 1962, at the age of thirty-one, the poet explored his passion for the East. Then, as a genial Hindu guru and icon of the counterculture, he went on to dominate a movement that reshaped Western consciousness. Dylan considered him to be the single greatest influence on the American poetic voice since Whitman. The Beat poet Ferlinghetti called him "the great spellbinder". In his search for new methods of expression, he moved his poetry away from the memory of past visions toward "the actual awareness of *now*". The Intrepids were his free-spirited and hallucinatory foot-soldiers, weaving in his footsteps toward enlightenment. Now, my trip on their tails begins to share their sense of regeneration.

A bare-legged *sadhu* in raw saffron cloak, a turbanned Sikh with a purple parasol, a flamboyant bridegroom in a candle-lit temple under a flyover: India's shifting splendors thrill me after the outward privations of Islam. In Amritsar, hundreds of tiled shrines and thousands of television shops, all with their sets tuned to different stations, spiral around the

Golden Temple. In Tangra, parrots quarrel on strings of winking lights. In Jalandhar, the pilgrims wear flip-flops in goldfish shops. At Laksar station, neither the rains nor the crush of travelers disturbs the sleep of a toothless grandmother, snoring on her sacking bed. In Lucknow, a beggar sits next to the ash-covered torso of a dead baby on a toy trolley. No sight can surprise me, even if a sacred cow stands on its hind legs and takes to the air.

At dawn, my train reaches one of the oldest cities in the world; "... older than history, older than tradition, older even than legend, and looks twice as old as all of them put together," wrote Mark Twain on his visit in 1896. Varanasi, he went on to record, is the beginning-place of Creation, where the god Vishnu stood an upright *lingam* – a phallic symbol representing the male and female energies of the universe – in the midst of a shoreless ocean.

This morning, the whole world seems to be cleansing itself. Parts of the city are submerged under the monsoon's waters. In the half-light I climb into a low open skiff near the station and am rowed through the narrow lanes, past the upper windows of tiny shops, over the tops of sunken handcarts. The flood, according to the boatman, is the worst for a decade. Out of the liquid shadows rise the sounds of drums, cymbals and chanting. Around me, bells ring and firecrackers crack to awaken the gods. Murky swells lap against balconies and spill over temple walls, creating a clangorous Hindu Venice of sewers and saints. Then we sweep out of the swamped warren, away from the stunning stench and on to a grand curve of the Ganges.

The sun soars tangerine-red above the Amazon-wide river. Miniature oil-lamps scuttle on the current. Garlands of marigolds catch in the ropes of flat-bottom ferry boats. Old Varanasi towers above the torrent, a press of buildings crusting a hill with slim minarets and temple towers. Beneath the pilgrims' platforms which flank the city's riverbank, thousands of bathers – dressed in white, in rags, in no clothes at all – descend the ghats' steps and, waist-deep in water, eyes closed, lips moving in prayer, face the rising sun. To bathe in the holy Ganges washes away a pilgrim's sins. To die here releases Hindus from the cycle of reincarnation.

The boatman puts me ashore at Dasaswamedh ghat, a few alleyways from where Ginsberg lived. I push through the glistening mass, flanked by wet skin the color of chocolate, parchment and paper, and step on to thick muddy steps littered with broken clay offering-pots. Oily incense smoke curls through the leaves of a banyan tree around which the faithful circle, as does a street-sweeper brushing up their red hibiscus offerings. A barefoot flower-vendor turns away and a goat steals lotus blooms from her stall. Beyond a shrine to Sitala, goddess of smallpox, one of the city's thirty civic drains discharges effluent into the swollen river.

Ginsberg called India his promised land, writing in his journal, "it's like a new earth – I'm happy." In a prayer hall, he experienced "a kind of Euphoria with my body relaxed cross-legged and eyes fixed and mind happy and aware of the long trail from New York to Tangier to that spot of wet on the floor". Like Hesse and W. B. Yeats, he found "in that East something ancestral in ourselves, something we must bring into the light". His journey was key to the emotional and intellectual counterculture renaissance.

He lived in a whitewashed, nine-doored room with a long balcony open "to trees, monkeys, market below one side, beggar street to ghats on the other". As dawn widens into morning, I set out to find it. I follow a press of water carriers, copper pots balanced on their shoulders, climbing the steep steps. I duck into the maze of filthy lanes, pass one-chair barber shops and cubby-holes serving thimble cups of milky tea. At a café, I pause for breakfast and consult my copy of *Indian Journals*.

Over fried potatoes and onions, I read that Ginsberg's room was both a few alleyways down river from Manikarnika ghat and in a Brahmin's house above a path leading to Dasaswamedh ghat. The contradiction doesn't make my search any easier, but it is my first lesson on India's view of certainty. Unlike Islam, Hindu theology accepts that there are many roads leading to nirvana. Hinduism, a tolerant, all-encompassing 4,000-year-old religion without central authority or rigid moral code, never countenanced exclusivity.

The sun sears the cobblestones, driving naked children and pigs into the shadows. Washing dries around post-box shrines. Hovel shanties obscure stagnant temple pools. All morning, I snoop beneath hundreds of balconies, count doorways, circle every "green ganja sadhu leper's park". I try to find the "huge black tree" which loomed over his window and obliterated half the square. I listen out for the street sounds which he recorded: the tin pan and rat-a-tat drums, the bicycle bells of the rickshaw wallahs, the clattering pails of a milk shop. I find the son of Chai baba – "Mr. Tea" – who once owned a tea shop in Chaumahni at the Assi crossing. His father, a handsome man who wore natural oils "which smelled like the soil after the first rain", knew Ginsberg, as well as Alain Delon and the Beatles. But the sweet-smelling old man is long dead and his son has no idea of the address of the nine-doored room. So I search on, watching a pilgrim with sparse topknot bargain for a single apple, idling past squatting radish-sellers, gazing at Ginsberg's black-and-white photographs and realizing his stained balcony could be anywhere in this city.

But if not the man himself, at least I find his legacy is all around me: in the posters for an Indo-pop fusion concert at the Bread of Life Bakery, in Sunil Ganguly's poetry at the Book Net Café, in the hundreds of Westerners who live here, not far from Madonna's and Sting's houses, learning Sanskrit or the sitar, in the airhead speed freaks who forget both youth's promise and the lyrics of "Mr Tambourine Man".

The sixties travelers arrived in India with a feeling of homecoming, as much to themselves as to the country. After the long and narrow overland trail, the road broadened out into the subcontinent's hundred cities and thousand choices. The Intrepids, carried forward by Ginsberg's first article on India in *City Lights Review* and Kerouac's vision of a Rucksack Revolution, fanned out, slowed down, looked to find a place of their own. Some headed south to Rajasthan, with its pink medieval city of Jaipur rising out of a yellow desert. Others went north to Kashmir's lakes. Most traveled straight to Delhi, usually asleep on third-class carriage luggage racks. There, the inner quest usually began at the Crown, a rose-scented, bug-infested hotel with shacks on the roof. Almost everyone turned up, tuned in and dropped out. Drugs were thought to prepare the mind, to initiate the transformation away from the physical realm toward self-knowledge, assuming one wasn't thrown off course by an overdose or a fortnight in prison. A smoldering chillum helped to fuse the newcomer's fragmented awareness, as well as to pass the time while waiting for money from home or queuing at the railway booking office.

Then, with a (forged) student card in hand, the typical Dharma bum set off to search for a guru, God and a long, slow Tantric fuck. He – or she – might begin in Varanasi, in a houseboat or ashram on the banks of the Mother Ganges. Or at Rishikesh, like the Beatles. Or in Pune dressed in orange robes as a disciple of Bhagwan Rajneesh, later to become Osho, in whose hedonistic community thousands bonked their way to spiritual fulfilment. Or they checked out Hardwar, where the plump, thirteen-year-old Guru Maharaj ji promised to Give Knowledge (and graduated to hiring the Houston Astrodome to spread his teachings). Other spiritual tourists might head for the northern hills to study Buddhism or ramble south to Puttaparthi, where Sai Baba conjured holy ash – *vibutti* – out of thin air before rows of astonished, white faces.

Of course, not everyone came to India for Truth, dope and sex. Many came just to keep up with their friends. In 1967, Norman Flach, a nineteen-year-old from Rosetown, Saskatchewan, went traveling because he admired storytellers and wanted to have his own tales to tell. After two years on the road, working on a kibbutz and singing Tom Jones hits with Turkish bus drivers, he walked into a tiny Delhi ice-cream parlor and two former classmates. "Hey, man, want to share a banana split?" they asked him, as if meeting after school at the Rosetown Rio.

No one knows how many young men and women followed the overland trail between 1962 and 1979. The Indian government estimated there were ten thousand "youthful" foreigners in the country in 1967. Five years later, after the Beatles had popularized the route, that same number crossed the Wagah border from Pakistan in a single week. In 1973, there were 250,000 French nationals alone in India. In Varanasi, I met an old hippie who guessed that close to two million Intrepids had – like him – reached India by land.

My first Ganges day ends as did so many of Ginsberg's, sitting inside the red-stone eyrie above smoke-stained Manikarnika ghat. An awareness of death, or of life's transience, pervades the embankment. Here, mortality meets immortality, sanctity cohabits with poverty. Here, also, the question of whether to live as one has always lived or to decide to reinvent oneself and start anew is easily addressed. Behind me, axemen hack and split tree trunks into fire wood. The oily pilgrims' shed, a poor house for the dying, rises on my right, overlooking the burning platforms.

It is the hour of *aarti*, when the gods are praised with incense and fire. As I watch, a green bamboo stretcher is carried down the narrow lanes. The corpse is tinsel-wrapped in a vermilion shroud. The *doms*, the ghat's funereal outcasts, spread branches on top of the body, as well as *ghee* and five combustible, sacred elements. A young male relative touches a thick straw taper to the wood. The curls of smoke shiver the muslin shroud, flashing its golden foil lining, and the flames lick the sole of a foot.

"Burning, some red juices dribbling out of nose or eye, down cheek, dropping off bright red hot ear," Ginsberg wrote more than a generation ago. "Scalp split and cream color skull still smooth and dry in the heat peeping through the blackened hair."

As he watched the Manikarnika cremations, he imagined the fires burning his fear away, "burning the dross inside me". He contemplated release from the Wheel of Existence and trips to the "ultimate unknown".

I don't think I would have much liked Ginsberg, the first holy soul, jelly-roll, drop-out traveler. He was a cocky self-publicist, exaggerating his connections, doing so much morphine that his head spun. He liked to have himself photographed with beggars. His stay in Varanasi ended in disappointment; alone in the nine-door room, cold and exhausted from a cocktail of abuse, suffering from kidney attacks and "washed up desolate on the Ganges bank". But in India and afterwards in America, he remained *alive*, an original, transcending traveler full of hope and – through his writing – regeneration. He was the glittering link from Thoreau and Whitman, by way of Nietzsche and Kerouac, on a journey from Romanticism and idealism, through numb and mindless nihilism, from death to "this now life ... this here life".

I spend my evenings in Varanasi descending to the river at dusk to watch the lighting of the widow lamps, their cane baskets hoisted atop arched bamboo poles. I hear the crack of brazier coals, the lowing of cows and the cry of an owl. Funeral parties await their turn at the burning platform while along the shore hundreds of saffron-robed children sit crosslegged on mats, singing their evening prayers to the river.

My skepticism makes me doubt that I – unlike the faithful who come here to die – stand on the threshold of enlightenment. I don't wake each morning aware of a new cosmic truth. I'm not anticipating an imminent release from the cycle of birth and death. My dreams don't elevate me toward sublime, High Romantic visions and the stars. But I see here the importance the sixties placed on the individual, inner journey, as well as the decade's enduring legacy of transcendental – *transcending* – travel.

"Stop trying not to die," Ginsberg wrote during his sixteen-month Indian sojourn, "fly where you can fly."

Sky and water are the same luminous blue, and a rowboat, its oars dipping into and lifting out of the airy fluid, seems to be swept downstream by an invisible hand. I listen out for voices on the river and hear tourists float by the ghats.

24. BLACKBIRD

I backtrack 500 miles to reach the mother of pop ashrams, following the Ganges north-west until lines of slender hills rise out of the plain like the fingers of a Himalayan hand. On a knuckle of earth stands Hardwar, Gateway to the Gods. Hindus flock here in their millions to bathe in the ice-blue waters that rush out of the mountains. On the station platform I sidestep a troop of red-assed monkeys and hail an autorickshaw to take me the final few miles upstream. The road is jammed with weekend pilgrims. Ardent devotees fly spangled banners from overheated Ambassadors. Two-wheeled *sadhus* cycle with Char Dham prayer flags on their handlebars. The blare of klaxons and clang of bells echoes into the open pine woods and off the far dark cliffs.

Rishikesh, tucked into a cleft between steep hills, flanks the narrowing river. My driver drops me, deafened now by the mobile piety and his tortured engine, at a slender footbridge. A scruffy Carnaby Street spreads along the near bank. I push past its souvenir-and photo-shops and over the eddying water, my progress slowed by an idling calf, toward a sacred, retail precinct of tapering temples.

On the far shore, numberless holy men daub themselves with ash. Beggars ring their alms bowls with – depending on their age – the high rattle of youthful exuberance, a persistent, middle-aged *tick-tick* or a single, somber death knell. Day-trippers in colorful saris ignore them, as do their husbands, while buying ice cream. Shops sell plastic beakers for collecting the sacred water. A ragged, barefoot boy runs in front of me, pausing first at a sweet stall then a toy stand, at each stop holding out his hands. Between Ayurvedic chemists and spiritual bookshops (top sellers: *Christ Lived in India* and J. K. Rowling) a woman wraps her tame boa around bypassers' shoulders and earns a few rupees for each photograph.

In 1962, Ginsberg sampled this "pure and sacred atmosphere", writing in his diary about clear-skinned, shining-eyed youth and homeless women "dressed in orange robes and singing Sanskrit hymns to nirvana". Until then, Rishikesh was little known outside the Hindu world. Only a very few Intrepids had joined the ecstatic, once-in-a-lifetime pilgrims crossing the river by the open ferry. But the City of Saints rose to international attention in 1968 with the arrival of the Beatles, whose five-week stay changed forever the trail, Western fashion and our perception of India.

George Harrison had long been attracted to the East. In 1965, he first met Ginsberg and heard the sitar. Within a year, he was a student of Ravi Shankar, a great Indian sitar master. Harrison's haunting playing of the instrument on "Norwegian Wood" inspired Brian Jones to use it on the Rolling Stones' "Paint It Black". He invited Shankar to perform at the seminal Monterey Pop Festival. The sitar had a profound influence on the Beatles' work, as did Hinduism in Harrison's life. Sales of Indian instruments soared, along with popular interest in Eastern religion and philosophy.

In 1967, Ginsberg, wearing a Tibetan oracle ring and brandishing finger-cymbals, dropped in on Paul McCartney at his London house. Mick Jagger and Marianne Faithful happened to be there that day. They listened to his prayers and poetry and discussed Eastern mysticism: the need to reach beyond the material world, the Hindu belief in the World-Soul, Buddhism's "four noble truths". A few weeks later, all four Beatles, along with Jagger and Faithful, attended a weekend initiation seminar with the Maharishi Mahesh Yogi. The giggling guru was in the UK to promote his Westernized version of the ancient Vedic quest for unbounded bliss. "Expansion of happiness is the purpose of life, and evolution is the process through which it is fulfilled," he assured his audience. Five months later, the Beatles – along with Donovan, Mike Love of the Beach Boys and a trailer load of Hollywood movie stars – arrived at his Academy for Transcendental Meditation in Rishikesh.

"We wanted to try to expand spiritually," McCartney said of the experience, voicing the spiritual cravings of a generation, "or at least find some sort of format for all the various things we were interested in: Indian music, Allen Ginsberg, poetry, mantras, mandalas, tantra, all the stuff we'd seen."

Their stay was a mixed success, ending for Harrison and Lennon in mutual confusion, anger and accusation. Ringo hated the food and flies. But as well as filling – as McCartney said – "a little bit of emptiness in our souls, a lack of spiritual fulfilment", those few weeks were a period of remarkable creativity. Almost all the songs that would appear on the *White Album* and *Abbey Road* were composed beside the Ganges. The phenomenal success of the Beatles and their music conjured India and Nepal into *the* hip destination.

In Rishikesh I set out to find the Academy. At first, no local seems familiar with Transcendental Meditation. The manager of the Green Hotel not only doesn't know of the Maharishi, he has never heard of the Beatles. Perhaps my pronunciation confuses him. At the Swarg ashram, one of the dozens in town, an aged ascetic tells me to walk along the Ganges, "past the yellow house". As every third house is a dirty shade of yellow, his advice isn't particularly helpful. But outside the Sri Ved Niketan ashram I stop a tall white yoga teacher. "Follow the path over the bridge, then turn up a dry riverbed," says Australian Michelle. "Ahh, the *swami* here will take you."

At my arm appears a spindle-thin, silver-haired holy man dressed in a cotton robe. His forehead is banded by ash. In his right hand is a bucket of Ganges water. In his left he carries a staff. I didn't hear him approach, but he nods to me and I follow, walking one step behind him in silence away from the town.

The *swami* moves like a leggy girl, elegant and effete, his slender, brown feet barely leaving an impression in the soft sand. After half a mile we reach the riverbed and turn inland. A high brick wall encircles acres of wooded hill. He gestures toward it with a gracious twist of his hand. We pass through a Hobbit-like gatehouse, glide up a snaking concrete avenue and squeeze through a line of barbed wire into the vast compound. Vines smother the main buildings. Saplings displace the cobblestones. The terraced gardens are wild with weeds and howling monkeys. Around us mushroom 120 river-stone meditation houses. The Academy is deserted.

The Maharishi Mahesh Yogi developed his tidy meditation technique while living as a recluse in the Himalayas in the 1950s. The repetition of a simple mantra for twenty minutes twice a day was said to unlock one's "inner genius". In India, Transcendental Meditation met with little success so, in 1958, the Maharishi took it abroad. In 1965, forty students at UCLA enrolled on an early course. Ten years later – after the Beatles' flirtation with TM – there were 600,000 adherents in the US. Today, 4 million people are said to practice around the world. Maharishi Vedic City, "Capital for the Global Country for World Peace", with schools, university and massive 2,000-seat Halls of Bliss, strives for an earthly utopia in the heart of the Iowa cornbelt. The Maharishi himself controlled this billion-dollar corporate empire into his nineties.

At his meditation mushroom, beneath a great overhanging oak, the long-limbed *swami* sits, tucks his left leg underneath him and says nothing. Behind him, I pick out the original lecture hall where the Beatles received instruction from the Maharishi. I also spot the ruined bungalow where Prudence, Mia Farrow's reclusive sister, stayed. At her front door, Lennon wrote, then sang with McCartney, "Dear Prudence, won't you come out to play..."

A *mauna* or vow of silence can last for years so, in lieu of conversation, the *swami* agrees to mime answers to my questions. I ask him first if anyone still practices TM at the abandoned compound. He laughs without a sound and draws a definitive "X" in space. Next I ask if the Beatles' cottages are still standing. Each boasted a four-poster bed, a dressing table and occasional hot running water. He draws another "X" between us. Not a guitar string remains to be found. Finally, I ask if the local tailor who dressed the Maharishi's pupils in distinctive pyjamas and tinselly waistcoats, creating a look which was adopted by all flower children, is alive. A third big "X".

Then the *swami* clutches his stomach.

"Are you feeling unwell?" I ask him.

He shakes his head and points at me.

"Am I unwell? No. I'm fine."

He throws his head back in laughter, again in silence, and makes a gesture of listening to his chest with a stethoscope.

"A doctor? You want to see a doctor? *I* want to see a doctor?"

Finally, he pretends to strum a guitar while tossing his head back and forth as if singing a pop song.

"A musical doctor?" I ask. "The Beatles' doctor!"

The *swami* leans back on a huge orange cushion and smiles with divine satisfaction.

I descend back to town, the name and address of the Beatles' doctor written on a scrap of paper. Mangy *sadhus*, believers who renounce all worldly goods in their spiritual quest, puff hashish on the narrow, corridor-like streets. A revered *mahant* in beads and blossoms blows a conch shell. Israelis in dreadlocks float off to yoga class. A stoned German reads Tolkien under a hand-painted sign which warns "Western Tourist Murdered by Chillum Smokers".

I cross to the west bank and plunge into a frantic mêlée of pilgrims' buses and rickshaw repair shops. On Railway Road, between a nursing home and a men's outfitters ("Excite inner wear for the sensuous man"), I find the red-brick Guru-Dev-poly Clinic.

"Welcome," says Dr K. P. Singh, holding out his hand. "Please come in." He is a compact, energetic sixty-year-old with pencil moustache and beak-like nose. "I offer spiritual treatment alongside full modern Western medicine."

His surgery is a two-room, neon-lit, cross-cultural refuge. Holistic Ayurvedic health care is provided in the left-hand room. In his right-hand office, Singh proffers Viagra, Canesten cream and ECGs. "VAT, aches and pain, tone up and sexual disorders" are his areas of speciality.

I explain that my needs aren't medical, and Singh, courteous and mannerly, invites me to sit down.

"Ah, the four mop-tops," he says, offering me a cup of his Himalayan tea. "The *swami* never speaks an untruth."

"He never speaks," I remind him.

"I served as the Maharishi's medical officer during the Beatles' stay at the Academy."

As a child in Gorakhpur, Singh contracted polio. His parents prayed for his health, promising to make him a doctor if he recovered. His survival was to them a miracle, a rebirth, and they encouraged Singh "to serve the people and nation". After graduation in early 1968, Singh's first posting was Rishikesh.

"I knew of the Beatles from newspapers but I had never heard their music," he says, pushing the thinning grey curls back from his ears. "I sat with them on the banks of the Ganga most days. You see, they had no one to talk English with but the Maharishi and me."

"Were you with them that evening when the whole ashram walked to the traveling cinema?" I ask. A procession of about a hundred people, decked in hibiscus and frangipani, strolled down the path into town.

"When McCartney first played "Ob-La-Di Ob-La-Da'?"

He nods, answering, "They were not allowed to make very large music during their stay."

"And did you join them the night they drifted downstream in boats under the stars singing together?"

"In the mornings and evenings the Beatles played on the roof of their cottages, but most of the time they were silent, living just in their rooms."

And writing more than forty songs including "Blackbird", "I Will" and "Across the Universe".

The Academy had no rules or timetables but breakfast tended to be followed by meditation. Afternoons were free for sunbathing and sightseeing. One day, at the long communal table, McCartney started composing "Back in the USSR" on his acoustic guitar and Mike Love – amused by the take-off of Beach Boys harmonies – suggested adding some lines about Russian girls. He wrote "Rocky Racoon" sitting on the ashram roof with Lennon and Donovan.

"I understand they came here to find a path away from drugs," I say.

Since turned on to pot by Dylan in 1964, the Beatles – like almost every sixties rock 'n' roll group – had embarked on a heady exploration of hallucinogenics. By 1968, they wanted to cross the universe without LSD.

"Mr Harrison aspired to reach God through music. He said that material things had become unimportant to him. They all tried to find a world apart from that of money and business. So they talked to me of spirituality, and how to make donations to orphans and the handicapped."

The Maharishi gave two lectures each day and, in return, he asked the Beatles' advice on how best to promote TM. Singh often sat at the back of the lecture hall pondering how best to deal with Ringo's flatulence (he had brought a suitcase of baked beans from the UK).

"They were very affectionate to me. And it was a new experience to treat the richest men of the world. Years later, Mr Harrison sent his eternal thoughts to me," he says. Then he adds, "Do you enjoy my tea? It improves freshness in the blood, concentration, memory and eyesight."

"How did their visit change Rishikesh?" I ask, nodding my approval and wondering if the Beatles had drunk it too.

"Their visit brought knowledge of yoga to many Western people. Now they come to Rishikesh every day looking – like you – for health and peace of mind."

"Looking for nirvana too?"

"That is a little more difficult to find. Especially because..." he hesitates. "Much of a doctor's business here is with narcotics abuse. Unfortunately, many of the visitors seem unaware that the four mop-tops renounced drugs."

I buy a jar of his tea. Singh gives me a second to pass on to Paul McCartney "when you next see him". On the wall behind him is an American Medical Association lumbar-spine-exercise chart and a plaque from the Divine Light Society. His clinic's name – Guru-Dev-poly – combines the ancient Greek word for "many" with the name of his and the Maharishi's guru. As I stand to leave, he asks me to photograph him outside his clinic.

"One day, two monks were looking at a flag pole," he says as I take out my camera. "The first one said that the flag was moving. The second responded that the wind was moving. The Sixth Patriarch happened to be passing by and, hearing their argument, told them, 'It's neither the flag nor the wind. It is the mind that is moving.'"

I whistle "Ob-La-Di Ob-La-Da" back over the Ganges and up the path along which it had first been sung. A damp patchwork of brilliant saris and ochre cloaks dries on the stone steps. Marigold petals line the water's sandy edge as if the river itself radiates an orange aura. The *swami* – whose name is Narayananda Saraswati – has no objection to me spending a night in one of the deserted mushrooms. At least, he doesn't express any reservation. At dusk we sit together in silence watching camphor candles float past us on our hilltop, twinkling points of light and memory sweeping away on the black current toward the indistinct horizon.

I lie down to sleep on an old meditation mat, planning to leave for Delhi in the morning. In the dead of night a blackbird sings.

25. REVOLUTION

To be first in the queue, I reach Hardwar station before dawn. But the ticket hall, waiting rooms and platforms are already knee-deep in bodies. Three or four thousand people appear to have fled a storm and taken refuge in the station. Except this storm will never pass. It rages without stop, night after night, in the land of a billion souls.

Narrow pathways snake between sleepers lying on the concrete, beside steel trunks, with and without blankets. I step around dozing pilgrims and beggar children curved together in protective embrace. Next to them, a young woman stretches herself awake, shaking the red plastic bangles on her wrists, arching her back like a scarlet cat. Behind her is the booking office.

"Sir, you must attend to Room 5 Platform 1," says the clerk. The sign above his head reads, "All tickets can be bought here."

Room 5 Platform 1 is closed. As arrows of light pierce the grey sky, a kindly school boy takes my hand and walks me over the bridge to the advance booking office. I queue for thirty minutes at the Inquiries window to learn that there is one seat left on the first Delhi train. On a torn slip of paper I write the train number, the date and my details, then join the booking queue. An hour later, when I am only two places from the front, all of Indian Railways' employees – 1.44 million by the last count – take a collective tea break.

"Your train's booking is now closed," says a helpful stranger beside the deserted information desk. She and her three plump daughters in fruity-colored saris sit on a mat like scoops of ice cream on a plate: banana, lime and cherry. Geckos scuttle on the beams above their heads. "You must go to Room 5 Platform 1 in one hour."

One hour later, both the first and second Delhi trains have left. At Room 5 Platform 1 – a paneled office of wooden desks and twine-tied bundles of canceled tickets – I am allocated a seat on the next train (having changed my class of travel; there are eleven different classes on Indian Railways). I return to the first booking office with a new scrap of paper and buy my ticket. I go back to Room 5, pay a 25-rupee supplement and am allocated a seat.

All the sleepers are on their feet now, drinking plastic bottles of Krishna mineral water ("Taste of Purity"), shitting behind the goods sheds. I sit on a stack of burlap sacks, swatting away mina birds, waiting for my train. As I take a sleeve of crackers from my pack, a dozen local children scramble around me, dirty hands outstretched. They've been fighting for the chance to unload a freight car and earn a few piastes. I give a cracker to a boy with a lazy eye, another to the toddler standing next to him, distributing the food evenly around the hungry semicircle. Taller kids appear behind the children, crowding them forward. A girl – maybe twelve years old, with a baby on her hip – reaches over their heads and grabs the package from my hand. She is as startled by her action as me. Then she runs away with the crackers, leaving the others still begging and me with no food left to give.

"For your kind attention..." is all I catch of a muffled announcement. I join the throng sweeping toward the Bandra Express, a mile-long tube of filthy, two-tone-blue carriages. Every day, 14 million passengers travel on India's railways. This morning, half of them seem to be on my train. Five hours late, I lurch out of Hardwar – and a fellow traveler falls off the luggage rack and on to my lap.

My compartment is an unswept cell. Its bench seats are sardined with people. At any moment, I expect its revolving fan to snap off the ceiling and slice me like salami. Across from me sit a policeman heading to Laksar to deliver a summons, a young businessman with a nose as long and sharp as a needle and two quiet brothers from Bijnor. Beside me, a walrus-like Sikh, dressed in elegant white with a magnificent turban, stares at his miniature mobile phone. Dozens of eyes gaze in from the corridor as I'm the only foreigner in the carriage. Until a lean Westerner in pyjama bottoms pushes his sitar case through the steel door and drops into the pinch of space beside me.

"You the writer?" he asks me, inches from my nose, looking down into my notebook.

"How do you know?" I say as we shudder over a set of points.

"This is India," he shrugs. "Once you jump on the tiger's back, it's hard to jump off."

Jonathan's accent tells me he's Welsh. His greying hair is swept back from his crown and tied into a neat ponytail. His long face has firm skin and precise, neat features. He must have spoken to Australian Michelle. Or the silent *swami*.

"I'm following the old overland trail," I tell him.

"The long and winding road," he nods.

"When did you do it?" I ask.

"Still on it," he answers.

Jonathan tells me he was born on Anglesey, the son of a lighthouse keeper and a CND activist who filled their tubulous home with alternative blasts of bebop and Brahms. To get away from the racket, Jonathan joined the local Labor Party rambling club, climbed all the Cambrian mountains, stood on top of a dozen peaks and ached to escape Wales.

"Then it was the 1960s, even in Bangor."

"So you started hanging out at the Cavern Club?" I say. Seeing the sitar. Thinking Beatles.

"The Philharmonic Hall," he says. "At first, Europe seemed exotic. Amsterdam was a big scene. I heard Callas in Venice. But I felt a misfit in the West. I realized that if I was going to live life I couldn't stay wrapped in cotton wool, listening to the Monkees."

In 1968, Jonathan reached India and – like others before him – felt at home. He dressed in a bright orange *kurta*, bell bottoms and a Chairman Mao cap.

"Life was one *lassi* to the next. A rupee bought four *chipatis* and a dried-pea curry. An extra 50 piastres bought a bowl of yoghurt," he says, recounting his first years with warm ease. "When money got tight, there was a sack of brown rice in the van. But the poverty, dear God, that transformed me."

The young businessman switches on a well-traveled laptop. The two brothers look over his shoulder. The Sikh holds his mobile between the bars of the window to get a better signal. Beyond him spreads the Ganges, or at least its muddy riverbed. The holy water has been diverted through Neeldhara for a couple of weeks to enable a new sewer to be built. Beneath a rail bridge, thousands of lean men, women and children squat in the slime, scooping up handfuls of silt, sieving it through their fingers, searching for devotional gold medallions or even a single copper penny.

"In '68, 95 per cent of Indians lived in poverty," says Jonathan. "Religion held back *realpolitik*. The caste system stagnated social change. The country's desperation turned me on to the Marxist interpretation of society."

As I recall Chatwin's comments on travelers driving Afghans into the arms of communists, the businessman raises his sharp nose. "Yet you – with your dollars – were content to bum around this 'desperate' place?" he says to Jonathan. The laptop's screen is reflected in his dark glasses.

"*Namaste*," he replies, pressing his hands together in the respectful manner of an older India. Meaning "I bow to you" in Sanskrit. "Not every Westerner was middle class, you know."

"Even the poorest Welshman was rich beyond most Indian's dreams."

"I hated to see the exploitation."

"Your lofty ideals were never much appreciated," says the businessman, affecting a striking balance between polite curiosity and hostility. He's in his mid-thirties, stocky and strong, with deep brown eyes and oily, trimmer-clipped hair. He wears jeans and boots.

"I've read that our influence wasn't welcomed by everyone," I tell him.

"It's true that, in the sixties, India hadn't opened its eyes," he goes on in the tone of an MBA graduate. "Most Indians were happy with their lot, believing that God lived among the poor, that a guest was your god, that it was *our* religious duty to help the traveler. Hippies were attracted to this 'simple' contentment. But we had survived long enough on curd and bananas. Now, if you'll excuse me."

I want to ask the businessman more but he cuts us off, turning his attention back to his work. So I twist my head – there's not enough room to turn my body – to Jonathan.

"And the sitar?" I ask, nodding at his case.

"When the Bangladesh war closed the borders, I couldn't afford to fly home," he says, distracted, an eye on our neighbor. "To make money I got into mix music."

"Mix music?"

"The Royal Liverpool was one of the first orchestras to mix Indian soloists with a Western symphony. In 1955, the tabla master Ali Akbar Khan cut an album with Yehudi Menuhin. Then Shankar and Menuhin played together in '66, around the time that Mayer started Indo-Jazz Fusions." As the train settles into its rhythm, Jonathan too regains his momentum. "I loved the sound, that crossover, so I started studying Indian technique."

As the Beatles introduced the sitar to pop, classical musicians melded East and West, breaking away from the traditional structure of the chord sequence, laying the foundations of world music.

"Britain offered me a job, a mortgage, the Bee Gees. I didn't want to spend my life paying for crap, listening to crap. That wasn't my scene. India gave me room to breathe, to find myself. For that I am deeply grateful."

In a low marsh alongside the rails, naked boys pull at water-lily roots, collecting snails for supper. Behind them, their fathers harvest modest rice paddies by hand. A water buffalo, with only its head visible, stands motionless in the water. As our filthy metal tube clatters past the fields, its whistle blowing off-key, an egret lifts into the sky, a flash of white against the emerald shoots.

The businessman, whose name is Arun, looks again at Jonathan. "So we've known India for the same number of years," he says, an edge of anger in his voice. "I was born about the time you decided that life was a succession of *lassis*."

"Not for everyone," I say.

In 1968, the year of Arun's birth and Jonathan's arrival, India teetered on the cusp of revolution. After Independence and Partition, with its appalling loss of life, Nehru came to power championing a vision of a secular, tolerant India. His socialist democracy set about abolishing feudal estates and building steel mills. His dream caught the imagination of India's youth, who made him an icon of the optimistic new age. But, in private, Nehru saw himself only as "a traveler, limping along in the dark night" and, by his death in 1964, much that he fought for proved illusory. His grand economic policies were overambitious. A massive influx of refugees, mostly from east Pakistan, precipitated a national crisis. Rice, wheat and sugar had to be rationed following a failed monsoon and severe droughts. China seized parts of the North-East Frontier. A staggering 60 million unemployed – about 10 per cent of the population – harbored huge resentment against the system.

In their frustration, many young Indians turned to spiritual cults or extremist militant groups. A peasant uprising in Naxalbari in Darjeeling became the flashpoint for armed revolt. The Naxal guerrillas imported communist ideals and aimed to force revolution on India. They rejected electoral politics and called for a return to an agrarian economy.

Five years later, the "Emergency", when wide powers were given to the prime minister, finally crushed the movement by suspending fundamental rights. Thousands were held without trial. The press was censored. In a joke printed at the time in the underground newspaper the *Battledrum*, Gandhi rose from the dead to ask Indira, now leader, what had happened to his India.

"Where are my spectacles?" he asked her.

"We gave them to the hippies."

"Where is my *dhoti?*" His homespun loin-cloth.

"We gave it to the hippies."

"Where is my stick?"

"That we've kept to ram up the rectums of Indians."

Arun looks at his Rolex and says, "I suppose we should be grateful to you for perpetrating the myth of self-discovery." His dark eyes are resolute yet dart about the hot compartment. "That at least did wonders for our foreign-currency reserves."

"Why are you so hard on him?" I ask.

"Because his generation was so naive," Arun says to me. "No wonder Bhagwan and the Maharishi managed to fleece them so successfully. I do admire those gurus. They sold themselves with the same smart marketing that sold flower power." He goes on, "You know Sai Baba used to pull a stream of ash and watches from the air? When the Mumbai magician P. C. Sorcar Jnr met him, he conjured up a watch, an alarm clock and a plate of *rassogolla*, a milky sweet dripping with syrup."

"Sai Baba was a charlatan," says Jonathan, now irritated. "Bhagwan fled his ashram, leaving behind ninety-three Rolls-Royces. The Maharishi also failed because of materialism. All he wanted was a Western mind and washing machines."

"You can't say he failed, not with his annual turnover," says Arun. "The gurus' mistake was not having an exit strategy."

"I once heard a story about an American student flying into Delhi," I say. "He dropped some LSD, then stripped off all his clothes and started to run up and down the aisle, claiming to have been a *sadhu* in his past life, crying out, 'Daddy, I'm coming home!' The stewards and stewardesses sat on him to restrain him."

Arun smiles. "Those were the days when Air India promised nirvana to tourists for $10 a day."

"Costs a bit more today," I say.

As we speak, the train thunders across another bridge, the noise halting conversations, the shadows of girders strobing across our faces. The smells of scorched metal and spices waft into our carriage, mixing with the coarse heat of bodies. A tray of nuts and seeds appears in the doorway of the compartment, held aloft by a skinny, serious boy. Jonathan cuts across his sales cry, saying, "Once, I was traveling alone on a train. I got out to stretch my legs and came back to find my backpack had been stolen. 'Do not worry, sir, there are many poor people in India,' the conductor told me. So I learnt that money didn't matter."

Arun gapes at him – the modern Indian unable to understand the romantic Welsh convert – then looks out of the window.

The sun burns through the thin clouds, delivering a noontime heat at half-past nine in the morning. Poor, line-side homes open on to the rails. Our sweltering express runs between their front rooms and blue-tile temples. At Laksar, the platform is so long that, as the train slows, announcements are heard over seven or eight times along the run of tannoys. Shoeless sweepers press their brooms between the crowds. A porter loses his load of green bananas. The distant locomotive's departure whistle can hardly be heard above the rattle of the carriage's fans.

"Hippies weren't considered bad hats at first," says Arun, still peering out of the window. "The majority of Indians knew nothing about them and their drug culture until *Haré Rama Haré Krishna*."

Now Jonathan looks away with a sigh. "Dreams died with that movie," he admits, playing with his fingers in obvious anxiety.

In 1971 Bollywood produced an unexpected blockbuster. In the film,

Zeenat Aman – a former Miss India – ran away from home to follow the hippie trail to Nepal. The hit song *"Dum Maro Dum"* caused a sensation, as did the sight of stoned Westerners twisting and kissing in a candle-lit Kathmandu night-club. "Dope Take Dope" began with a whoosh of exhaled smoke and swelled into a Doors-like rhythm as Aman, lost and disillusioned, danced with the flower children. A Hendrix lookalike played the guitar. "Free Love" was tattooed on a man stripped to the waist. Later, Aman killed herself; a first cinematic casualty in the fusion of East and West.

Jonathan says, "At every tea stall, in every bazaar, people chanted *'Dum Maro Dum'*."

"And when we tired of singing the song, you became her murderers," Arun says to Jonathan.

In India and Pakistan, newspapers started to turn against the transcendental intruders. Indira Gandhi, having once welcomed the hippies as "children of India", now criticized their careless dressing and hedonism. The *Rawalpindi Sun* wrote, "It is tragic indeed that our youth should indiscriminately try to ape Western values."

"When we hear about the so-called independence of the Western woman – bouncing around in mini-skirts and bell-bottoms trying to take a last go at life, let us not close our eyes to their ordeals," continued the article, "Imagine a girl in a snow storm and bone-chilling winds waiting at a bus-stop in order to reach her office in time to avoid the dirty looks of her boss. Imagine her sitting on typewriter for eight hours, coming back wet and tired to her apartment, with no one to welcome her. What can this independent girl do but take a double Scotch and start cooking the dinner?"

The correspondent concluded, "I fail to understand the reasons which prompt our boys and girls to be lured by the so-called advanced Western civilization."

"Do you know Gandhi's comment on Western civilization?" asks Jonathan. "He said he thought it was a good idea. *Haré Rama Haré Krishna* was part of the commercial crap we'd tried to leave behind."

A laugh escapes from Arun. "The paradox is you brought it with you," he says.

"And you embraced it," replies Jonathan.

The train runs on. The Ganges plain spreads toward the horizon, its large, fertile fields surrounded by poplars. Cow pats dry for winter fuel beneath the high-tension pylons. Within a few hours' journey are four of Hinduism's holiest sites, as well as the city where the Buddha first preached his message. Across from the Taj Mahal, there stands – as in Istanbul – a Pizza Hut.

"*Rishi Bhoomi*," says Jonathan, looking out of the window. "The Land of Sages is what Indians call this country. There's meant to be a sage destined to teach enlightenment to every seeker."

Arun raises his eyebrows and glances up from his laptop. He says, "A devotee asks his guru, 'What should I seek in the cradle of civilization?' The guru looks at the man with infinite compassion and answers, 'Zanussi'."

26. TICKET TO RIDE

At a hundred oval work stations, students in saris and baseball caps book flights from Gatwick and JFK to Johannesburg and Sydney. Calls from Paris, Dublin and Frankfurt are routed to Delhi. Beneath posters of Spanish footballers and notices about a pending Royal Mail strike, the young sales staff work four-hour shifts, usually after class, reading their horoscopes and loading Ganesh idol screen-savers between calls. A technician, having inadvertently stubbed his toe against a hard drive, touches his forehead and heart with his right hand to pay respect to Saraswati, the goddess of learning. I'm reminded that Indians have a gift for transforming the prosaic into the extraordinary, whereas the travel industry ferrets out the unique and turns it into the mundane.

Arun is a tourism consultant. On the phone, he becomes Arnie. Next to him, French-speaking Manisha is Monique. Beyond a potted palm sits Jaideep.

"Call me Jerry," he says, holding out his hand.

Their employer is Tecnovat Data, the Indian subsidiary of ebookers, a European dot.com owned by the American travel-and-property-services provider Cendant. Its open-plan operations floor, with screens and keyboards, could be in Croydon or Kalamazoo. In the back office, another five hundred employees issue tickets, settle accounts and crunch numbers for a dozen other European and American travel agencies. In the free staff canteen, Team UK watch BBC World, read the British papers and try to keep up with events on *Coronation Street*. The German team discusses the *Füssball Weltmeisterschaft* and Air Berlin's new schedule.

"The European markets are still sensitive to overseas call centers," says Arun, slipping on his headset. "So we try to give the impression of being a local operation."

"What about *Big Brother*?" a pretty operator recites into her headset. "Wasn't last night outrageous?"

Only Suomi proved to be a language beyond the abilities of native linguists. So Finnish graduates are enticed to Delhi by the offer of free flights and accommodation in exchange for a year's work at the call center. Their blond heads bob in a far corner of the office, speaking to Helsinki and Turku, flogging vacations in the exotic East.

"We're not just selling a product which lets people cross the world," Arun tells me. "We're selling dreams."

"Just like the sixties gurus," I say.

Arun is lucid, ambitious and generous. On the train I asked him to explain his "myth" of self-discovery, and he invited me to stay at his Delhi house. I while away the afternoon at Tecnovat talking to his workmates, collecting my email and booking my flight out of Kathmandu. Sixty years ago, Nehru wrote that India was a bundle of contradictions held together by strong and invisible threads. Today, those threads are likely to be the digital cables which link the world.

Under the neon lights, at birch-veneer desks, multilingual operators tout Star Alliance around-the-world tickets and Lonely Planet international phone cards. I feel churlish recalling Geoff Crowther's advice to travellers in his second BIT newsletter. In 1972, he asked them to minimize their part in the expansion of Western materialism, writing, "Many places on the way to Nepal have already become little more than extensions of Portobello Road." I'm relieved when Arun finishes for the day and we pack up to go home to India.

"So you think the attainment of self-knowledge is illusory?" I say to him as we drive through leafy, booming Okhla Industrial Estate.

"Not illusory but deluding," he replies, our taxi avoiding a golf cart which glides between the headquarters of BMW and Land Rover India.

"An American poet named Wallace Stevens wrote that the last illusion is disillusion." In Hindu and Buddhist philosophy, the traveller follows the mental path beyond life's everyday illusions to reach perfect knowledge. "I don't buy that."

"You believe modern man has moved beyond disillusion?" asks Arun.

"I think we have to. In the West, we've dismantled civil society and deconstructed ourselves, which is one reason why Islam is advancing as a moral force. I think the sixties generation recognized the need to find a new way forward – through self-discovery."

"A pretty notion," says Arun, as we pull out into the evening rush hour. Outside the perimeter fence squat homeless transients, sleeping under makeshift shelters. Pigs sift empty plastic bags in gutters. "But do you know the story of Buddha's disciples planning to build the first temple to him? To guide them, Buddha placed one empty alms bowl over another. Every stupa came to be based on that simple design. His point is the bowl covers emptiness with emptiness." He concludes, "Self-discovery is a myth because there is nothing to find."

I think of the West's spiritual emptiness, its incipient commercialism, the culture of laziness and ask, "So how does society move beyond disillusion?"

"By being realistic."

"And learning from other's mistakes."

"Thank you for the advice, but India is too big to be changed by incomers' ideas."

"You've embraced the twin gods of capitalism and material prosperity."

"You give meaning to life by preserving it in words. I give it meaning by securing my family's future. It is a simple choice. Anything beyond that is illusory."

Arun is a champion of India's astonishing march to affluence. His brother, on the other hand, is one of its auditors. We eat together with their parents, wives and two children in a worn, pebbledash bungalow in Chittaranjan Park, beneath a flight path a dozen miles south of Old Delhi. Here, too, East and West are woven into a complex mosaic. After dinner, we sit together on hard sofas in their front room, drinking herbal tea beside their new white refrigerator. The tax-inspector brother drills me with an endless stream of statistical questions. Does Britain use pounds or kilos? Do Amtrak trains run on time? What is the mean temperature of Irish post offices?

"Why on earth do you want to know that?" I ask.

"To see if air conditioners are an allowable expense for cooling their computer equipment."

"India's old problems will be healed by prosperity," says Arun, picking up our conversation from the train. "Both poverty and the conflict between the Hindu and Muslim are economic matters. As was the conflict between Christians and Jews in twentieth-century Europe."

"By which date does Revenue Canada require the submission of completed income-tax returns?" asks his brother.

Their wives refill my cup, offer me more sliced mango and tell me that they are Brahmins, the caste said to have emerged from the mouth of Lord Brahma at the moment of creation.

"Ours is an inter-caste marriage arranged by our parents," explains Arun's wife, her hair escaping in long strands from its pins. "Would you care for another After Eight?"

"I had other offers and could not decide on a husband," says the second woman, a telecom economist. "So my family's guru compared the astrological charts of my suitors."

"My boys eat *roti* with a knife and fork," says the mother with pride.

Arun's children watch *Atomic Betty* on the Cartoon Network. Wax drips from a shrine on to the television set. The evening breeze wafts through the grilles. The fourteen-year-old *ayah*, who is frightened of ghosts, eats alone in the kitchen, squatting on a newspaper on the floor.

"Your flower children believed that happiness was a yardstick for living," Arun says to me, shaking his head. "More important is repaying our debt."

"Which debt?" I ask.

"At birth we are given energy, an animal strength that is creative, moral and spiritual. Our task is to enhance it, to make it grow, to pay back the providence that gave us life."

"Every human must unleash the power which lies dormant within him like a coiled serpent," says his wife.

"One day I hope to visit the headquarters of the World Bank," says his brother.

The next morning, I wander around the neighborhood. When "my" flower children first hit India, Chittaranjan Park was jungle. Now, it is a colony of Bengali refugees, who – like Arun and his family – were displaced from east Pakistan by the Bangladesh war. In the sunlight, barefoot, retired civil servants walk around the J-block ornamental gardens feeling the dew between their toes. Six or seven members of the colony's "Laughing Club" stand in a circle chuckling on cue. One beaming practitioner assures me that ten minutes of laughter is more therapeutic than an hour's jogging. Overhead, an El Al Boeing descends on its final approach to Indira Gandhi International. Along the main road, hand-painted lorries with the sacred "*om*" on their bonnets rattle past broadband internet booths.

I head across town to meet the man who touched – and enlightened – more Intrepids than any other Indian; a living connection to the early days of the trail.

A bug-eyed three-wheeler buzzes me along broad roads lined with palm trees, opulent office blocks and rotting slums. Here, in the filthy, brown air, is Delhi in all its "nagging symbolism," as wrote the travel writer Jan Morris. "Tombs of emperors stand beside traffic junctions, forgotten fortresses command suburbs, the titles of lost dynasties are woven into the vernacular, if only as street names." Mughal leaders once rode out on bejewelled elephants from the Red Fort. Now, at traffic signals, most drivers switch off their engines to save petrol. When the lights turn green, the motorcyclists jump up like clockwork toys to kickstart their bikes.

My rickshaw drops me at the south gate of the Jama Masjid and, as arranged, I walk through the bustling, congested lanes to Karim's cafeteria. The close, urban heat clings to me like a damp kaftan. I watch a grocer weigh out potatoes twice on his hand scale. A boy brushes past his stall, slips a cucumber into his sock then washes it out of sight at a spigot.

Even in the crush of diners at Karim's, no one could miss Rama Tiwari. He is a remarkable-looking man; a hairy cherub with broad Mongol face, smooth domed head and a glossy black ruff of locks which tumble forward into his salt-and-pepper beard. As I enter, he leaps up from his table and strides toward me with stubby arms outstretched, roaring, "People is like oxygen for me! I breathe you into my heart."

I love him at first sight. Under the cool fluorescent light, his face glows with eager warmth. He wears a loose salmon shirt with matching cotton trousers. His skin appears to be the color of polished cherry wood.

"We talk now. Talk talk talk. Then, later, we will dance," he says, wrapping an arm around my waist. He stands no taller than my shoulder. "Come sit. *Sit.* You are kind and sweet to take an interest in my life. I want you to ask me anything. *Everything.* And what I do not know I will make up for you in a great Indian epic full of beautiful partners and good sex. *Sex,*" he repeats in a breathless, panting laugh which seems to erupt from his core.

Rama plops down on a cushion, kicks off his shoes and tucks his feet under him like a lissom child. I sit beside him but, before I can ask my first question, he places his arm on my leg.

"Before talk I will order life-nurturing food. And before food, water. *Water.*" He pours two glasses and hands one to me. "We will toast together because our bodies are 70 per cent liquid. To life, my friend. To *life.*"

Rama is no shrinking violet. Over forty years, he forged a meandering chain of marvellous book shops for foreign travellers. He owns bibliophilic homes in Varanasi and Kathmandu. He operates library-like offices in Delhi and on Venice Beach. He's due to fly to California in the morning.

"Now we make another toast," he hurries on, gripping my wrist, refilling my glass. "This time to writers, to poets in the eye of the storm." He lifts his glass above his head. "May you find stillness in the midst of chaos."

Rama's is a rags-to-riches (or pulp fiction to first edition) story. He was born in a poor village between Lucknow and Kanpur, "where you can smell the soil and the rain". Books fascinated him from the earliest age, not least because of his parents' acquisitive passion for holistic tomes. At that time, it was the custom to throw sacred scriptures into the Ganges as an offering. Rama was appalled by the waste and began to call on neighbors, then on nearby villages, offering to buy and to preserve their manuscripts.

"I rode my bicycle because my father wouldn't let me borrow the bullock cart," he remembers. "In a day, I would buy maybe one hundred books. I'd take them home and flip through every one, all for my self-satisfaction, to see how writers displayed knowledge, how with every page they tried to extend that knowledge. I'd sit in my room for fourteen or sixteen hours with my feet swelling and forgetting my food and water." He smiles. "Maybe, in my last life, I worked in a library and just got a heart attack."

At the age of twelve, Rama's first job was cleaning floors in a Varanasi bookseller's. In time, he worked his way up from office boy to salesman and then department manager. When the first Intrepids reached the city, he noticed both the paperbacks they bought and those which were carried with them.

"When I heard the words 'hippie man' I thought 'happy man'. You see, Varanasi was always a factory of happiness. Kabir wrote his *dohas* and Tulsidas his *Ramayana* there. Mirabai left her palace and husband to wander around the city with the *sadhus* and get realized. Even Buddha came to Sarnath to give his first sermon. So, when the hippies followed everlasting Krishna and the Beatles to our holy city of learning, I saw a chance to feed their appetite with my passion."

Rama began by trading books on the pavement outside the Tourist Bungalow. At first, he couldn't afford a blanket on which to display his stock.

"The books were shown on cardboard. Of course, later, I got a blanket, then I got boxes, then actually trunks and, when the trunks got heavier, I built a little stall."

Rama exchanged Ginsberg for Gandhi, *The Dharma Bums* for *Bhagavat-Gita*, *Autobiography of a Yogi* for *Zen and the Art of Motorcycle Maintenance*. He also sold classic works – D. T. Suzuki's *Introduction to Buddhism*, the Vedas and the Koran, as well as many of the sacred texts he collected as a boy. Newcomers, hungry for knowledge of the East, surrendered their Western titles along with 50 rupees. Rama then sold on the dog-eared copies of *Catch 22* and *Naked Lunch* to kids heading home.

"The arriving hippies wanted to leave behind the loaded mechanical mind. They wanted to search in themselves to find heart-*chakra*. So they read my books and found mystics and teachers with good approaches. We pilgrims grew together."

I ask him if that is the reason his wordy empire is named "Pilgrims"?

"It is more a question to myself; who I am, what my relationship is with this world, with other brothers and sisters," he replies, dipping his head in thought. "The simple answer is, I'm on a pilgrimage and I see everyone else as a pilgrim, too." He smiles at me, cocking his head inquisitively. "And you?"

"Not a pilgrim," I answer.

"All my life, I believe in one earth, one people, one family, one god," Rama goes on, his eyes crinkling with optimism. "I wanted to create a book house to help people learn about meditation, yoga, magic, tantra, sex."

"More sex?"

"More and *more* sex," he cries with his panting laughter. "I wanted to welcome and *namaste* all oxygen-giving pilgrims."

As he relates his story, our meal arrives: chicken *mughali*, *makhani daal*, *palak paneer*. "Now we say a little prayer for the food," he gasps, catching his breath. "Oh, Lord, it is yours – and we will offer it back to you tomorrow morning," he chortles. "Now *eat*."

I cannot recall meeting a more joyful man in my life. I want to adopt him as my guru.

"I remember on the road to Rishikesh there once lived a Fire Baba," he tells me, wiping a smear of *daal* from his beard. "His cheerful charm and chillums gave comfort to many hippies who stayed around him. One day, a German disciple came to him and said he had a visa problem and had to leave India. Fire Baba said, 'That is no problem. Give me your passport.' The German fellow handed it to Babaji, who opened it and made the sound, '*Om* one, two, three, all India is free.' Then he tore the passport in half and put it on the fire. 'From today your name is no longer Günther,' Fire Baba said. 'I am giving you holy name Sant Samosa Ram. Now chant "*Om Shanti, Shanti, Shanti*" and be happy.'"

Rama puts his arm around my waist again and roars at his story. *Sant Samosa Ram* translates as Saint Little Pastry.

"Sounds to me like Fire Baba was full of hot air," I say.

"Always there were a lot of things going on in those years," he chuckles. "I listened, I understood and I lived for the moment – so forgive me if I don't remember much else."

His path to self-realization wasn't without disillusionments or puffs of elated amnesia. In Varanasi, his landlord doubled the rent, so, like most of his customers, Rama turned his back on the heat, dust and crush of India. In a dream, he'd seen the need for a shop specializing in holistic and spiritual books for tourists in Nepal. A decade before Mind, Body and Spirit publishing found its niche in the West, Rama made a modest start in Pokhara. Later, he moved Pilgrims to larger premises in Kathmandu.

"I dreamed of building a mountain of books, a Himalaya of books and, since that day, my life has been happy bread and butter. Every moment is now like Christmas and *Holi* and *Diwali* rolling together in a big soft bed."

Some of his early customers became partners: a Vietnam veteran who structured the first business plan, a wandering Welshman who edited Pilgrims Publishing's new titles, an Australian librarian who taught Rama about the international book trade and still runs the company's website. Today, the Thamel store rambles over twenty-four rooms. His Patan shop carries over 20,000 rare and antiquarian volumes in English, German, Hindi, Sanskrit and Nepali. His Feed 'n' Read restaurant serves burgers alongside Ayurvedic herbal remedies. Rama even reopened a store in Varanasi, designed to look like a Victorian English library. Pilgrims grew and changed with its clients, adding New Age titles, trekking maps and luxury travel guides to its religious primers and series of Himalayan classics.

"When I came back to Varanasi, I said to the tourism minister, let us turn the city into a world-literature library. To contain all knowledge. According to our Hindu philosophy, God is infinite. The entire space and beyond is part of the infinite God. Which means every page of every book is part of God. So I told the minister, 'Put all the statues out of the temples and replace them with books! *Books*.'" He hurries on, "I like to read between the chapters, between the paragraphs, even between the lines. In that empty space I try to sense what the writer is saying. Why did she choose this word? Who is the person behind these sentences? Also, of course, I love the older editions of books, with the beautiful bindings, the beautiful papers, the fascinating ink colors, which for me are just like ... yogi's semen."

"I've never seen yogi's semen," I joke.

Rama's head rolls back and his mouth opens to expose a fat pink tongue. "You haven't? Then, my friend, you have not *lived*!" He is roaring now, play-acting, babbling, "Oh, when the yogis hear of this they will come and beat me. All their lives they are chaste and celibate and now we joke of their semen."

Rama's laughter is contagious, rippling out of him, shaking the table, spilling the water from our glasses. He rises to his feet declaring, "We must go now to the temple and ask to see blissful Shiva semen."

"Or we could just look in books."

He slaps my back with such enthusiasm that the cook glances up from the kitchen. Then he wraps his arms around my neck and howls, "You and

I are not so different from hippie seekers. Or Indian wanderers of first millennium BC. All want just to be happy as children. But hippies made one mistake and it broke them. Now dancing," he announces, clapping his hands, startling me as much as the other diners. "We go now to Ruby Tuesday's to dance and sing. I breathe *oxygen*."

"What was their mistake?" I say, taking hold of his hand to pull him into his seat. "You searched and were not broken."

"They imagined peace of mind was not with their families or in their home countries," says Rama Tiwari. "They didn't see we can only live in happiness if we conquer the restless dream that paradise is in a world other than our own."

As the waiter clears away our dishes, Rama calls – *yells* – for the bill. He is known at the cafeteria and indulged like an ebullient, much-loved boy.

"I believe books need to be about truth, the *truth* of experience," he goes on. "Writing shouldn't be about ego or money or fame but about selfless sharing and helping others. We all live under one sky so, when we do something positive for others, we are in fact doing it for ourselves. The diamond is made from the clay, all comes from Mother Earth, all belongs to the One."

Rama snatches the bill when it arrives and, as I try to pay, he tells me, "Every day I pray to Lord Tourist, 'You have given to me and now I give back to you. Thank you for sharing with me.'"

On the street, India assaults us in temple bells, mounds of turmeric and blaring Hindu-pop. Countless shoving bodies compress our personal space. Crows pick at the rust-red soil. Street musicians pound drums and ring cymbals.

As we walk, Rama says, "No people have time any more to listen to a little music, to go to dance room, to have sex and go to sleep. No time to get up early, at sunrise, and go for a little stroll. People now work, take a short holiday, have such poor dreams." We turn a corner, and he asks, "After your travel book, you next should write about what people all over the world do with their hands: wash babies, cook dinner, pet the dog."

"Not hands," I say. "Hearts."

"That is even better," he roars, the laughter rippling out of him again. "Write to help people find their way back home."

I don't think it's that simple.

"Do you know the poet Tagore?" Rama goes on. "'The traveller has to knock at every alien door to come to his own, and one has to wander through all the outer worlds to reach the innermost shrine at the end.'"

Rabindranath Tagore's poem is called "Journey Home".

It is time for me to leave India. There remains one last border I have to cross. A part of me still believes that my destination lies in the pure, clean Himalayas, or at least in a world other than my own. Earlier, I told my host that I will leave for Nepal at the end of the week. In his hand he carries a suitcase for me to deliver to his Pokhara shop.

"Inside are only books and clothes and old things. No bombs," he laughs. "Not from this old hippie."

"Nepal has enough bombs of its own," I point out.

"Now," he cheers, hailing a passing rickshaw and wiggling his hips like a teenager, "we *will* go dancing!"

Nepal

27. FLOWERS IN THE RAIN

Nepal. Divine home of the gods. Snow-capped mountain kingdom. Spiritual center of the universe where – in some districts – mortal life expectancy hovers around forty-seven years. Rocky strip of land that brothers have squabbled over for centuries. Nepotistic apartheid state of spectacular inequality. Last battleground of Maoist guerrillas. The End of the Road.

I brush away Gorakhpur's touts and mosquitoes to catch an overloaded bus to the border. The tattered rattletrap judders forward, collecting another dozen dusty-faced passengers, bedding rolls and baskets. Inside, it is impossible to move, even to fall down and, beyond the cracked windows, India appears to be almost as airless and chaotic, with overheated lorries and swaying tongas jamming the road and suffocating progress. Our teenage ticket collector spits betel, calls out destinations, swings out of a window and over the roof like an acrobat to chide his captives into giving up their coins. In the aisle, a woman peels an orange in strips, removing the pips, placing the segments one by one in her son's mouth. The child, then, is sick on my knees.

At least there is space onboard to think. As we cross an ashen flatland of thatched villages and stagnant ponds, I realize that my role – as Rama suggested – isn't to help people to find their way back home. Home doesn't lie at the end of my road, it remains years and miles behind me. I have no desire to return to beginnings, to geographical familiarity, to complacency. I want to move forward, to reach for the unknown, even in a world where every corner is known.

Old Nepali farmers have a saying to discourage people from leaving their land: "To those who stay, the soil. To those who leave, the pathway." A farming culture naturally prizes the soil over the open road. But modernity has transformed not only Nepal into a land of migrants – of people moving out of the countryside or out of the country, leaving behind the settled culture, the soil. Perhaps it's my last illusion, but the new horizon rouses my joy of life. I can't turn back now.

The border runs through the middle of squalid Sunauli. I have to wake up the dozing official to stamp me out of India. One hundred yards on, I join the queue at the Nepalese immigration post. An inspector asks me to open Rama's suitcase. I've already flipped through its contents: dog-eared copies of Ian Macdonald's *Revolution in the Head*, *World Without Borders* and *The Great Rock and Roll Trivia Quiz*, as well as six pairs of yellow shoes and a white kaftan. He considers the dated contents and, with a sceptical lift of the eyebrow, asks me, "Sir, you are having no Beatles LPs?"

I'm happy to be on the threshold of Nepal. In the sixties, the Intrepids pushed the frontier of the exotic back to this line. Here, their search for an individual paradise must have seemed a real possibility, away from India's crowds, in the clear mountain air, among a people of legendary hospitality.

"Your old road is rapidly agein'," sings the woman ahead of me in the queue. In English. Not under her breath. "Please get out of the new one if you can't lend your hand..."

I recognize the slim, skittle-shaped body, the seal-grey hair, the wide feline eyes. My heart skips a beat.

"Penny!"

"Hey, Jack," says Penny.

I give her a huge hug, her bangles ringing against my ears.

"I can't believe it," I tell her.

"Good karma," she says with an indulgent, complicit smile. "Like I said, there's a connection between us."

"Penny, you look great."

"Jack, this guy says I don't have enough money to come into Nepal," she says, turning back to the immigration officer. "I mean, I lived in Kathmandu before he was even born."

"We're fellow travelers," I tell the official, laughing, showing my passport and wallet. Three months have passed since I left her in her cave. "What happened in Turkey?"

"All sorts of weirdness," she says as our visas are stamped. "The police kicked me out of Cappadocia. Even though it's a World Heritage Site and I'm an ancient relic. I grabbed a bus to Tehran, but it was so damn hot I flew to Delhi. No way I could walk around Iran inside a tent. Been chilling out in Pune ever since."

"And now?"

"Going for a swim," she says, "in Pokhara."

'That's my first stop too," I laugh.

Penny fixes me with her jade-green eyes and squeezes my hand. Her moonstone and *I Ching* rings flash in the mid-morning sun. "Jack, did I ever tell you," she says, "you're a typical Scorpio."

Ten minutes later, our clattering Tata coach groans into gear.

Nepal immediately looks different from India. There are fewer people and the land seems softer, a pleasing patchwork of family banana plantations, dappled forests and low-lying floodplains thick with weed. Its neat brick houses are covered in yellow-flowered creepers and surrounded by picket fences. A sleek black water buffalo wades in a fast, clear river. A strip of luminous cloud marks the northern horizon. Penny holds her head out the window, gazing forward at the sky, happy and humming to herself.

"I first reached Shangri La La La in 1970," she says, picking up her easy monologue, unfazed by the time that's passed. "Sixty-eight had been a bad year, a *very* bad year. Things improved with Woodstock but, other than that, man, those days were the pits."

1968. The year the sixties soured. The single most turbulent year since the end of the Second World War. The year when vague ideals of a better world, of more participatory democracy, of liberation, met with sharp realities.

That glad, confident year had dawned in colors psychedelic. Women went bra-less, tank tops were tie-dyed, "Everlasting Love" boomed out of transistors from Littleworth to Big Sur. Berkeley professors came to class barefoot with flowers in their hair. The peace symbol replaced the crucifix and Star of David for millions of young believers. People power aspired to stop the draft, to legalize grass and to levitate the Pentagon on the collective will of a generation.

Then, Martin Luther King, civil-rights activist and an apostle of non-violence, was murdered in Memphis, touching off a wave of rioting in US cities. Two months later in Los Angeles, Robert Kennedy, the one leader whose appeal crossed America's racial divide, was killed. The bombing of North Vietnam after the Tet offensive inflamed hatred of the establishment, uniting world youth in revulsion and rebellion. In May, in Paris, ten of thousands of students took to the streets. Their graffiti proclaimed, "We will invent a new original world." But their optimism was perverted by political extremists and the dogma of Sartre and Foucault. In August, Warsaw Pact armies invaded Czechoslovakia. Anti-war protesters were beaten and maced during the Democratic National Convention in Chicago. In November, Richard Nixon was elected US president.

By year end, 1,200 students had been arrested on American campuses. Tokyo University was occupied for three months and the LSE shut down. The embittered New Left splintered into the Weathermen, the Red Brigade and Baader-Meinhof. The flower children's innocent spiritual trip was hijacked by Timothy Leary, whose half-baked chemical theories contributed to heroin's ruinous ascendancy over mescaline and LSD. Jefferson Airplane sold out to commercialism, singing "White Levi's" to the tune of "White Rabbit". The Monkees hit number one with "Daydream Believer".

"Hope was the casualty," says Penny.

In August 1969, she was at Woodstock. She helped to set up the music festival's main stage, laid in stocks of muesli, collected bread and milk from Max Yasgur. She watched the Hindu *swami* Satchidananda, seated in white robes on the big stage, give the opening prayer invocation. She listened to John Sebastian sing "I Had a Dream" and Jimi Hendrix play "Star-Spangled Banner". She sang along to "Marrakech Express" with half a million other kids. She slipped on the mud while taking Janis Joplin to the stage and played out the rest of the supreme sixties feelgood celebration with a broken toe.

Within months, Hendrix, Joplin and Jim Morrison of The Doors were dead. Alcohol abuse finally caught up with Jack Kerouac, killing him in Florida. Ken Kesey "left literature behind" to move to a blueberry farm in Oregon. The hippie vibe was knocked off key and many heard its requiem.

That bitter winter, Penny and Orrin – pop painter, performance artist and her "final and best husband" – picked up sticks and split the States to join the thousands following the trail across Asia.

"I remember the sun shining on the water paddies and the mountains reflected in the lake," Penny says to me, her voice full of emotion. "The houses had peacock windows and pumpkin roofs. At night when the oil-lamps were lit, the mountains were clear and sharp against the sky. I'd read my *Hobbit*. I felt I'd arrived in Middle Earth. Nepal was paradise on earth."

She continues both holding my hand and staring at the ice-white clouds. Only then do I realize that the clouds haven't moved, that they are the Himalayas rising above the road ahead of us.

"Our days passed in a haze of beauty," she sighs.

Their first stop in Nepal was Pokhara. An image of cool alpine fastness had sustained them along the dusty 6,000-mile journey from disillusionment and Istanbul (by way of the Auroville ashram in Pondicherry). Penny and Orrin wanted to swim in Pokhara's highland lake.

"We rowed a *dungaa* out into the middle of Phewa Tal," she tells me, intoxicated by the memory. *Dungaas* are leaky, flat-bottomed, barge-like rowing boats. "Another boat was returning to the village full of wildflowers. I was wearing a pair of ridiculous little white sockettes. I'd saved them in the bottom of my pack for this special occasion. The boatman saw them and called out in English, 'Flowers! Flowers for the lady!' In exchange for my socks, he filled our boat with blooms." Penny is laughing but there are tears in her eyes. "Later, when we were alone, we lay down on our floating floral bed and popped our corks."

The road rises above the Indian plain and into dense, subtropical foothills. Our Magic Bus shudders to a stop at a village on the lip of a steep ravine backed by grey stone cliffs. The passengers step down to buy paper cones of peanuts and cheeseballs from a huddle of bamboo stalls. A flock of bulbuls wheel above their tin roofs and the setting sun. I smell fried cumin, coriander and woodsmoke, each aroma caught in a separate layer of cool air. I adjust my focus from India's heat and crush, reach for clarity. Angular men lash to our roof rack heavy hands of tiny green bananas and a goat. I buy Penny a cup of fragrant milk tea.

As evening falls, the bus edges around steep hillsides of terraced fields.

We turn north at Narayangadh and climb high above the Trisuli, a tributary of the Ganges. Nepal's main north–south road – a twenty-mile dirt ribbon between plain and plateau – is knotted with heavy traffic. The monsoon rains have washed away much of the embankment and, in the half-light, trucks inch around cavernous pot-holes and cottage-sized boulders which have crashed down from the upper slopes. Drivers stretch out beneath their stranded lorries, repairing gearboxes by torchlight. Mechanics drag jacks and tools between the breakdowns. Penny and I lean together against the bus's violent motion like drunken sailors, trying to keep ourselves on an even keel, numbed by the tortuous ride, transfixed by the glacial blue river churning hundreds of feet beneath us. Here and there, the twisted remains of the crash barrier poke above the current. The goat bleats in terror.

Around midnight, we shudder into Mugling, a *daal bhaat*-and-prostitute stop for long-distance drivers. The Nepali passengers file off the bus for another security check. Our six-hour drive has already doubled in duration. Now it stops altogether because of the curfew.

The night is black and moonless. Headlights sweep across sleeping faces in dozens of trucks and buses. A tea shop owner snores behind his refrigerator. A slender teenager in a modest pleated *fariya* draws near to my side, brushing her back against me. When I step away, she moves on, accosting two young drivers for a cigarette. Dogs bark at every new vehicle that squeals into town. Penny groans, "I don't remember this place."

Dawn reveals *himal* peaks above us. Our promised 4 a.m. departure slips away, the driver sleeping on across the front seats. Two hours later, the conductors manage to wake him. He pushes back his bandanna and waves a stick of incense over the steering wheel. A minute later, we are off, horn blaring, music wailing, the patient passengers stretching themselves awake. The boys run forward to pay tolls, call out to girls, hammer on the metal body to stop and collect more fares. Only at army checkpoints do they snap off the tape player and fall silent.

The bus turns west to follow the deep valleys of the Trisuli and fast-flowing Marsyangdi rivers. Curved terraces of rice step up to hilltops of gum and bottlebrush trees spun in fine morning mist. Ears of corn dry on the balconies of three-story Baahun and Chhetri farmhouses. Women draw water in humble thatched Tamang and Magar hamlets. Spacious new houses made of Chinese bricks belong to Gurkhas retired from the British or Indian armies. Into this landscape of sixty different ethnic and caste groups tripped the Intrepids, too many of them disregarding the proprieties of class and race in sheer stoned incomprehension.

An hour later, the road lifts into the broad Seti valley. Beyond an upland of tree-lined mustard fields rise the Annapurnas. Nowhere else on earth do mountains climb to such a height in such a short distance. Machhapuchare, the razor-edged "Fishtail", seems to erupt from the plateau, only twenty miles to the north and filling the skyline. I don't want to drop my eyes back to earth, especially in the dirty expanse of chaos at Pokhara's public bus park.

We catch a taxi to Lakeside and, as Penny did almost forty years before, walk down to the shore. The morning is sparkling clear. The altitude magnifies the mountains, exaggerating their size and color: the frost-white of the snow, the vast grey flanks, the luminous light and stainless sky.

"This way," she says, leading me around Phewa Tal, between the trees and away from the houses.

In a forest of oaks and evergreens, she lays down her cane, then strips off her purple embroidered shift and sarong. I avert my eyes but, when I glance back, she's smiling at me, striking a carefree pose, lacing a marigold into her hair. She slips naked into the water, gasps at the shocking cold, paddles away from the shore. I find a stone *chautara* resting platform under a gnarled banyan tree. In the distance I hear the tinkling of temple bells.

As I watch, Penny's loose, white skin seems to tighten and shimmer beneath the surface. The years slip away with each stroke. The ripples ruffle the reflection of the Himalayas as they must have when she and Orrin first swam together in their new-found paradise. At once I understand Hesse's words that the East "was not only a country and something geographical, but it was the home and youth of the soul".

Penny is about one hundred yards out when she starts to laugh.

"It still tastes of ice," she calls back to me. "Of new ice and old, old earth. What a gas."

28. WHILE MY GUITAR GENTLY WEEPS

Nepal was closed to foreigners until 1951. The wheel wasn't seen in Pokhara until the first DC-3 landed in 1952. No road linked Kathmandu to the outside world until 1956. Before then, VIPs had to be carried to the capital by palanquin. The king's cars were portered from India by teams of coolies. In 1962, the US Peace Corps arrived in the medieval kingdom, digging tube wells, dispensing smallpox vaccine and opening Aunt Jane's, the first restaurant in the Himalayas serving milkshakes and apple pie. About the same time, the first tourists dropped into nirvana, and changed it for ever. Every morning, a ten-year-old boy named Ranji met new arrivals at Kathmandu's Royal Hotel – one of only four in the country – and offered to be their guide. As payment, he asked for an English dictionary, which the tourists bought for him at the capital's only foreign book shop. Each evening, Ranji then sold the same dictionary back to the store. Six years later, Ranji – the country's original independent travel guide – fell in with a stoned band of space cadets and became the first Nepali to die from a hallucinogen overdose.

Four decades later, many of Nepal's 400,000 annual visitors are smoking joints at Pokhara's German Bakery. Next door at the Boomerang Kosher Restaurant, Israeli girls order French toast and agree it is impossible to stick to the Atkin's Diet in Asia. A Jamaican in dreadlocks on a mountain bike sails past vanloads of trekkers heading off for the Annapurna Circuit. Tibetan refugees, displaced by the Chinese and resident in Nepal for a generation, sell Native American prayer wheels and Buddhist *thangka* paintings outside the Holistic Barber Salon. A child presses into my hand a flyer for Oktoberfest at the Fulbari Resort ("an unlimited free flow of San Miguel") and whispers, "Hashhhhh, Mister?"

The outside world's intrusions do not end at Zorba's Restaurant and the edge of town. In the mountains, moraines crumble on trekkers' "highways". Foothills have been denuded of trees, in part to fuel hungry guests' cooking fires. At Khumbu's Saturday markets, only lodge-owners can afford to buy eggs, passing on the hefty price to mountaineers. The few short decades of tourism have turned much of Nepal into a vulnerable Himalayan theme park.

Alone, I hurry out of the laid-back holiday haven, past earthen-walled farmhouses transformed into cafés by new front porches, following the lake's gentle curve into an embrace of hills. I have no illusions about finding the remains of the "real" Nepal. I don't kid myself that I'm traveling on the edge. After the long journey from India, I – like most travelers – choose not to trek to the far western Humla district, where four out of every ten children die before their fifth birthday. Instead, I settle on the short climb to Sarangkot, a viewpoint on the ridge north of the lake.

Beyond a chestnut forest, the garden walls are hedged with thorny spurge. Mustard fields are lined with flowering cacti. At a painted marker, I fork away from the cool water and climb a stony path between hillside hamlets. Half a dozen children chewing sugar-cane sticks follow me with their light-golden eyes. Pots of lentils boil in single-room houses with mismatched windows. A farmer clears the weeds from a vegetable patch. At a tea stall, I pause beneath posters of Hindi cinema stars and the god Saraswati to look back at the green terraced shores. Sailboats drift across the glittering lake. Shadows of hang-gliders slide over the rice paddies. Ahead of me, razor-edged Machhapuchare is hidden from view by the hill.

"May I walk with you?" asks a man.

"Thank you. I'm not looking for a guide," I say.

"I want to practice my English. It's a two-hour walk to the top and the paths can be confusing for you."

I walk on. Rishi stubs out his Yak cigarette and clings to my side, asking the usual questions. Where am I from? Where am I staying? How do I like his town? His country? My freedom?

"My freedom?" I repeat. This isn't a usual question.

He spits at the undergrowth before answering me. "To walk anywhere. To travel anywhere."

"I'm not looking for a guide," I say again, pushing ahead.

"This way," he says, indicating the obvious path. He falls into step behind me as I climb through thickets of rhododendron and laurel, their waxy leaves glistening with the last brush of dew. His slippers flip-flop in the dust. After a hundred steep yards, he calls after me, "On television last night I saw a man being arrested in London." His English is fluent and confident. "The police treated him with dignity and I thought, yes, that is correct. But in Nepal, if a policeman catches a thief, the first thing he does is slap, slap, give me a hundred rupees. I have done it myself. I beat the thieves because I thought that's what you do."

I glance back at Rishi's compact build, his sharp features, his grave, sunken eyes. His manner is assured, but I have no wish to subject myself to his droning patter. We walk a dozen more steps before he adds, "But the worst thing is when you have the chance to kill someone after you have taken him.'"

I stop in my tracks, alarmed. If this is a sales pitch, then it's very effective.

"Don't be so surprised," shrugs Rishi. "I'm a soldier."

Nepal is a yam between two boulders, a rugged land straddling the icy boundary between India and China. The country is an ethnological crossroads, traditionally tolerant yet not cohesive, where Hinduism and Buddhism intertwine with animist rites and shamanistic practices. Four separate New Year's Days are celebrated within its borders. Its vital bonds are of family and caste, not nation. Never colonized because of its inaccessibility, Nepal didn't inherit a functioning bureaucracy and judiciary. Instead, its enduring legacy is one of autocratic dynasties which ignore their subjects' needs in the pursuit of personal gain. The Royal Nepalese Army has long sustained the status quo. Ninety-eight per cent of its officer class are of the Chhetri caste, from which most of the ruling families are also drawn. The rule of royal authority, the army and successive corrupt governments was so absolute as to go unchallenged until 1996.

"Once, my unit captured a big guy in the Maoists. We knew that whoever killed him would get a medal," explains Rishi. I assume he's on leave, trying to earn a few extra dollars. "And a medal means promotion, money. The commander gave the order just to hold him, but any of us could have finished off the man, at one o'clock in the morning, saying, you know, he was running away."

In 1996, after years of injustice, compounded by the frustration following a dismal flirtation with democracy, the tiny Communist Party of Nepal (Maoist) declared a "People's War" on the state. The government's brutal and indiscriminate response alienated many countrypeople and drove thousands to join the insurgency. In less than a decade, the nascent movement went from attacks with ancient muskets on rural police stations to blockading the capital.

"Maybe you think this is strange, but I went to the temple that night and lit candles and prayed that the Maoist would not be shot. In the morning, I was happy that he was still alive."

"I don't think it's strange," I say.

"Months later, I was going through his village, and I met a man who was his spitting image. It was his father." He shrugs at my surprise. "Nepal is not a large country. We are used to such coincidences. He took me inside his house and showed me photographs of his son. I knew then, if I had killed that man, I could not have faced that day."

As we climb the terraces, new mountain ridges are revealed behind us. Across Phewa Tal, I catch sight of the World Peace Pagoda. Then a green canopy of trees closes over us, snatching it from view. In the doorway of a bamboo shack, a woman picks stones from rice.

"Maybe you also think it strange that I wanted to see action from close quarters," he says, now moving ahead of me as the path narrows. "All my life I dreamt of winning the battles for my country. But Nepal had no foreigners to fight other than tourists, and we can't fight you. There are too many," he laughs. "This way," he says, showing me a shortcut up the wooded hill. He pauses at the crest for me to catch my breath. "The insurgency brought the chance for me to see action."

Over ten years, the bloody conflict has claimed more than 12,000 lives, two-thirds at the hands of the soldiers like Rishi. In the course of waging their "revolutionary struggle", the rebels – motivated by a grass-roots idealism and the Naxalites across the border – resorted to torture and murder. Their leaders ordered the conscription of children and the execution of school teachers, landowners and village headmen. To try to contain the violence, the government spends $100,000 a day on the military – in a country where the average annual income is $230. In its hunger for revenge, the RNA has acted with equal ruthlessness, killing innocents forced to shelter

Maoists and burning villages in the mountains. In police "search-and-kill" operations, like the recent Kilo Sierra Two, hundreds of women are alleged to have been raped. But Nepal is not only losing its people to bullets and pressure-cooker bombs. In some months, as many as 100,000 young Nepalis cross the border into India, desperate to escape the daily extortion of money by the rebels and of information by the army.

"I was posted to the Mountain Warfare School and the 4th Brigade in Nepalganj," says Rishi, pausing on a wall to light another Yak.

"You learnt your English there?"

"From the British advisers," he nods. "I always volunteered for seek-and-destroy missions. My unit received reliable information about a Maoist camp in the Mugu valley. With forty soldiers, I moved across the *lekhs* for three days and nights. In the small hours of the third morning, we intercepted a rebel group. I chased their leader and pinned him down after a hand-to-hand fight."

Rishi flicks ash on to the dry stones. I listen, his story interrupted only by the calls of cuckoos.

"We took defensive positions against counter attack. But we weren't prepared for being surrounded by nearly three hundred women. They claimed that the captured men were their innocent husbands and sons. This was a trick situation, of course; the militants played very smartly, because the villagers blocked our exit routes and tried to force their way through our cordon."

"We couldn't fire on them but we had to move out before the situation became violent. There was no possibility of air evacuation – my country has only six helicopters – so I made a decision to climb down from the mountain at night. We started around midnight, cutting through the forest to avoid both the women and potential ambush sites, changing our routes so as not to be trailed. The Maoists assumed we'd try to get back to the main camp, so we headed instead in the opposite direction to a police checkpost. It was across difficult terrain, but it was the safest."

"Later we learnt that the man I'd caught was a district commander. He had been going home to meet his newborn son and celebrate with his family. For the first time, I saw the human face of insurgents, and I went to our unit temple and prayed for him."

He tosses aside his cigarette.

"My brigade commander recommended me for a medal. 'So, tiger, you have tasted blood,' he said to me. I felt like a tiger, roaring for more: more action, more honor..."

"More money?" I ask.

"Of course. I hear the Mugu valley will be reopened to trekkers soon," he replies and starts to climb again.

As the day warms, a diaphanous haze gathers in the valleys. We walk above it and the woods through an encampment of handicraft- and tea-stalls. A few other travellers join us here, though none has passed us on the path.

Foreigners had not yet been targeted by the Maoists but, as almost all the trekking routes pass through their areas, many are required to pay a 1,000-rupee "donation" – about $13 – to the cause. Only last month, the Minister of Tourism assured the world that Nepal was safe for visitors. The next day, the Gaida Wildlife Jungle Camp was burnt to the ground and four bombs were dropped on the tennis courts of Kathmandu's Soaltee Crowne Plaza Hotel. That same week, in a lodge in Gangdrak, an American trekker watched a government Puma helicopter gunship swoop down on a populated valley, shooting "at everything that moved".

Back along the trail in Morocco, Penny's first little paradise, forty-three people were killed a few months ago when suicide bombers attacked a tourist restaurant, a five-star hotel and the Belgian Consulate. Like the Luxor massacre and Yemen kidnappings, the Casablanca bombings marked the start of an international campaign targeting Western travellers and the expansion of domestic terror campaigns to Bali, Mombassa, Sharm el-Sheikh, Mumbai and beyond.

Rishi and I walk past the last restaurant beneath the summit of Sarangkot. A grand sweep of mountains suddenly appears before us, pure white peaks rising steeply above stone-blue flanks, dazzling the horizon and my eyes. I stagger back, unbalanced by the sight, grabbing a metal railing. Beneath a boundless sky, no one speaks, and the silence, broken only by the distant rush of water, heightens the sense of timelessness.

"You see now why we have to fight?" says Rishi. "For this paradise."

"This paradise is a war zone," I say.

A Japanese tour group appears at the look-out. A young Nepali puffs up ahead of his chubby English girlfriend, carrying their motorcycle helmets. Only then do I realize that on the opposite side of the hill a paved tourist road snakes up to Sarangkot.

"I have brought you to the most beautiful view in the world," says Rishi, nirvana's warrior. "I wouldn't say no to a tip."

That evening, a story circulates around Pokhara about the latest government action in Doti district. In response to a provocative "cultural revolution entertainment" show at the Sharada Higher Secondary School in Mudbhara, the army surrounded the building, pulled off its roof tiles and started firing into the classrooms. Eleven Maoists and four school children were killed in the firefight, and more than a dozen others left wounded.

"The injured students have not been treated as of yet," reported the *Kathmandu Times*. "Bullets have not been removed from their bodies due to lack of money."

29. IT'S ALL OVER NOW, BABY BLUE

"When that Thunderclap Newman song 'Something in the Air' came out, I thought it was a signal," says Penny, "to go back on to the streets and restart the revolution. I was gutted to realize it was just a song."

We're sitting by the lake at Mike's Breakfast. A twisted band of cloud separates the foothills from the mountains, as if levitating the silver peaks above the earth. A seasoned *dharma* bum with orange protection cord and hiking boots sits at the next table. Penny slept through the previous day and following night but woke from her dreams in an irritable temper. Earlier this morning, she grumbled at the bathroom mirror, "You know, Jack, I preferred being young and impressionable." I hadn't counted on a free restaurant newspaper further darkening her mood. Or on it evoking an extraordinary story.

"Did you read this?" she asks me, shaking both the *Nepali Times* and her head.

"About Sharada School?"

"About Charles Sobhraj," she says. She swallows her coffee in a gulp. "He's been arrested in Kathmandu."

In the summer of 1970, a personable young Indo-Vietnamese and his pregnant French wife drove an old Triumph Herald along the trail to India. The charismatic couple had met in Paris two years earlier, the twenty-four-year-old Sobhraj proposing to Chantal behind the barricades that tumultuous May. But unlike many of their contemporaries, they weren't heading east to work on their karma. Sobhraj, a petty thief and compulsive gambler, was on the run from the police.

In Mumbai, Sobhraj – intelligent, arrogant and rebellious – graduated from cashing bad cheques to black-marketeering. Born in Saigon to a prosperous Sindh businessman and his Vietnamese mistress, he aspired to live the wealthy life which the family had lost on emigrating to France. With his mixed features and gift for languages, Sobhraj was able to disguise his identity, travel on pickpocketed passports, smuggle duty-free Rolex and Cartier watches across borders. He advanced to stealing Alfa Romeos and BMWs to order, driven from Europe and around India's import ban by backpackers. Those backpackers – and passports – were usually acquired at a crowded, hippie café called Dipti's House of Pure Drinks on Ormiston Road.

Sobhraj had no sympathy for the overlanders' pleasure in recreational drugs or their rejection of parental conservatism. As an outsider, he wanted to snake his way into established society, not to reject it. But he realized that many young travelers were gullible and that he could use them. He manipulated their vague ideals and enlisted their help by giving an air of revolutionary glamor to gem-smuggling and the robbery of 'bourgeois' tourists.

Sobhraj was a ruthless, amoral and ambitious con-artist. In the course of his travels, he escaped from half a dozen police lock-ups, smuggled arms into Iran, sold passports to the PLO, abducted his own child and abandoned his wife in a Kabul jail. When Chantal divorced him, he hardened himself against attachment and offered his services to the major operator in the Chinese heroin trade.

By the mid-seventies, amateur drug-smugglers had disrupted the business of the larger organizations. Naive kids carried half-keys across borders, got caught and attracted unwanted publicity. Sobhraj was commissioned to discourage small-time couriers and dealers. The method he decided to use was killing them. In India, he had learnt to use pharmaceutical drugs – Librium, Largactyl and Quaaludes – to disable and pacify his prison guards. Now, he applied his knowledge to young travelers, often on the spurious assumption that they were involved in smuggling, sneaking laxatives into their drinks to induce illness and then soporifics to numb them.

His first victim – after he suffocated a Pakistani driver in the back of a Chevrolet – was André Breugnot, a Frenchman who may have worked for a European heroin ring in Chiang Mai. Next, he abducted Teresa Knowlton, a twenty-two-year-old American en route from Seattle to Nepal for a meditation course. He offered to take her to the beach at Pattaya. There, he and an accomplice drugged her with 150 milligrams of Mogadon, dressed her in a bikini and swam out into the South China Sea to let her drown. He battered and incinerated a flamboyant Turkish pusher and a young Amsterdam couple who had saved for five years for their "trip of a lifetime". Their charred and smouldering bodies were found dumped on a Thai roadside. In Kathmandu, he killed a burly Canadian trekker named Laurent Carrière and the Californian junkie Connie Jo Bronzich, who had arrived on a bus from London a few days earlier. Her blackened, naked body was found beside the Bhagmati river.

In each case, Sobhraj's gracious outward manner won his victims' initial friendship. He presented himself as an urbane gem-dealer and once bragged, "As long as I can talk to people I can manipulate them." By 1977, he had cast a pall over the Asian trail and was wanted for at least twenty murders in Thailand, Malaysia, Indonesia, India, Pakistan and Nepal. He was caught only after drugging an entire busload of French tourists at Delhi's Vikram Hotel.

During his sentence for robbery and manslaughter in the high-security Tihar jail, Sobhraj – who also used the name Alain Gautier – escaped twice, once by feigning appendicitis and, then, in 1986, by throwing a birthday party and feeding grapes and biscuits injected with sleeping pills to his guards. On both occasions he was recaptured, yet he remained outspoken and defiant, managing to have a telephone and fax installed in his cell. In 1997, after serving twenty-one years, he was deported to France. According to the *Nepali Times*, Asia's premier serial killer had now returned and was arrested at the Yak and Yeti Casino on Friday.

"He swore that he never killed good people," says Penny, "but isn't there goodness in everyone?"

The sunken black eyes of a sullen man gaze out from her newspaper. His motivation remains a mystery. Bitterness at the opportunities of Western youth? Revenge against the father who failed to help him to build a future? A lack of feeling or too much feeling? Sobhraj once confessed – then later retracted the boast – that his sadistic murders were "cleanings" for "fun". He never admitted to feeling remorse. "Does a professional soldier feel remorse after having killed a hundred men with a machine-gun?" he once asked. "Did the American pilots feel remorse after dropping napalm on my homeland?"

Sobhraj – a cunning psychopath who brought terror to the hippie trail – was to stand trial and serve a life sentence in Kathmandu, convicted at last for murder.

But Sobhraj alone had not cast a dark shadow on paradise.

Many Intrepids reached Nepal and found themselves at a loss. Was the sacred mountain landscape really their spiritual haven? Could isolated Nepal actually sustain a harmonious fusion of East and West? And if Kathmandu, hidden by a ring of snow-covered peaks, wasn't paradise, then where was it? No one had asked where to go after the End of the Road. Travelers came in search of a perfect society, trusting to find it at the end of the longest bus ride, beneath the white mountains, surrounded by prayer flags and tinkling bells.

Some of the lost souls of Kathmandu committed suicide. Others turned to heroin, smuggled into the kingdom by stewards on the first Royal Nepali flights from Bangkok. Most simply let go of their disappointed dreams and went home.

To expedite their return, Western governments forced Nepal in 1973 both to revoke long-term tourist visas and to make cannabis use illegal. America, Germany and Britain had seen enough of their citizens come back with fried brains. Life in the East became not only less trippy but more expensive. Kathmandu's Chief of Police started demanding a 1,000-rupee bribe every month to extend a visa.

Penny and Orrin clung to their romantic utopia until 1979. That year – as revolution swept through Iran, as the US ambassador to Afghanistan was killed and its Islamabad embassy set on fire – the original flower child's "best and last" husband died of cancer.

"We'd prepared for it, of course," she says, sucking on a cheap *bede*. "At the monastery, we'd done our *samsara* – journeying – visualizations and followed the steps through death. But I was frightened. All I had left in the world was possessions..."

30. KATHMANDU

"A fine class of day," says Roddy Finnegan, stretching himself awake in the sunshine, "with flowers and mountains and…" An explosion rumbles in the distance. "…a few bombs. Into every ointment a fly will crash."

Roddy's eyes are moss-green. His skin is copper-brown. He has a thick white walrus moustache and long silver-grey hair, combed and well kept, which reaches down his back in a plait. His Irishness is worn lightly, like his contentment and good-natured irreverence. He looks a decade younger than his sixty years.

"On mornings like today, I get these incandescent visions of all the things I've seen in my life: the Serengeti plain, the *dhows* on the Malabar coast, the innocence of Kathmandu."

"Innocence?' interrupts Penny. "Or innocents?"

"Looking beautiful, girls," he calls over the wall to a passing modesty of neighborhood women: swaying floral *fariya*, chubby babies on slender hips, full-moon lustre in their young faces.

"For sure, this is still a grand place to live," he says, aware of the bombs, stretching again and turning back to us. "With little kids, old temples and teenage girls who I *wish* would take off their clothes so I could adore them one last time."

On her final journey, Penny wanted to see "wonderful, magical Roddy", her friend, fellow Intrepid and Nepal's most musical foreign resident. We arrived not five minutes before, after an eventful ride from Pokhara. On a wooded stretch of the Prithvi Highway forty miles short of the capital, a small band of armed Maoists had stopped the bus, taken off all the passengers, apologized for the inconvenience and set fire to the vehicle. The guerrillas claimed to have seized the countryside and encircled Kathmandu. With the air of busy and confident hosts, they then flagged down the next bus, installed us aboard and dispatched us to our destination. We reached the city four hours late, descending a tortuous road over jumbled foothills into the valley. A taxi delivered us around the army's barbed-wire barricades to the white house at the foot of Swayambhu. We woke Roddy, hedonistic guitar-picker and freak-next-door, who leapt, long, lean and naked out of bed to embrace Penny.

"I find it hard to convey my exhilaration today," he enthuses, touching her cheek, "seeing you again, remembering those days." He has thrown a sarong around his waist. Penny sits between us in his terraced garden above the spreading plain, listening to cooing doves and another explosion, looking from Roddy to me and back again, her eyes glistening with pleasure. Our chairs are set in the sun around a kettle of tea and tatter of music sheets. Behind us rises Swayambhu's sacred hill, its lines of fluttering prayer flags like birds' wings suspended in flight. "For sure, it's *fine* to see you again," he adds for good measure.

"And for you two to meet," Penny says, nodding in my direction and mentioning my book.

"I will tell you for a start why we could never communicate with our fathers' generation," Roddy volunteers, offering to fill me in on the origins of the sixties. "Because of the war. Because of all those young years wasted in that spectacular war."

"Which one?" I ask.

Vietnam? Palestine? Afghanistan? Gulf One or Two? Nepal? The proliferation of wars along the trail has foreshortened my long view of history.

"The Second *World* War," Roddy says without pausing for breath, "when eighteen-year-old boys murdered with sanction and fucked French girls in dusty barns for the price of a cigarette. After which they went home to Dresden or Donegal crying out, 'Give me suburbia.' They wanted to forget their horrible memories. They wanted to watch their children grow up listening to bland music on the phonograph. *Our* generation was born under the shadow of that war, under the mushroom cloud, listening to Doris Day. It mutated us."

"Write this down," Penny tells me, pointing at my notebook, basking in the glow of Roddy's excitable monologue.

"The sixties were the last gasp of the spiritual age," he pronounces, adopting a learned air. "God swept his hand across the world and gave us the cosmic break of our lives. Along with the monkey virus."

"The monkey virus?"

"That first run of the Salk vaccine was a trial," he hisses with delightful drama, sitting forward on his chair, brushing a line of talc across his chest. "The scientists hadn't finished the research. All around the world, millions of God's children were injected with the stuff."

"The polio vaccine," I realize. Roddy has muddled the facts. In 1952, an American medical researcher, Jonas Salk, discovered how to prevent poliomyelitis. He didn't use primates in his research, but another scientist, Albert Sabin, improved the vaccine by experimenting on more than 9,000 monkeys and 100 chimpanzees. According to Roddy, scientific innovation and divine intervention conspired to create the counterculture.

"During the research, a virus crossed from monkeys to humans and took away our ambition. It diluted our respect for authority. It turned us off the consumer society. It made us want to lie together in a big heap and not wash. In fact, it made us hippies."

"That was the cosmic break?" I ask.

"As the mushroom cloud rose above us, God looked down and gave us three great gifts," he replies, lifting his hands toward heaven. Warmed by both our attention and the sun, he grows even more animated. "First, He gave us the electric guitar. Second, He gave us Chuck Berry. He saw we had no attention span because of the monkey virus, so he gave us short songs."

I'm making notes now, scribbling down the words as fast as Roddy utters them in his soft burr, losing count.

"Short songs was the third gift?" I ask.

"The third gift was ... dope. *That* was the greatest gift. The greatest moment in rock 'n' roll. We breathed deep and *annexed* time. That is where the sixties – and so the overland trail – began."

Roddy was born in Ireland, probably Dublin, but he won't say exactly where. In 1960, aged sixteen, he moved to England to work in a Bird's Eye fish-finger factory and – with the monkey virus pumping through his veins – he bought a guitar.

"And an *amp*. No fucking acoustic for me, man."

Two years later, he returned home to form the Wakeful Finn, the first – according to him – Irish rock band.

"We wanted to make music like Charlie Parker and Thelonius Monk, big black heroes who'd been in jail for murder, playing saxophones and twelve-string guitars."

In no time at all, he found Ireland too small. He took off again, first for Sweden, then Ibiza, which was already "a bit crowded" in 1964. He missed Ginsberg in Tangiers but fell in with the Beat poet Gregory Corso in Athens, traveling without destination or money, inventing the unpackaged tour.

"Those mutated genes had kicked in, and I abandoned everything: my parents, money, television. I was good at rejecting crap."

In 1965, he settled in London for a spell, hanging out with Barry Miles at the Indica Gallery (where John Lennon first met Yoko Ono), working with Mark Boyle and the Sense Laboratory, doing the light-show for Hendrix and Cream's farewell concert. His Ladbroke Grove flat was busted on the day Dylan's *Blonde on Blonde* was released. As the drug squad tore open pillows and emptied boxes of cereal, Roddy walked through the feathers and flakes to change the record, "because it was a double album and it was *so* good."

"Being an Irishman, I like words. I sing lyrics that move me. I don't do songs which are glib. That gift of music is a grand thing, a happy thing, for sure. Mr Molotov and Mr Kalashnikov may get their names in the history books, but couldn't they have invented something a little better for mankind?"

By 1968, Roddy was restless, a shadow of pessimism and acquisitiveness lengthening across London and toward the "Me" decade. The music was "showing signs of strain" too. Then, kids started coming back from India, skinny, smiling, wearing pyjamas and *chitrali* hats and saying, "Have a little toke of this shit."

"I did, and I woke up a day later. 'Where did you say this came from?' I asked them. 'Masr? And how much did it cost? $15 a *kilo*?!'"

Roddy was back on the road.

His first trip to the East was by air. He bought a one-way ticket to Mumbai for £48 on Basco, the South Yemeni airline. Its puny, overloaded DC-6 barely cleared the perimeter trees at Brussels. At Cairo, the pilot was refused permission to land because of unpaid fees. He ran out of fuel above a military airfield in Luxor. The crew and passengers were arrested as spies and the aircraft impounded. Roddy and six other freaks stumped up the cash for bribes and fuel (the Indian businessmen had hidden in the toilets). In Aden, they made an unscheduled stopover to replace an engine. Three days later, the DC-6 touched down in Mumbai.

"The door opened and I smelt India – a *mikniva* of shit and urine. I walked around Colaba in wonder, watching the *puja*, seeing the light, feeling no fear, thinking I'd landed in my mother's lap."

For a year, Roddy tripped around the subcontinent, hitched back to Europe, returned to Asia, his cool Carnaby Street boots patched and "Indianized". He hung out in Rishikesh, floated down the Ganges, sat on beaches and *himals*, passed around chillum and guitar, reached through drugs and music for a spiritual life beyond Western materialism.

"The road was a great leveler. It took everyone: guys, girls, poor, posh. No one had heard of AIDS. It cost us nothing to live. Those days were like a warp in time."

Roddy turned up in Kathmandu a few months after Penny and Orrin. The air smelt of jasmine. Bougainvillaea bloomed by wayside shrines. Ponds were full of blue lotus flowers. On their walk into town, the only buildings passed were clay-and-thatch Newar farmhouses. Scavenging pigs wandered in and out of Boris's Hotel. Orrin opened the Dreamweaver gallery on Freak Street. Penny painted the garuda, lion and peacock statues in the monastery. Roddy resurrected the Wakeful Finn.

"We made Nepal our home and stuck a dagger of pure fear into the heart of the Machine," he roars on, the sinews in his neck bulging. "'No, Da, we're not coming back to buy a house and improve the economy. No, we don't need an answering machine. We want to *talk* to people.'"

"We studied Buddhism, Hinduism, Tantrism, the tabla..." says Penny, beaming at me.

"You may even have put your foot on the right path for a moment," I venture.

"We grabbed hold of the hem of heaven and danced. *Danced*," exclaims Roddy. "I've not been back to Europe since the day the Sex Pistols broke up."

Morning melts into noon, tea is transformed into rice and *daal*, Roddy shifts his chair across the garden and we chase after him and the sun. As he talks, he twists in his seat, stands up, changes accents. He winks at Penny, strokes her hair, claps an arm around my shoulders. He appears carefree, impulsive and healthy, his day unfolding like ten thousand others before it. I know I'm envious of him and his liberty, of the flash of years when an optimistic generation first opened their eyes, of their recognition of opportunity, of their ideals rippling across the surface of a pool of cool water: shallow, perhaps, yet alive.

"I always knew that when I got sick, I could come back to Kathmandu and Roddy would look after me," Penny says, suddenly serious. "He'd arrange for the lamas to cremate me properly."

"Are you sick, girl?"

"What do you think? Living in a dark box in London."

"Until you abandoned it," I point out.

"This is *kali yuga*," she tells us.

According to Hindu philosophy, *kali yuga* is the last era before destruction and rebirth.

"What you need is a bed, Penny, not a burning ghat," Roddy replies, taking her hands, fussing her to her feet, cupping his palm on her bottom to guide her into the house. "You should cop some Zs."

Five minutes later, he returns without a smile. He's thrown a cotton shift over his torso and suggests a walk to buy food for the evening.

Beyond the gate, Kimdol, once the domain of tigers, reveals itself as a neighborhood of cobbled lanes and old Tibetan burial grounds. A grocer sells cauliflowers from his bicycle. Housewives look up from grinding lentils to smile.

In Roddy's eyes is a new, sober look.

"I'll tell you a story," he says. "No one ever spent winters in Kathmandu; it was too damn cold. Everyone went south to Goa to catch some rays. The first year, Penny, Orrin and I sat together in a circle on the beach playing guitars. The second year, some new guy brought a cassette deck and rigged it up to a car battery. The third year, another guy came with bigger speakers, then with amplifiers. In the fifth year, a stage was set up and some kid asked me for my backstage pass. My backstage pass! What happened to our sacred beach, man? It was time to move on."

"And now from Nepal?" I ask.

"Kathmandu's full of people reading the Lonely Planet guide to Vietnam. They sit in internet cafés sending each other text messages. I mean, at their age we wanted to get into each other and society, not to live in a meltdown world. We didn't have guidebooks, we didn't even know the *name* of the next country. 'What's this place called? Bhutan? Where the hell is Bhutan?'" he shouts, his voice filled with angry energy. "We'd see a new city from the back of a truck. We'd see the lights. We'd think, 'Behind one of those lights is a little room, and a bed, and maybe, if I get lucky, a warm body.' We were dropped off. We trusted in fate. We were blowing in the wind. Now, a big jumbo jet dumps you at the corner."

We reach the foot of Swayambhu's conical hill and climb the stone steps of the great Buddhist temple, past deities smeared with vermilion and rice, to the platform and sweeping view of the city. Before us, a broad valley of terracotta roofs and bone-white concrete spreads in every direction toward the ring of hazy mountains, visible through the leaden veil of polluted air. Red-robed monks pad around the alms bowl dome which contains nothing. Above it, the spire rises through thirteen gilded rings representing Buddhism's thirteen steps to enlightenment and nirvana.

"They say you come to Nepal for the mountains and stay for the people. When I arrived, I fell in love with those peaks," Roddy says, nodding in the direction of the Himalayas. "I wanted to know the name of every one, and the names of the gods who live there. Way over there somewhere..." he gestures towards Tibet "...is Mount Kailasa, the spiritual center of the universe. Man, it's from there that the gods descend from heaven. A stairway *from* heaven to my doorstep."

Roddy drops his gaze away from the horizon and fixes his eyes on me.

"I've lived a life of genteel poverty. I write poems. I sing songs. As for checking out of Nepal, there's no way I'm going back to the West. In Ireland today you need a supply of mobile phones to throw at muggers. And those guys who stayed behind to change the system from within? 'Thanks, buddy. You did a great job.' No, I'm staying on the edge of the abyss with the Nepalese."

"At the End of the Road."

"I'll die here, man. They'll take me to the Kali temple burning ghat and watch my toes curl. Or I'll go like the Tibetans, cut up and fed to the birds. 'I can fly at last! LSD didn't do it but death sure does...'" His laughter has a suggestion of tears. "Nirvana is a Buddhist concept. Idealism is part of life here. The Nepalese speak of hunger while they dream bright dreams. But this isn't nirvana and maybe Penny has forgotten that. In nirvana, there's no loss or regret or misery because there are no more journeys to make. And who wants to be stuck on their butt in paradise with no stories to tell?"

Roddy lowers his eyes and turns away without uttering another word.

We leave the faithful spinning banks of prayer wheels and return to his sanctuary of birds and bamboo, the terrace suspended between the stupa and the city, between the sacred and the profane. The shadows have crossed the garden, casting all but the patio into shade. A single candle burns in an upper window of the tall white house.

Penny is awake again, sitting back in a cane armchair, at home.

"I remember the first time Orrin and I flew back to the States for his mother's funeral," she says, freeing us from the clutches of silence, restoring our good humor. She's wearing moccasins sewn together with string and there's a flower in her hair. "At LAX we were shoved into a little room with a dozen long-hairs and fellow undesirables. This button-down guy in uniform calls us to his desk, ready to give us the third degree. 'You been out of the country for *nine* years,' he said, like it was a crime. I half-expected him to send us to Alcatraz. 'Nine years,' he repeated, flicking through our passports, looking at the visas. 'You've been living in...' then he stopped and this weirdness came over him. '...Kathmandu,' he said under his breath, over and over again. 'Kathmandu.' I don't know if it was the name, or if he'd been here, or if he just dreamt about Nepal during his tour of Vietnam, but he looked up at us like there was some sort of holy light shining out of our backsides. He closed our passports really slowly, handed them back to us and just said, 'Wow.'"

Roddy sits down beside her and strokes her hair. Her purple bangles ring as she reaches for his hand. I notice once more the beauty of her high cheekbones and her seal-grey hair.

"What a long, strange trip it's been," she says. Then she's quiet for a long minute. "Jack," she adds, turning to face me, "Roddy and I are going to talk about our retirement plans."

"We are?"

One by one, Penny takes hold of Roddy's guitar-picking fingers.

"My old mother from Guernica had a saying. '*La esperanza muere última.*' Hope dies last. Lose hope and you've lost everything."

"Just split for a couple of hours, will you?" Roddy asks me, the light flashing again in his eyes. "There's a bicycle under the banyan tree."

I freewheel downhill into the fading light, laughing until my shoulders shake, almost colliding with a passing Sherpa.

The sixties marked a shift of consciousness. Ordinary people did extraordinary things. A generation rejected old, unfeeling ways, questioned established practices, searched for new values. Then, in the seventies, the oil crisis and later Reagan economics forced on them a financial reality-check. Jobs became scarce. Time grew expensive. Borders closed. Hippie chicks swelled into earth mothers and their children needed new shoes. Lonely Planet, Greenpeace, Apple and MTV went from alternative to mainstream. Revolutionaries reinvented themselves as CEOs. Some kids couldn't adapt, of course, retreating to log cabins in the Sierras or making a last stand as ecowarriors in mid-Wales. But most of them – like Penny and Roddy – found peace in themselves, even as the rainbow bridges were brought down by bombs and rueful self-interest; and the New Conservatives, born of the alliance between big business and "hard-hat" working-class Americans, unpicked the liberal legacy.

Around me, the sprawling, modern suburbs bring to mind a dozen other Asian capitals rather than a one-time idea of paradise. I'm on a foot-bridge over the meandering Vishumati when the street lights flicker and fade. The city's electricity fails, due to a Maoist grenade or an overdue bribe, and Kathmandu is plunged into darkness. I swing off the bike to get my bearings. The flashing billboard for Virgin Blended Scotch ("There is nothing like a virgin") no longer lights my way. The road back to Swayambhu is equally dark. So I push into the disorienting press of bodies, listening to the mixed languages of old Nepal – Tamang, Magar, Gurung, Hindi – following my nose toward the heart of the old city.

In the twilight, bicycle rickshaws clatter through the maze of cobbled streets, their drivers hissing a path between the faceless crowds. Tilting wooden houses rise above half-seen holy men and dogs. The calls of peddlers echo off crumbling buildings. Great weeping stands of bamboo loom over the red walls of the Royal Palace.

I reach Durbar – or Palace – Square as the oil-lamps are lit. A dozen extraordinary, time-worn temples, some dating back to the twelfth century, appear to dance in the glimmering flames. They rise on tiered brick steps, their asymmetrical position heightening the sense of movement. Shiva and his consort, Parvati, gaze out from high windows, their faces turning in the shifting shadows. Stone lions paw the ground outside the House of the Living Goddess. The erotic carvings on Maju Deval's roof struts seem to rock together in eternal copulation.

In the flickering half-light, it's easy to wish away the present. I hear no English spoken. All the hotel signs are blacked out. No cars pollute the alleyways. The jumbled medieval city seems remote from modernity again, ready to be discovered anew.

In the sixties, the magic buses used to park along Basantapur Square. Their drivers – Chattanooga Bob, Jon Benyon and Blossom – drank Guinness on the upper decks. Rudy and Speedy Eddie smoked Mustang and Manali downstairs at the Eden Hash Center, lighting their pipes with Flying Horse matches which exploded and burnt holes in their trousers. Their passengers let go of time at the Dupo Dope ("Your Old and Favorite Joint"). Cat Stevens wrote songs in a chai shop in Asantol. Michael Hollingshead, the Englishman who had introduced Timothy Leary to LSD, swept along Freak Street pontificating on the aspirations of the great psychedelic revolution. In the Cabin, Roddy tuned his guitar and sang about the first social movement in history propelled by students. Orrin took in travelers' problems and rucksacks at Dreamweaver. Rama Tiwari arrived in town with his trunk to build a "Himalaya" of books.

Kids checked into the Inn Eden, the Hotchpotch and the Matchbox, dirty warrens of cell-like rooms with low, ornamental, head-cracking doorways, and debated how best to heal the world. At the Bakery (with its sacred *dhuni* fire, mosaics of the zodiac and *I Ching* hexagrams, as well as the best record-player in Nepal), many newcomers sold their jeans for strings of amber and red-felt boots embroidered with flowers. On their first night in town, Tony and Maureen Wheeler splurged on a two-dollar hotel. Their second night was in a budget one-dollar room next door. Newari snake-charmers played their flutes outside the central post office from where travelers sent home traditional wooden statues, hollowed out and filled with "temple balls" of hash. Crows squabbled in the old palace trees, their black wings sweeping over the terracotta rooftops, Union Jacks, Stars and Stripes and hand-drawn "Kathmandu or Bust" signs. Beneath them, the Intrepids tripped out of smoky black rooms, popped into the mud-floored market to buy bananas, paused to meet friends at a curd shop to hear the news from home, then returned to the Tibetan Blue to refill their pipes and ask in a tone of rising panic, "Where to now, man? Where to now?"

The lights come on. I'm in Thamel, the concrete-and-brass-Bhudda center of tourist Nepal. Around me I see no lotus ponds. White faces blink at the false neon dawn. Sound systems and shop radios crackle back to life. The DJ on a local station drops English words into her Nepali patter: "cool, slipping back, combat dress, Magnum rifle". Then she spins a Bob Seger track. A song which my father used to play. A song about the ever-enthusing, forever deluding dream of a better place.

My hair stands on end as party people at Paddy Foley's Irish Pub sing along to "Katmandu". In the Himalayan Java coffee lounge, laidback Japanese tap their feet while ordering American-style hash browns. Intoxicated Russian tourists sway to the music outside the Moon Stay Lodge and Monumental Paradise. No one takes much notice of the distant crack of a rifle shot.

Goa

31. THE LONG AND WINDING ROAD

From 20,000 feet, I can follow the frothy, palm-fringed arc of India's western seaboard to the horizon. Then, with a lift of the imagination, I can see further up the coast to Gujarat and dust-red Rajasthan. I can reach back over the Khyber, along the trail through Afghanistan, around sacred Bamiyan and beyond the shadow of the lost Buddhas. I can follow the arrow-straight pipelines across sad Middle Eastern borders, catch sight of turquoise Isfahan sparkling in the sun, sense Khomeini raging in his black tomb, even hear glass chimes tinkling in Cappadocia's ashen valleys. The Anatolian steppe rises across my path, raw and timeless, leading me down to the blue Mediterranean and the gates of Europe. Beyond them, back thousands of miles and a good generation, I can just glimpse (if I squint against the glare of the setting sun) Penny at Dover, straggle-haired Ginsberg at JFK and Ken Kesey firing up *Furthur* at Big Sur.

A scimitar of golden sand shimmers beneath the silver belly of the Airbus. We descend over Goa, the first Portuguese possession in Asia. When the Old Conquest colonists left in 1961, the Intrepids established the trippy winter retreat here beside the calm waters of the Arabian Sea. Over a generation its full-moon beach parties morphed from guitar-picking singsongs and psychedelic happenings to the Goa Trance scene. Ravers took over the northern shore. Thousands copulated on Calingute Beach. Local Indians found themselves unwelcome in the waterside cafés. Wasted lowlifers, off their heads and with no "philosophical flowers" in their hair, bartered away their passports and dignity at the Wednesday flea market. I'm about to face the man who set in train the chain of events which helped to bring them all here. My aircraft banks over the ocean. The landing gear grinds down and locks.

The evening light is plump and golden outside the terminal, perhaps because of the smog of hash smoke. I catch a taxi north from Dabolim through lush green fields surrounded by hamlets with white-painted churches. At Mapusa we turn west toward the string of former fishing villages which line the coast. In Anjuna's back lanes low-built houses are tucked beneath overhanging coconut groves. Orchids grow in husks lashed to tree trunks. The barking of wild dogs rises above the singing of the tree frogs. Every second porch displays a "To Let" sign. Fireflies glow under the satellite dishes. I knock at a screen door. Its cement frame is encrusted with sea shells. Alice opens the door.

"We thought you'd be here earlier," she says.

I'm right on time.

She's tall and shiny-faced with a nervous thinness. Her mouth is set and her body tense. She moves aside, not so much to usher me into the house as not to stand in my way. I step into the dim front room. "This is Joanne," she says, introducing her twelve-year-old Samburu daughter.

The room was once painted sky-blue. Backpacks and old leather suitcases gather dust on top of a metal wardrobe. Empty tubes of cooking spices are locked in a metal-mesh cupboard above a tableful of seasonal fruit. In the corner shrine, candles pool at Bhairab's feet. A line of incense ash falls on a crucifix. Joanne's bed is a thin mattress on the concrete floor.

A melon moves on the glass table. A haggard man, tired of life, lifts his head, pushing aside unread newspapers and unopened envelopes. His eyes are dull and slightly hooded. His white beard is stained nicotine-yellow. I walk towards him. He wavers to his feet and steadies himself by grabbing my hand. His bald head – the melon – is overlaid with forward-combed threads of thin hair. I notice his bent back, bowed legs and the tight dome of a swollen belly. "I've brought you whisky," I say. "Johnny Walker Black, right?"

"You star," he says, and slumps back down into his chair.

I sit across from the first independent travel guide writer. I start to tell him about my trip, the retracing of his original journey, and how his – and Tony Wheeler's – work taught a generation to move through the world alone and with confidence. He snaps open the bottle, lights his last B&H Extra Mild and says nothing in response. My heart sinks as the whisky level drops. After an hour, he pushes aside a rejected application from American Express, lays his head back down with the soft fruit and falls asleep. Above him buckle shelves of his five dozen guides: BIT's *Overland*

Through Africa, Lonely Planet's *South America on a Shoestring*, the *Kenya* and *Uganda* guides which Alice helped him research, all his Asian volumes, undertaken with his second wife, Poon, every book rotting in the tropical humidity. I notice also Newby's *Traveller's Tales*, works by R. D. Laing and Carlos Castaneda, *The Many Ways of Being* and *Drugs of Hallucination*. I can't see a copy of the original *Overland to India*.

In the adjoining kitchen, Alice and Joanne whisper in Swahili. When Crowther starts to snore, anger and disappointment swell inside me. I stand. I pick up my pack. I'm about to walk out. Then, Alice appears at my side. "Take him to the bar in the morning," she says. "Buy him a drink."

"Is that meant to make me feel better?"

"It'll make him talk."

In the spare bedroom I fold myself under the mosquito net. The sounds of unknown creatures rise out of the dark. The beating of the overhead fan blocks out the sound of the sea. I drop into sleep. In the middle of the night I surface from a dream. I'm disorientated, detached from the familiar, not yet connected to the new. In my dream I imagine scrawling words across Crowther's face with a felt-tip marker; words from Roddy's parting prediction at Kathmandu's Tribhuvan airport.

"My vision of the end of the planet is everyone taking a holiday in the same week," he said. "All the aircraft crash into each other in one great fireball. No more travel agents. No more pimple-faced immigration officers. Just a single, surviving traveler who arrives at his hotel with a singed copy of *Lonely Planet* crying out, 'What do you mean, there's no internet café?'"

Geoff Crowther was born in Todmorden near Halifax on the day the Americans dropped the first atomic bomb on Hiroshima. After school and a spell working for the Humberside water board, he hit the road. In London at BIT, he collated his travel notes into the Intrepids' first, impulsive guide. He and Tony Wheeler collaborated to produce the original Lonely Planet *India* handbook. His journeys informed the imprint's first African and South American guides. With their success, he bought acre by acre, check by check, an old banana plantation in northern New South Wales. In the rainforest he created a writers' retreat and nudist commune (the only clothes permitted were Wellington boots because of the snakes). He left his common-law English wife for Poon and built her a Korean-temple-cum-bushwhacker's-chalet on a mountainside. Crowther traveled as he lived, his excesses mirroring those of the age. Every time he returned from a spell on the road, Poon made him have a venereal disease test. Then he drove around the commune collecting his partners for a group visit to the clinic. He drank in those days, too, a six-pack of beer set beside the IBM to see him through the morning. The story of his life was legend among guide writers.

In the morning, Alice points me towards the ocean. Crowther left the house early. I walk barefoot along a sandy lane, through the soft embracing heat, past St Anthony's Church (patron saint of lost travelers). Coconut palms rise above the paddy fields. A heavy blossom drops from a tree, plummeting to earth like a falling bird. Waves whisper along the beach like lovers sharing secrets.

The Guru Bar overlooks the rocky bay. Crowther sits alone under its palm-frond balcony with his daily crossword. Only geckos keep him company. Beyond him the Arabian Sea glints in the morning sun.

"Is a symbolic tale an allegory?" he asks me without lifting his eyes. The wire arms of his pilot spectacles ride halfway up his temples. "*Nairobi Times* is best, a crossword without clues, but I can't get it. So *Indian Express* has to do." His hand shakes as he fills in the boxes. At his side are a bottle of Wite Out, a dictionary and an empty glass.

"Allegory is spelt with two 'l's," I say.

Crowther leans back on his chair and laughs at himself. A raw grinding of gravel and phlegm. His flat feet are splayed on oversize flip-flops. He wears a pair of old shorts and a floppy, faded sweatshirt.

"Nobody comes to visit me here," he says.

"Can I top up your beer?" I ask.

"You star."

I buy two for him, one for me. The drink loosens his tongue.

"Kathmandu," he says. "You've just come from Kathmandu."

I nod.

"From Delhi catch the Upper India Express – platform 13, 8.10 p.m. – to Patna. Cycle rickshaw to steamer *Mahendra Ghat* and Ganges. The Raxaul train leaves at 10.20 p.m. Cost in 1969: 17.50 rupees with student reduction."

"Very good," I admit.

"In Durbar, hash cookies were on every menu. The Cabin restaurant's telephone number was 14724."

It's my turn to laugh. "You have a good memory."

"I *never* let go of my journals. Slept with them. Drew maps by hand. No laptops back then. No photocopiers in Africa. If you lost a journal you were royally screwed."

He stamps the table with his fist, misses the fly, knocks over the bottles. I buy him another beer.

"Got screwed by lice too. On a bus, your neighbor's head would be crawling with them. They'd drop on to your lap. You'd feel them biting the back of your neck. Crabs were a pain in the ass too. Literally."

"I guess it was all part of the experience."

"A dollar bought 12.50 rupees in 1970," he adds, eager to share again his archaic knowledge.

As he talks, the day's heat gathers around us, coiling between the chairs and tables, thickening and condensing before our eyes. Shadows of sea birds sweep across the bamboo sunscreen, as does a black spider the size of a walnut. Backgammon tiles begin to click at other tables. Teaspoons clink on china cups beneath toadstool umbrellas. Loud Germans drop by for a late *frühstück*, complain about stale *brötchen* and coffee that's *nicht gut*. English tranceheads in ripped loincloths fall into the sea. Crowther snaps a flame to his cigarette. "I only started smoking when the dope ran out. Possession got you ten years in Turkey." Then he details the ride-by-ride bus fares from Istanbul to India. Total 1971 cost: $15 to cross Asia.

His recall does impress me. His interest in my questions eases my anger. He suggests that I read Pope's *Persian Architecture* and Naipaul on India (who wrote off the hippies' fascination with Hinduism as a "sentimental wallow"). He speaks of the world as if it truly were a village; dawn in Sri Lanka, house prices in Bali, sundowners in Marin County book shops.

Around noon, when I buy him his sixth drink, Crowther says, "Siggy's served the coldest beers in Iran."

"Siggy's was in Kabul."

"Don't fucking tell me about Siggy,' he spits back. "*I* knew him, knew his place; not you."

I let it drop, but he goes on, "There were bottlenecks on the trail, places everybody turned up and hung out: the Pudding Shop, the Amir Kabir, Siggy's place. Siggy's was in an alleyway behind the White Palace so I'm not about to forget it." The White Palace was in Tehran. "We'd hang out with Siggy, then crash at the Yogi Lodge." The Yogi had been in Varanasi.

When he starts to slur his words, I leave him at the bar. His lucidity has darkened for the day. Along the beach are fishermen, volleyball players, tourists smoking, sunbathing and scolding their children. Underfoot the sand is oil-stained and litter washes into the coves. I find a quiet beach-house café, order grilled fish and write up my notes.

Later, at the house, Alice tells me he hasn't come home yet. She invites me to share a plate of maize meal and greens with her and Joanne. We are asleep when he comes in.

On the second morning, he's back at the Guru, a stack of cloth-bound foolscap notebooks alongside his crosswords. I buy him two beers and he talks me through the pages. Here are the room rates of Kandahar's first freak hotel. On the next pages are the departure times of every bus from Jalalabad to Peshawar, with chai and chillum breaks noted, and a precise plan of Amritsar. Crowther walked every street for every map in his early guides. In the margin he had written in copperplate handwriting, "Golden Temple dorm free but treat hospitality with respect as many bad scenes with Westerners smoking."

I ask him if he has a copy of the original BIT *Overland to India* guide. He says that he's lost it.

"At the end of each trip, I typed up my notes at the commune in the company of pythons and kookaburras. Then I'd head down to Melbourne with the pages. Andy Neilson, LP's first employee and as mad as a snake, sat with her baby and a glass of strawberry Nesquik pasting up the lay-out. Maureen proofread while breast-feeding Tashi. As soon as one book was put to bed, Tony and I would take off again, visiting the countries we wanted to see, writing books for real travelers."

Crowther researched and wrote many *Travel Survival Kits* during Lonely Planet's first eighteen years, educating readers without patronizing them.

"But every time we returned to Melbourne we'd find a new employee, then two more, then a staff canteen. Those desk jockeys started to judge us, and our sanity, by the thickness of our socks. The thicker the socks, the longer we'd been on the road. After five years' travel, most of us went feral."

Crowther lifts the bottle to his lips, drains it, heaves it toward the sea. "Something got lost," he says, his body tense, his eyes closed. "Something essential. Doing the third edition of the Thailand guide I started feeling ... trapped. My last job, I was asked to write a 'Highlights' section for 'mature adventurers'."

The millions Crowther made by trailblazing the globe were pissed away on alcohol, alimony and a three-bed suburban unit near Surfer's Paradise. He, Alice and Joanne arrived penniless in Goa six months ago.

A girl brings him a couple of boiled eggs, which he rolls in his hands to cool. As he eats, I look at the typescript of his first Nepal guide, the letters typed with such manifest urgency that the "o"s punched little holes through the tissue-thin foolscap. His photograph in the front of *Africa on a Shoestring* shows a bright-eyed, curious twenty-seven-year-old with a wild beard reaching down to his chest.

"Tony loaned me his first computer – a Kaypros – in 1984," he remembers, calm once more. "Then we moved over to DOS and Windows 3.1, Windows 95..."

I hope that the food will extend our conversation, but he soon begins repeating himself.

"...No laptops back then. No photocopiers in Africa. In the sixties you had to believe in a better world. Now, who's got the time? Man, the Karakoram Highway was beautiful."

I leave him with his crossword and walk beyond Dando Vaddo for a swim.

On the third morning, Crowther isn't at the Guru. Alice tells me he didn't come home that night. On the fourth morning, he is back at his corner table, offering no explanation for his absence.

"China's the future," he says, before I've even sat down. "Those billions of golden boys and girls with spending power are about to hit the beach. They won't *defer* to other cultures. They don't want to be *transformed*. They

want adventures without risk. Forty years ago, we put on kaftans and headed east," he says. "Now the East is coming back at us dressed in DKNY."

Over the next week, we meet at the beach bar every morning, talking
until noon when he becomes abusive, insensible or comatose. Often he falls
silent and gazes at his newspaper for twenty or thirty minutes. One day he
says nothing at all. For my part, I try not to develop too much of a taste for
a morning beer.

"At the start of every trip I used to get a mental picture of the end,"
Crowther says on our final morning together. "I always knew things would
be OK if I could imagine myself arriving at my destination. That last flight
from Brisbane with Alice, it didn't happen. At first, I thought it was just
my bloody mind. Then half an hour out of Mumbai the lights went dim.
Captain came on saying we had hydraulics problems. He couldn't lower
the undercarriage. We ditched fuel over the sea. The stewardesses strapped
themselves in. The whole of the airfield was a mass of flashing blue and
red lights. I thought, 'This is my crash landing. This is the end.'" Crowther
looks out at the waves. "I settled down," he says, almost as an afterthought.
"I let go of what I loved."

Later that week I take a small house a few miles up the coast and start to
organize my thoughts. As Goa's autumn storms gather out at sea, their
broad sweeps of lightning silhouetting the palms, I rebuild the overland
journey in my head. I see Kerouac and Ginsberg listening to the Beatles. I
hear John Butt singing Dylan again. I picture eighteen-year-old girls from
Brooklyn raise their thumbs to hitch alone across Anatolia. I watch Nicolas Bouvier write in his journal, "A journey does not need reasons. Before
long, it proves to be reason enough in itself. One thinks that one is going
to make a journey, yet soon it is the journey that makes or unmakes you." I
think of Rudy's sense of belonging to the world and Laleh's fear of belonging nowhere. I remember again Hesse's "home and youth of the soul"
and Chatwin's assertion that the hippies wrecked Afghanistan. I imagine
Ahmed strapping a dynamite girdle around his waist. I hold Penny as she
kisses me goodbye in Kathmandu.

In the silence of this room, I begin to rework experience, looking at
the shadows of the unseen, trying to find an order in the pattern. I'm not

filled with melancholia, pining for a distant time or place which has been lost. I'm feeling my way over new ground, gazing inside myself as much as at geography, wandering and wondering away from certainty toward something open and flowing, toward a new destination.

"The trail across Asia is narrow and there's only one road, one way to go," wrote Douglas Brown in the conclusion to his 1971 guidebook. "When it broadens out in India, and you see the hundreds of cities marked in a very small area of the map, you will have at last the chance to go wherever you want, and find a place to rest and get into a way of life that will satisfy you. The one path has become many."

Those paths spin out from this room like the threads of a vast spider's web. In a thousand departure lounges a fresh generation of Intrepids stands on the brink of the world. Icelandic trekkers in flip-flops eye Gulf Air stewardesses in blue pencil skirts and high heels. Mumbai boys in transit chat up Filipino salesgirls at duty-free shops. A continent away, Argentinian kids board double-decker sleeper buses to cross the Andes and reach Pacific beaches. Uruguayan architecture students drive VW Campers on year-long study tours from Europe to India. In Tanzania, fledgling pilots buzz dirt runways to clear away giraffes, then try to avoid their aircraft being trampled by wildebeest. Malaysian teens fly to Hong Kong for shopping weekends. American undergrads jet into the Sorbonne for travel writing workshops. Gap-year Scots learn to enter Mongolian yurts by shouting "*Nokhoi khor*" – "Hold the dog!" Egyptian newlyweds sleep under the stars in the Namibian desert. From the stark horizons of the Arctic tundra to the tourist deck of a Caribbean mail-boat, the new voyagers stand to greet the sunrise, Youssou N'Dour singing "Mr. Everywhere" in their ears.

Like them, I am a foreigner, an open-hearted, sole traveler, spiralling out from where I was born, curious for the world and taking nothing for granted: not belonging, not possessing, at home in my skin and reinventing myself at every border. Moving on. That's our legacy from the sixties. Not simply "this now life ... this here life". Not just the raw experience of being. But living both in the moment and in the mind, striving to understand – and to express – how it feels to be alive.

The momentum of the sea marks off the days. Autumn makes way for winter. A bird nests under the eaves. The party people move on to Yang-

ONCE IN A LIFETIME

When *Magic Bus* was published in the UK and France, and the first reviews appeared in the press, something unexpected happened. Trail "veterans" started writing to me. They'd headed east in the Sixties or Seventies and – motivated by reading the book – now they embarked on a new trek, up the stairs to the attic to unearth old boxes and dusty journals. Within a couple of months I'd been sent over 500 photographs, and enough new material to write the book all over again. With their permission I started relaying those stories, along with those I'd already collected, in articles, talks and on the website www.magicbus.info. As a result the letters and emails multiplied again: Australian grandmothers recognised their earlier selves in old snapshots ("It is weird to see a photo you didn't know existed, in the newspaper, out of the blue 31 years later"); Parisien *soixante-huitards* reminisced about the political changes which had made them desert Montreuil for Mumbai; a Texan from Dallas even asked me if I could help him to find his old flame (Rosa Muscat, if you read this do email me via the website and I'll put you in touch with Dave).

© Kami Kanetsuka

In every case the trail had so marked these travelers that they wanted to share – and so relive -- their journey. Take one email from Scotland. David Cooper traveled for ten years to reach India, leaving Crieff in 1968, breaking off to go to university, spending time along the way with Ginsberg on Iona and Donovan and Lennon in the States. The Maharishi trained him to teach TM. R.D. Laing once slept in his apartment. "My trips had an indelible impact on my life, he wrote. "There was no way on earth I could ever be anything other than self employed as a result." Chilton Thomson's story moved me too. When the Khmer Rouge threatened to destroy Angkor Wat, he quit his job at a London bank to drive a bus across Asia determined to see the temple. "I will rejoice to the end of my life that I had a chance to wander around the lakes at Band-e-Amir and see Herat and Isfahan." At the end of his trip he married one of his passengers. "We are still together so my life was changed by the journey as effectively as by any ashram." Two Dutchmen, a Quebecoise and six Americans also wrote to tell me that they had married their traveling companion.

© David Smith

Their photographs were especially evocative. Traveling lightly with limited funds and often for years at a time was not conducive to carrying a camera. Valuable items tended to be stolen or traded. Sand and dust destroyed mechanical shutters. Film was expensive and – once exposed – occupied precious space in a backpack. I pored over every picture, hoping to catch sight of a mosque or line of hills that I'd seen during my research trip.

© Chris Weeks

The greatest journey of that age was – for many – its greatest learning experience. "I loved almost every minute of being an expedition leader. It changed my whole outlook on life," Chris Weeks told me. Chris drove Intertrek Bedford trucks to India and is now an antique furniture restorer in the English West Country. "But I saw that most people here have not got a clue about how the third world lives, about the real hardship there, the deprivation, the corruption, the lack of medical care and water. Really what life is about." Californian Joan Rippe – who went east in the Seventies and now manages a Santa Cruz construction firm while indulging a passion for belly-dancing learnt in Tehran -- was also humbled by her travels. "Doing the trail was possibly the best thing I ever did for myself. I came home better equipped to understand multicultural issues. I gained an appreciation for Islam and Arab cultures." Curt Gibbs, whose 18 month journey inspired his creativity in the revitalization of Los Angeles, remembers Goa as a paradise. "We found a little piece of heaven. We didn't realize then that our actions would be remembered long after we were gone."

The overland travelers were baby boomers, turning 19 or 20, questioning and rebelling like the world itself. They came of age during a period of political and social revolution, in parallel with the space race, in step with the banishing of borders by Boeing and of pregnancy by the Pill. They set out to find a new way of living, hitching alone to West Bank kibbutzes, drifting through Afghanistan, welcomed as honored guests in Baghdad. Today a Western passport, once respected, is a liability in much of the Middle East. No sane tourist holidays in Mosul or Kandahar. The Intrepids' journeys did change the world. That world has continued to change, and in dramatic ways that none of them could ever have imagined.

© Chris Weeks

SELECT BIBLIOGRAPHY

Books

Bouvier, Nicolas: *The Way of the World -- l'Usage du Monde* (Paris, Editions La Découverte 1963, 1985)

Brown, Douglas: *Overland to India* (Toronto, New Press, 1971)

Byron, Robert: *The Road to Oxiana* (London, Penguin, 1992)

Chatwin, Bruce: *What am I Doing Here?* (London, Picador, 1990)

Crowther, Geoff and others: *Overland to India* (London, BIT, 1970 and Crisis-BIT Trust, 1975)

Dupree, Nancy Hatch: *An Historical Guide to Kabul* (Kabul, Afghan Tourist Organization, 1965)

Ginsberg, Allen: *Indian Journals* (New York, Grove Press, 1996)

Gloaguen, Philippe: *Guide du routard* (Paris, Hachette, various dates)

Gray, Michael and Bauldie, John (eds.), *All Across the Telegraph: A Bob Dylan Handbook* (London, Sidgwick and Jackson, 1987)

Green, Jonathon: *All Dressed Up* (London, Pimlico, 1999)

Grissmann, Carla: *Dinner of Herbs* (London, Arcadia Books, 2001)

Hesse, Hermann: *The Journey to the East* (London, Grafton, 1972) and *Siddhartha* (London, Picador, 1973)

Holmes, John Clellon: *Go* (New York, Charles Scribner, 1952)

James, Bill: *Top Deck Daze* (Avalon, NSW, Halbooks, 1999)

Karlin, Danny: *Allen Ginsberg and Bob Dylan: At Kerouac's Grave and Beyond* (unpublished paper given at Shakespeare & Co. Literary Festival, Paris, 2003)

Kerouac, Jack: *On the Road* (New York, Viking Press, 1957)

Macdonald, Ian: *Revolution in the Head* (London, Fourth Estate, 1994)

Miles, Barry: *Many Years from Now* (London, Vintage, 1998)

Morris, Jan: *Destinations: Essays from 'Rolling Stone'* (Oxford, OUP, 1980)

Neville, Richard and Clarke, Julie: *The Life and Crimes of Charles Sobhraj* (London, Jonathan Cape, 1979)

Saunders, Nicholas: *Alternative London* (London, Saunders, 1970)

Schultz, Mik: *Asia for the Hitchhiker* (Copenhagen, Bramsen and Hjort, 1973)

Shephard, Sam: *Rolling Thunder Logbook* (London, Viking, 1977)

Thapa, Deepak: *A Kingdom Under Siege* (Kathmandu, the printhouse, 2003)

Twain, Mark: *Following the Equator* (Hartford, The American Publishing Company, 1897)

Wheeler, Tony: *Across Asia on the Cheap* (Sydney, Lonely Planet, 1973)

White, Kenneth: *The Wanderer and his Charts* (Edinburgh, Polygon, 2004)

Wolfe, Tom: *The Electric Kool-Aid Acid Test* (New York, Farrar, Straus and Giroux, 1968)

Periodicals

'Light Years from New York', Maureen Freely (Istanbul, *Cornucopia*, 2001)

'Moving Freely', Maureen Freely (Istanbul, *Cornucopia*, 2002)

'The New Indiaman', Frank Riley (London, *Meccano*, October 1959)

'Music Scene', Linda Solomon (New York, *The Village Voice*, 28 March 1963)

FIVE BOOKS WHICH MADE THE INTREPIDS TRAVEL

Books passed freely between travelers on the road in keeping with the Sixties' openness to new experiences. Top reads included More's *Utopia*, Kafka's *The Metamorphosis* and Orwell's *Down and Out in Paris and London*. Dog-eared copies of the novels of Hermann Hesse went back and forth from west to east countless times, as did Ginsberg's *Howl*, Paul Bowles' *The Sheltering Sky*, Flann O'Brien's *The Third Policeman* and Isaac Asimov's *Foundation* trilogy. Latecomers on the road to nirvana would have carried Carlos Castaneda, Knut Hamsun, Tom Wolfe (*The Electric Kool-Aid Acid Test*) and – in increasing numbers -- Tony Wheeler's *Across Asia on the Cheap*. My selection is inevitably personal but these are the five books I would have stuffed into my backpack in 1967.

On the Road

Jack Kerouac's restless, seminal, Benzedrine-fueled American adventure blended fiction and autobiography to define the "Beat" generation. Its influence in propelling countless kids onto the road cannot be overstated.

Siddhartha

Hesse's story of spiritual awakening is a classic of twentieth-century fiction. A man living in India at the time of the Buddha deserts his wealthy Brahmin family, discarding first a contemplative and then a hedonistic life, to find a new understanding of suffering, a growing sense of peace, and, finally, wisdom.

Walden

Henry David Thoreau's account of his time spent in solitude in the woods by Walden Pond in 19th century Massachusetts is a treasure. "I went into the woods," he wrote, "because I wished to live deliberately, to front only the essential facts of life, and see if I could not learn what it had to teach, and not, when I came to die, discover that I had not lived." The same spirit of discovery -- including self-discovery -- defined many Sixties travelers' quest.

Brave New World

Far in the future, the World Controllers have created the ideal society. Aldous Huxley's bewitching, insidious and prophetic masterpiece describes a haunting utopia, albeit an ironic one, where humanity is carefree because family, cultural diversity, art, literature, science, religion and philosophy have been eliminated.

The Way of the World

Nicolas Bouvier's passionate and exhilarating travel stories inspired a generation of young Europeans. "I dropped this wonderful moment into the bottom of my memory, like a sheet-anchor that one day I could draw up again," he wrote while traveling through Turkey. "The bedrock of existence is not made up of the family, or work, or what others say and think of you, but of moments like this when you are exalted by a transcendent power that is more serene than love." Although this account of his 1950s journey was not published until 1985, *The Way of the World* (*L'Usage du Monde*) is one of the definitive Sixties travel books.

ACKNOWLEDGEMENTS

Many people climbed on to the Magic Bus to help it on its way. In London, Colin Thubron was first aboard with early enthusiasm and gentle friendship. Philip Marsden and Bruce Palling opened the bus's rear doors. Jonathon Green stepped on, bringing his original interviews from *Days in the Life* and *All Dressed Up* in a tie-dyed shoulder bag. Hetty MacLise was enormously helpful with research and all errors and inaccuracies are due to my enthusiasm for her remarkable stories. Judy Astley, Ondine Barrow, Simon Calder, David Chater, Marlie and Michael Ferenczi, Christine Gettins, Gwyneth Henderson, David Jenkins, Sue Lascelles, Richard Ingrams, Tim Mackintosh-Smith, Jessie Marshall, Towyn Mason, Desmond O' Flattery, Mary Price, Hawa Rawat and JoAnne Robertson took their seats alongside Christine Walker of the *Sunday Times* and Toby Latta and Josh Mandel of Control Risks Group. Joanna Prior and Barry Blackmore sat in the back, rocking to the greatest playlist of all time. On the pavement outside, Verona Bass packed us off with her 1967 diaries and banana-loaf lunches.

In New York, the Magic Bus paused to collect Joy Press and Hervay Petion from *Village Voice*. In Massachusetts, Danny Karlin led the way to Kerouac's grave and bridged the Beats and the sixties. In Paris, George and Sylvia Whitman put us up between the stacks at Shakespeare and Company. In Amsterdam, Clive and Rebecca Tanquery reopened the Magic Inn, while in Berlin Dr Willi Steul helped to unpick the social fabric of Pashtun society.

In Turkey, I will never forget the kindness of the remarkable Freely family: John, Delores, Brendon and Maureen (who let me quote from her *Cornucopia* article on Carla Grissmann). Great thanks to them, to Jeremy Seal, Fatih Hatay, Pat Yale and to Nurdogan Sengüler of Les Arts Turcs.

Caution prevents me from naming the many generous Iranians who welcomed me both into their hearts and their extraordinary country. In Afghanistan, I openly acknowledge the assistance of my fellow Intrepids

Paul Clammer, Jason Elliot, Christina Lamb, Rory Stewart, Sanjar Qiam and Tahir Shah. In Kabul, John West gave me a place to sleep. Former Indian Army Major Sunil Shetty, SM, ensured I didn't get shot. Author and journalist Ahmed Rashid explained why no one would bother to waste the bullet.

In Pakistan, Meriel Beattie and Usman Homaira sped the Magic Bus further along the trail, as did Caro Coltman and Peter Berkeley, Norman Flach and Lory Thiessen, Fayyaz Ali Khan, Jonaid Shah of GTZ Peshawar, Neelofer Khan and Tariq Qurashi of the Canadian International Development Agency. Makhdoom Shahabuddin, gentleman and *Pir*, also treated me with great kindness.

Rosie Goldsmith helped me motor into India. Many thanks, as always, to her, to William Dalrymple and to Jayanta Roy Chowdhury, who guided me from Naxal to nirvana by way of Nehru. In Nepal, I am grateful to Daniel Lak and Manjushree Thapa, as well as to Ruth and Mark Segal for the great family breakfasts.

At Lonely Planet's offices in Melbourne and London, Tony and Maureen Wheeler could not have been more helpful, as were Simon Westcott, Jennifer Cox and Andy Neilson. Along with Bill Dalton of Moon Publications, Philippe Gloaguen of *Guides du routard*, Stefan and Renate Loose of *Stefan Loose Verlag* and Mark Ellingham of Rough Guides, they changed the way we travel the world. I am grateful to drivers and enthusiasts Jonathan Benyon, Graham Bourne, Kevin Buckley, David "Blossom" Johnson, Geoff Hann, Jim D. Holden, Geoffrey Morant, Brian Page, John Shearman and Chris Weeks.

Finally, with the Magic Bus now safely parked in my garage (alongside an East German Trabant, a Canadian birch-bark canoe and a light, white Cretan flying-machine), I wish to acknowledge the guidance and navigational skills of my agents Peter Straus and Melanie Jackson, my British editor, Mary Mount, my American publishers Elizabeth Clementson and Robert Lasner, and – most of all – my wife, Katrin. As they say, I get by with a little help from my friends.

www.rorymaclean.com
www.magicbus.info

HAVE YOU READ?

Stalin's Nose: Across the Face of Europe (1992, 2008)

According to the *New York Times*, Rory's first book is "a surreal, zanily nihilistic comedy", describing a journey from Berlin to Moscow, through Czechoslovakia, Hungary, Poland and Romania only weeks after the fall of the Berlin Wall. A UK Top Ten best-seller and shortlisted for the Thomas Cook Travel Book Prize, this is a story of the then forgotten half of Europe: black, comic, surreal yet painfully real, at once a documentary of a journey and a fantastical narrative. "A surreal masterpiece" Colin Thubron. "Outrageously funny...the kind of book that you might refuse to lend to your friends for fear they'd never return it." Houston Chronicle

The Oatmeal Ark: From the Scottish Isles to a Promised Land (1997, 2008)

A wave-rocked, wind-tossed adventure story which reaches from Scotland to Nova Scotia, across Canada by water, and through three generations of extraordinary family history. It weaves ghostly invention through true stories, stitching imaginary characters into real events, to unravel Canada's epic history. "A truly astonishing performance" wrote Jan Morris. "A fascinating family chronicle; challenging and satisfying" The Toronto Globe and Mail. Nominated for the International IMPAC Dublin Literary Award.

Under the Dragon: Travels in Burma (1998, 2008)

In 1988 the Burmese people rose up against their military government. The unarmed demonstrators were cut down, leaving more than 5,000 people dead. Under the Dragon recounts a journey through Burma some ten years later, meeting the victims - and the perpetrators - of that uprising. At the book's heart are the stories of four remarkable women, among them Aung San Suu Kyi, Nobel Peace laureate and elected leader, held under house arrest for over a decade. Winner of an Arts Council Writer's Award and shortlisted for the Thomas Cook Travel Book Prize. "Read it. Read it.

Read it." Fergal Keane (BBC London).

Next Exit Magic Kingdom: Florida Accidentally (2001, 2008)

Rory sets out to discover that Florida's greatest wonders are not to be found at Disney World but in the remarkable stories of ordinary men and women. On a quest that warms even Mickey's plastic heart, he considers the nature of human goodness in the sunshine state -- a place at once kooky and dangerous, superficial and sincere, sensationalist and dumb. "Zippy and fun, with heart and energy and a restless haphazard charm. MacLean has wrestled the Sunshine State like an alligator and stuffed and mounted it for our readerly pleasure." Louis Theroux. Shortlisted for the WHSmith Travel Book Award.

Falling for Icarus: A Journey among the Cretans (2004, 2010)

On a windy spring morning in an ancient village surrounded by mountains on Crete, Rory falls to earth. His mother had died a few months earlier and a single obsession had risen from his grief: the notion to build a feather-light flying machine. And so, on the island where Daedalus and Icarus had made man's maiden flight, Rory journeys back to beginnings, back into the Greek myths, and – with the help of effusive but irrepressible neighbours and plenty of wine – builds a plane and tries to fly... "Destined to become a classic," the Scotsman.